ALSO BY MARCIA ANGELL

Science on Trial

The Truth About
the Drug Companies

RANDOM HOUSE

NEW YORK

The Truth About the Drug Companies

HOW THEY DECEIVE US
AND WHAT TO DO ABOUT IT

MARCIA ANGELL, M.D.

All rights reserved under International and Pan-American
Copyright Conventions. Published in the United States by
Random House, an imprint of The Random House Publishing
Group, a division of Random House, Inc., New York, and
simultaneously in Canada by Random House of Canada
Limited, Toronto.

RANDOM HOUSE and colophon are registered trademarks
of Random House, Inc.

Library of Congress Cataloging-in-Publication Data
Angell, Marcia.
The truth about the drug companies: how they deceive us and
what to do about it / Marcia Angell.
p.   cm.
Includes bibliographical references and index.
ISBN 0-375-50846-5 (cloth: alk. paper)
1. Pharmaceutical industry—United States—Costs.
2. Drugs—Prices—United States.   3. Drugs—Research—
United States—Finance.   4. Prescription pricing—United
States.   5. Advertising—Drugs—United States.
6. Pharmaceutical policy—United States.
HD9666.5.D774   2004
338.4'36151'0973—dc22   2004041212

Printed in the United States of America on acid-free paper
Random House website address: www.atrandom.com
9 8 7 6 5 4 3 2

Book design by Victoria Wong

To Bud
and to
Lara and Elizabeth

Contents

Introduction:
Drugs Are Different

EVERY DAY AMERICANS ARE SUBJECTED to a barrage of advertising by the pharmaceutical industry. Mixed in with the pitches for a particular drug—usually featuring beautiful people enjoying themselves in the great outdoors—is a more general message. Boiled down to its essentials, it is this: "Yes, prescription drugs are expensive, but that shows how valuable they are. Besides, our research and development costs are enormous, and we need to cover them somehow. As 'research-based' companies, we turn out a steady stream of innovative medicines that lengthen life, enhance its quality, and avert more expensive medical care.

You are the beneficiaries of this ongoing achievement of the American free enterprise system, so be grateful, quit whining, and pay up." More prosaically, what the industry is saying is that you get what you pay for.

Your Money or Your Life

Is any of this true? Well, the first part certainly is. Prescription drug costs are indeed high—and rising fast. Americans now spend a staggering $200 billion a year on prescription drugs, and that figure is growing at about 12 percent a year (down from a high of 18 percent in 1999).[1] Drugs are the fastest-growing part of the health care bill—which itself is rising at an alarming rate. The increase in drug spending reflects, in almost equal parts, the facts that people are taking a lot more drugs than they used to, that those drugs are more likely to be expensive new ones instead of older, cheaper ones, and that the prices of the most heavily prescribed drugs are routinely jacked up, sometimes several times a year.

Before its patent ran out, for example, the price of Schering-Plough's top-selling allergy pill, Claritin, was raised thirteen times over five years, for a cumulative increase of more than 50 percent—over four times the rate of general inflation.[2] As a spokeswoman for one company explained, "Price increases are not uncommon in the industry and this allows us to be able to invest in R & D."[3] In 2002, the average price of the fifty drugs most used by senior citizens was nearly $1500 for a year's supply. (Pricing varies greatly, but this refers to what the companies call the average wholesale price, which is usually pretty close to what an individual without insurance pays at the pharmacy.)[4]

Paying for prescription drugs is no longer a problem just for poor people. As the economy continues to struggle, health insurance is shrinking. Employers are requiring workers to pay more of the costs themselves, and many businesses are dropping health benefits altogether. Since prescription drug costs are rising so fast, payers are particularly eager to get out from under them by shifting costs to individuals. The result is that more people have to pay a greater fraction of their drug bills out of pocket. And that packs a wallop.

Many of them simply can't do it. They trade off drugs against home heating or food. Some people try to string out their drugs by taking them less often than prescribed, or sharing them with a spouse. Others, too embarrassed to admit that they can't afford to pay for drugs, leave their doctors' offices with prescriptions in hand but don't have them filled. Not only do these patients go without needed treatment but their doctors sometimes wrongly conclude that the drugs they prescribed didn't work and prescribe yet others—thus compounding the problem.

The people hurting most are senior citizens. When Medicare was enacted in 1965, people took far fewer prescription drugs and they were cheap. For that reason, no one thought it necessary to include an outpatient prescription drug benefit in the program. In those days, senior citizens could generally afford to buy whatever drugs they needed out of pocket. Approximately half to two-thirds of seniors have supplementary insurance that partly covers prescription drugs, but that percentage is dropping as employers and insurers decide it is a losing proposition for them. At the end of 2003, Congress passed a Medicare reform bill that included a prescription drug benefit scheduled to begin in 2006, but as we will see later, its benefits are inadequate to begin with and will quickly be overtaken by rising prices and administrative costs.

For obvious reasons, senior citizens tend to need more prescription drugs than younger people—mainly for chronic conditions like arthritis, diabetes, high blood pressure, and elevated cholesterol. In 2001, nearly one in four seniors reported skipping doses or leaving prescriptions unfilled because of the cost.[5] (That fraction is almost certainly higher now.) Sadly, the frailest are the least likely to have supplementary insurance. At an average cost of $1500 a year for each drug, someone without supplementary insurance who takes six different prescription drugs—and this is not rare—would have to spend $9000 out of pocket. Not many frail seniors have such deep pockets.

Furthermore, in one of the more perverse of the pharmaceutical industry's practices, prices are much higher for precisely the people who most need the drugs and can least afford them. The industry charges Medicare recipients without supplementary insurance much more than it does favored customers, such as large HMOs or the Veterans Affairs (VA) system. Because the latter buy in bulk, they can bargain for steep discounts or rebates. People without insurance have no bargaining power, and so they pay the highest prices.

In the past two years, we have started to see, for the first time, the beginnings of public resistance to rapacious pricing and other dubious practices of the pharmaceutical industry. It is mainly because of this resistance that drug companies are now blanketing us with public relations messages. And the magic words, repeated over and over like an incantation, are *research, innovation,* and *American.* Research. Innovation. American. It makes a great story.

Rhetoric Versus Reality

But while the rhetoric is stirring, it has very little to do with reality. First, research and development (R & D) is a relatively small part of the budgets of the big drug companies—dwarfed by their vast expenditures for marketing and administration, and smaller even than profits. In fact, year after year, for over two decades, this industry has been far and away the most profitable in the United States. (In 2003, for the first time, the industry lost its first-place position, coming in third, behind "mining, crude-oil production" and "commercial banks.") The prices drug companies charge have little relationship to the costs of making the drugs and could be cut dramatically without coming anywhere close to threatening R & D.

Second, the pharmaceutical industry is not especially innovative. As hard as it is to believe, only a handful of truly important drugs have been brought to market in recent years, and they were mostly based on taxpayer-funded research at academic institutions, small biotechnology companies, or the National Institutes of Health (NIH). The great majority of "new" drugs are not new at all but merely variations of older drugs already on the market. These are called "me-too" drugs. The idea is to grab a share of an established, lucrative market by producing something very similar to a top-selling drug. For instance, we now have six statins (Mevacor, Lipitor, Zocor, Pravachol, Lescol, and the newest, Crestor) on the market to lower cholesterol, all variants of the first. As Dr. Sharon Levine, associate executive director of the Kaiser Permanente Medical Group, put it, "If I'm a manufacturer and I can change one molecule and get another twenty years of patent rights, and convince physicians to prescribe and consumers to demand the next form of Prilosec, or weekly Prozac instead of daily Prozac, just as my patent expires, then why would I be spending money on a lot less certain endeavor, which is looking for brand-new drugs?"[6]

Third, the industry is hardly a model of American free enterprise. To be sure, it *is* free to decide which drugs to develop (me-too drugs instead of innovative ones, for instance), and it is free to price them as high as the traffic will bear, but it is utterly dependent on government-granted monopolies—in the form of patents and Food and Drug Administration (FDA)–approved exclusive marketing rights. If it is not particularly innovative in discovering new drugs, it is highly innovative—and aggressive—in dreaming up ways to extend its monopoly rights.

And there is nothing peculiarly American about this industry. It is the very essence of a global enterprise. Roughly half of the largest drug companies are based in Europe. (The exact count shifts because of mergers.) In 2002, the top ten were the American companies Pfizer, Merck, Johnson & Johnson, Bristol-Myers Squibb, and Wyeth (formerly American Home Products); the British companies GlaxoSmithKline and AstraZeneca; the Swiss companies Novartis and Roche; and the French company Aventis.[7] (In 2004, Aventis merged with another French company, Sanofi-Synthelabo, which catapulted it to third place.) All are much alike in their operations. All price their drugs much higher here than in other markets. Since the United States is the major profit center, it is simply good public relations for drug companies to pass themselves off as American, whether they are or not. It is true, however, that some of the European companies are now locating their R & D operations in the United States. They claim it is because we don't regulate prices, as does much of the rest of the world. But more likely it is because they want to feed on the unparalleled research output of American universities and the NIH. In other words, it's not private enterprise that draws them here but the very opposite—our publicly sponsored research enterprise.

Getting It Straight

This book will expose the real pharmaceutical industry—an industry that over the past two decades has moved very far from its original high purpose of discovering and producing useful new drugs. Now primarily a marketing machine to sell drugs of dubious benefit, this industry uses its wealth and power to co-opt every institution that might stand in its way, including the U.S. Congress, the Food and Drug Administration, academic medical centers, and the medical profession itself. (Most of its marketing efforts are focused on influencing doctors, since they must write the prescriptions.)

I witnessed firsthand the influence of the industry on medical research during my two decades at *The New England Journal of Medicine*. The staple of the journal is research about causes of and treatments for disease. Increasingly, this work is sponsored by drug companies. I saw companies begin to exercise a level of control over the way research is done that was unheard of when I first came to the journal, and the aim was clearly to load the dice to make sure their drugs looked good. As an example, companies would require researchers to compare a new drug with a placebo (sugar pill) instead of with an older drug. That way, the new drug would look good even though it might actually be worse than the older one. There are other ways to bias research, and not all of them can be spotted, even by experts. Obviously, we rejected such papers when we recognized them, but often they would turn up in other journals. Sometimes companies don't allow researchers to publish their results at all if they are unfavorable to the companies' drugs. As I saw industry influence grow, I became increasingly troubled by the possibility that much published research is seriously flawed, leading doctors to believe new drugs are generally more effective and safer than they actually are.

There are now signs that the industry is in deep trouble, mainly because it has so few innovative drugs in its pipeline. In addition, the public is growing increasingly skeptical about its high-flown claims, and purchasers of drugs are beginning to complain loudly about the intolerable prices. Profits, while still enormous, are starting to fall off, and stock prices for some of the largest companies are dropping. But instead of investing more in innovative drugs and moderating prices, drug companies are pouring money into marketing, legal maneuvers to extend patent rights, and government lobbying to prevent any form of price regulation.

If prescription drugs were like ordinary consumer goods, all this might not matter very much. But drugs are different. People depend on them for their health and even their lives. In the words of Senator Debbie Stabenow (D-Mich.), "It's not like buying a car or tennis shoes or peanut butter."[8] People need to know that there are some checks and balances on this industry, so that its quest for profits doesn't push every other consideration aside. In Chapter 13, I will suggest ways the system could be reformed to ensure that we have access to good drugs at reasonable prices and that the reality of this industry is finally brought into line with its rhetoric.

Reform will have to extend beyond the industry to the agencies and institutions it has co-opted, including the FDA and the medical profession and its institutions. This sort of thoroughgoing change will take government action, which in turn will require strong public pressure. It will be tough. Drug companies have the largest lobby in Washington, and they give copiously to political campaigns. Legislators are now so beholden to the pharmaceutical industry that it will be exceedingly difficult to break its lock on them.

But the one thing legislators need more than campaign contributions is votes. That is why you should know what's really going on—and why I have written this book. Contrary to the industry's public relations, you don't get what you pay for. The fact is that this industry is taking us for a ride, and there will be no real reform without an aroused and determined public to make it happen.

The Truth About
the Drug Companies

1

The $200 Billion Colossus

What does the eight-hundred-pound gorilla do?
Anything it wants to.

WHAT'S TRUE OF THE EIGHT-HUNDRED-
pound gorilla is true of the colossus that is the
pharmaceutical industry. It is used to doing pretty
much what it wants to do. The watershed year
was 1980. Before then, it was a good business, but
afterward, it was a stupendous one. From 1960 to
1980, prescription drug sales were fairly static as a
percent of U.S. gross domestic product, but from
1980 to 2000, they tripled. They now stand at
more than $200 billion a year.[1] Furthermore, since
the early 1980s, this industry has consistently
ranked as the most profitable in the United
States—by a long shot.[2] (Only in 2003 did it fall

from that position to rank third among the forty-seven industries listed in the Fortune 500.) Of the many events that contributed to their sudden great and good fortune, none had to do with the quality of the drugs the companies were selling.

In this chapter I'll give you an overview of the pharmaceutical industry—its meteoric rise and the recent, early signs of either a coming fall or an overhaul. I will not go into much detail here, I'll leave that to later chapters. What I want to do now is provide a quick look at what's under this rock when it's lifted. It's not a pretty sight.

Before I begin, a few words about the facts and figures I will use throughout the book. In most cases, I use data from the year 2001, because it is the most recent year for which information is reasonably complete for all the aspects of the industry I will consider. If I stick with one year, it will make it easier to see the whole picture. But for some important facts, I will use figures from 2002 and, whenever possible, 2003. In all cases, I will make it clear what year I am talking about.[3]

I also need to explain what I mean when I say this is a $200 billion industry. According to government sources, that is roughly how much Americans spent on prescription drugs in 2002. That figure refers to direct consumer purchases at drugstores and mail order pharmacies (whether paid for out of pocket or not), and it includes the nearly 25 percent markup for wholesalers, pharmacists, and other middlemen and retailers. But it does *not* include the large amounts spent for drugs administered in hospitals, nursing homes, or doctors' offices (as is the case for many cancer drugs). In most analyses, they are allocated to costs for those facilities.

Drug company revenues (or sales) are a little different, at least as they are reported in summaries of corporate annual reports. They usually refer to a company's worldwide sales, including those to health facilities. But they do not include the revenues of middlemen and retailers.

Perhaps the most quoted source of statistics on the pharmaceutical industry, IMS Health, estimated total worldwide sales for prescription drugs to be about $400 billion in 2002. About half were in the United States. So the $200 billion colossus is really a $400 billion megacolossus, but my focus in this book will be mainly on how the drug companies operate in the United States.

You should understand, however, that it is virtually impossible to be precise about most of these figures. Before drugs reach consumers, they pass through many hands and are paid for in exceedingly complicated, often hidden, ways. It is easy to compare apples and oranges without knowing it. You need to ask, for example, whether a number refers just to prescription drugs or includes over-the-counter drugs and other consumer products made by drug companies; whether it includes revenues for middlemen and retailers or not; whether it refers just to outpatient consumer purchases or also to health facility purchases; and whether it includes mail order purchases.

Let the Good Times Roll

The election of Ronald Reagan in 1980 was perhaps the most fundamental element in the rapid rise of big pharma—the collective name for the largest drug companies. With the Reagan administration came a strong pro-business shift not only in government policies but in society at large. And with the shift, the public attitude toward great wealth changed. Before then, there was something faintly disreputable about really big fortunes. You could choose to do well or you could choose to do good, but most people who had any choice in the matter thought it difficult to do both. That belief was particularly strong among scientists and other intellectuals. They could choose to live a comfortable but not luxurious life in academia, hoping to do exciting cutting-edge research, or they could "sell out" to industry and do less important but more remunerative work. Starting in the Reagan years and continuing through the 1990s, Americans changed their tune. It became not only reputable to be wealthy, but something close to virtuous. There were "winners" and there were "losers," and the winners were rich and deserved to be. The gap between the rich and poor, which had been narrowing since World War II, suddenly began to widen again, until today it is a yawning chasm.

The pharmaceutical industry and its CEOs quickly joined the ranks of the winners as a result of a number of business-friendly government actions. I won't enumerate all of them, but two are especially important. Beginning in 1980, Congress enacted a series of laws designed to speed the translation of tax-supported basic research into useful new products—a process sometimes referred to as "technology transfer." The goal was also to improve the position of American-owned high-tech businesses in world markets. The most important of these laws is known as the Bayh-Dole Act, after its chief sponsors, Senator Birch Bayh (D-Ind.) and Senator Robert Dole (R-Kans.). Bayh-Dole enabled universities and small businesses to patent discoveries emanating from research sponsored by the National Institutes of Health (NIH), the major distributor of tax dollars for medical research, and then to grant exclusive licenses to drug companies. Until then, taxpayer-financed discoveries were in the public domain, available to any company that wanted to use them. But now universities, where most NIH-sponsored work is carried out, can patent and license their discoveries, and charge royalties. Similar legislation permitted the NIH itself to enter into deals with drug companies that would directly transfer NIH discoveries to industry.

Bayh-Dole gave a tremendous boost to the nascent biotechnology industry, as well as to big pharma. Small biotech companies, many of them founded by university researchers to exploit their discoveries, proliferated rapidly. They now ring the major academic research institutions and often carry out the initial phases of drug development, hoping for lucrative deals with big drug companies that can market the new drugs. Usually both academic researchers and their institutions own equity in the biotechnology companies they are involved with. Thus, when a patent held by a university or a small biotech company is eventually licensed to a big drug company, all parties cash in on the public investment in research.

These laws mean that drug companies no longer have to rely on their own research for new drugs, and few of the large ones do. Increasingly, they rely on academia, small biotech start-up companies, and the NIH for that.[4] At least a third of drugs marketed by the major drug companies are now licensed from universities or small biotech companies, and these tend to be the most innovative ones.[5] While Bayh-Dole was clearly a bonanza for big pharma and the biotech industry, whether it is a net benefit to the public is arguable (I'll come back to that).

The Reagan years and Bayh-Dole also transformed the ethos of medical schools and teaching hospitals. These non-profit institutions started to see themselves as "partners" of industry, and they became just as enthusiastic as any entrepreneur about the opportunities to parlay their discoveries into financial gain. Faculty researchers were encouraged to obtain patents on their work (which were assigned to their universities), and they shared in the royalties. Many medical schools and teaching hospitals set up "technology transfer" offices to help in this activity and capitalize on faculty discoveries. As the entrepreneurial spirit grew during the 1990s, medical school faculty entered into other lucrative financial arrangements with drug companies, as did their parent institutions. One of the results has been a growing pro-industry bias in medical research—exactly where such bias doesn't belong. Faculty members who had earlier contented themselves with what was once referred to as a "thread-bare but genteel" lifestyle began to ask themselves, in the words of my grandmother, "If you're so smart, why aren't you rich?" Medical schools and teaching hospitals, for their part, put more resources into searching for commercial opportunities.

Starting in 1984, with legislation known as the Hatch-Waxman Act, Congress passed another series of laws that were just as big a bonanza for the pharmaceutical industry. These laws extended monopoly rights for brand-name drugs. Exclusivity is the lifeblood of the industry because it means that no other company may sell the same drug for a set period. After exclusive marketing rights expire, copies (called generic drugs) enter the market, and the price usually falls to as little as 20 percent of what it was.[6] There are two forms of monopoly rights—patents granted by the U.S. Patent and Trademark Office (USPTO) and exclusivity granted by the Food and Drug Administration (FDA). While related, they operate somewhat independently, almost as backups for each other. Hatch-Waxman, named for Senator Orrin Hatch (R-Utah) and Representative Henry Waxman (D-Calif.), was meant mainly to stimulate the foundering generic industry by short-circuiting some of the FDA requirements for bringing generic drugs to market. While successful in doing that, Hatch-Waxman also lengthened the patent life for brand-name drugs. Since then, industry lawyers have manipulated some of its provisions to extend patents far longer than the lawmakers intended.

In the 1990s, Congress enacted other laws that further increased the patent life of brand-name drugs. Drug companies now employ small armies of lawyers to milk these laws for all they're worth—and they're worth a lot. The result is that the effective patent life of brand-name drugs increased from about eight years in 1980 to about fourteen years in 2000.[7] For a blockbuster—usually defined as a drug with sales of over a billion dollars a year (like Lipitor or Celebrex or Zoloft)—those six years of additional exclusivity are golden. They can add billions of dollars to sales—enough to buy a lot of lawyers and have plenty of change left over. No wonder big pharma will do almost anything to protect exclusive marketing rights, despite the fact that doing so flies in the face of all its rhetoric about the free market.

Riding High

As their profits skyrocketed during the 1980s and 1990s, so did the political clout of drug companies. By 1990, the industry had assumed its present contours as a business with unprecedented control over its own fortunes. For example, if it didn't like something about the FDA, the federal agency that is supposed to regulate the industry, it could change it through direct pressure or through its friends in Congress. The top ten drug companies (which included European companies) had profits of nearly 25 percent of sales in 1990, and except for a dip at the time of President Bill Clinton's health care reform proposal, profits as a percentage of sales remained about the same for the next decade. (Of course, in absolute terms, as sales mounted, so did profits.) In 2001, the ten *American* drug companies in the Fortune 500 list (not quite the same as the top ten worldwide, but their profit margins are much the same) ranked far above all other American industries in average net return, whether as a percentage of sales (18.5 percent), of assets (16.3 percent), or of shareholders' equity (33.2 percent). These are astonishing margins. For comparison, the median net return for all other industries in the Fortune 500 was only 3.3 percent of sales. Commercial banking, itself no slouch as an aggressive industry with many friends in high places, was a distant second, at 13.5 percent of sales.[8]

In 2002, as the economic downturn continued, big pharma showed only a slight drop in profits—from 18.5 to 17.0 percent of sales. The most startling fact about 2002 is that the combined profits for the ten drug companies in the Fortune 500 ($35.9 billion) were more than the profits for all the other 490 businesses put together ($33.7 billion).[9] In 2003, profits of the Fortune 500 drug companies dropped to 14.3 percent of sales, still well above the median for all industries of 4.6 percent for the year. When I say this is a profitable industry, I mean *really* profitable. It is difficult to conceive of how awash in money big pharma is.

Drug industry expenditures for research and development, while large, were consistently far less than profits. For the top ten companies, they amounted to only 11 percent of sales in 1990, rising slightly to 14 percent in 2000. The biggest single item in the budget is neither R & D nor even profits but something usually called "marketing and administration"—a name that varies slightly from company to company. In 1990, a staggering 36 percent of sales revenues went into this category, and that proportion remained about the same for over a decade.[10] Note that this is two and a half times the expenditures for R & D.

These figures are drawn from the industry's own annual reports to the Securities and Exchange Commission (SEC) and to stockholders, but what actually goes into these categories is not at all clear, because drug companies hold that information very close to their chests. It is likely, for instance, that R & D includes many activities most people would consider marketing, but no one can know for sure. For its part, "marketing and administration" is a gigantic black box that probably includes what the industry calls "education," as well as advertising and promotion, legal costs, and executive salaries—which are whopping. According to a report by the nonprofit group Families USA, the former chairman and CEO of Bristol-Myers Squibb, Charles A. Heimbold, Jr., made $74,890,918 in 2001, not counting his $76,095,611 worth of unexercised stock options. The chairman of Wyeth made $40,521,011, exclusive of his $40,629,459 in stock options. And so on. This is an industry that amply rewards its own.[11]

In recent years, the top ten companies have included five European giants—GlaxoSmithKline, AstraZeneca, Novartis, Roche, and Aventis. Their profit margins are similar to those of their

American counterparts, and so are their expenditures for R & D and marketing and administration. Furthermore, they are members of the industry's trade association, the misleadingly named Pharmaceutical Research and Manufacturers of America (PhRMA). Recently I heard Daniel Vasella, the chairman and CEO of Novartis, speak at a conference. He was clearly pleased with the American commercial and research climate. "Free pricing and fast approval secure rapid access to innovation without rationing," he said, sounding like the most red-blooded of Americans, despite his charming Swiss accent.[12] His company is now moving its research operations to a site near the Massachusetts Institute of Technology (MIT), a hotbed of basic research surrounded by biotechnology companies. I suspect the move has nothing to do with "free pricing and fast approval" at all, and everything to do with the opportunity to profit from U.S. taxpayer-funded research under the terms of Bayh-Dole, and from the proximity of U.S. medical scientists who do the research.

Trouble

If 1980 was a watershed year for the pharmaceutical industry, 2000 may very well turn out to have been another one—the year things began to go wrong. As the booming economy of the late 1990s turned sour, many successful businesses found themselves in trouble. And as tax revenues dropped, state governments also found themselves in trouble. In one respect, the pharmaceutical industry is well protected against the downturn,

13

since it has so much wealth and power. But in another respect, it is peculiarly vulnerable, since it depends on employer-sponsored insurance and state-run Medicaid programs for much of its revenues. When employers and states are in trouble, so is big pharma.

And sure enough, in just the past couple of years, employers and the private health insurers with whom they contract have started to push back against drug costs. Most big managed care plans now bargain for steep price discounts. Most have also instituted three-tiered coverage for prescription drugs—full coverage for generic drugs, partial coverage for useful brand-name drugs, and no coverage for expensive drugs that offer no added benefit over cheaper ones. These lists of preferred drugs are called formularies, and they are an increasingly important method for containing drug costs. Big pharma is feeling the effects of these measures, although not surprisingly, it has become adept at gaming the system—mainly by inducing (I'll discuss how later) doctors or health plans to put expensive, brand-name drugs on formularies.

State governments, too, are looking for ways to cut their drug costs. Some state legislatures are crafting measures that would permit them to regulate prescription drug prices for state employees, Medicaid recipients, and the uninsured. Like managed care plans, they are creating formularies of preferred drugs. The industry is fighting these efforts tooth and nail—mainly with its legions of lobbyists and lawyers. It fought the state of Maine all the way to the U.S. Supreme Court, which in

2003 upheld Maine's right to bargain with drug companies for lower prices, while leaving open the details. But that war has just begun, and it promises to go on for years and get very ugly.

Recently the public has shown signs of being fed up. The fact that Americans pay much more for prescription drugs than Europeans and Canadians is now widely known. An estimated 1 to 2 million Americans buy their medicines from Canadian drugstores over the Internet, despite the fact that in 1987, in response to heavy industry lobbying, a compliant Congress had made it illegal for anyone other than manufacturers to import prescription drugs from other countries.[13] In addition, there is a brisk traffic in bus trips for people in border states to travel to Canada or Mexico to buy prescription drugs. Most of those on the buses are senior citizens, who not only pay more for drugs than people in neighboring countries but also pay more than younger neighbors in their own hometowns. The resentment among senior citizens is palpable, and they constitute a powerful voter bloc—a fact not lost on Congress or state legislatures.

The industry faces other, less well-known problems. It happens that, by chance, some of the top-selling drugs—with combined sales of around $35 billion a year—are scheduled to go off patent within a few years of one another.[14] This drop over the cliff began in 2001, with the expiration of Eli Lilly's patent on its blockbuster antidepressant Prozac. In the same year, AstraZeneca lost its patent on Prilosec, the original "purple pill" for heartburn, which at its peak brought in a stunning $6 billion a year. Bristol-Myers Squibb lost its bestselling diabetes drug, Glucophage. The unusual cluster of expirations will continue for another couple of years. While it represents a huge loss to the industry as a whole, for some companies it's a disaster. Schering-Plough's blockbuster allergy drug, Claritin, brought in fully a third of that company's revenues before its patent expired in 2002.[15] Claritin is now sold over the counter for far less than its prescription price. So far, the company has been unable to make up for the loss by trying to switch Claritin users to Clarinex—a drug that is virtually identical but has the advantage of still being on patent.

Even worse is the fact that there are very few drugs in the pipeline ready to take the place of blockbusters going off patent. In fact, that is the biggest problem facing the industry today, and its darkest secret. All the public relations about innovation is meant to obscure precisely this fact. The stream of new drugs has slowed to a trickle, and few of them are innovative in any sense of that word. Instead, the great majority are variations of oldies but goodies—"me-too" drugs. Companies are merging to combine their pipelines or comarketing the same drug while scrambling to find drugs to license from the government, universities, and biotechnology companies. But these sources are themselves experiencing difficulties in coming up with new drugs.

Of the seventy-eight drugs approved by the FDA in 2002, only seventeen contained new active ingredients, and only seven of these were classified by the FDA as improvements over older drugs. The other seventy-one drugs approved that year were variations of old drugs or deemed no better than drugs already on the market. In other words, they were me-too drugs. Seven of seventy-eight is not much of a yield. Furthermore, of those seven, not one came from a major U.S. drug company.[16]

Losing Support

For the first time, this gigantic industry is finding itself in serious difficulty. It is facing, as one industry spokesman put it, "a perfect storm." To be sure, profits are still beyond anything most other industries could hope for, but they have recently fallen, and for some companies they fell a lot. And that is what matters to investors. Wall Street doesn't care how high profits are today, only how high they will be tomorrow. For some companies, stock prices have plummeted. Nevertheless, the industry keeps promising a bright new day. It bases its reassurances on the notion that the mapping of the human genome and the accompanying burst in genetic research will yield a cornucopia of important new drugs. Left unsaid is the fact that big pharma is depending on government, universities, and small biotech companies for that innovation. But the predictions are beginning to sound a lot like *Waiting for Godot,* Samuel Beckett's grim play about two men waiting and waiting for something, and telling each other that whatever it is will come any minute. While there is no doubt that genetic discoveries will lead to treatments, the fact remains that it will probably be years before the basic research pays off with new drugs. In the meantime, the once-solid foundations of the big pharma colossus are shaking.

The hints of trouble and the public's growing resentment over high prices are producing the first cracks in the industry's formerly firm support in Washington. In 2000, Congress passed legislation that would have closed some of the loopholes in Hatch-Waxman and also permitted American pharmacies, as well as individuals, to import drugs from certain countries where prices are lower. In particular, they could buy back FDA-approved drugs from Canada that had been exported there. It sounds silly to "reimport" drugs that are marketed in the United States, but even with the added transaction costs, doing so is cheaper than buying them here. But the bill required the secretary of Health and Human Services to certify that the practice would not pose any "added risk" to the public, and secretaries in both the Clinton and Bush administrations, under pressure from the industry, refused to do that. In 2003, the House approved a bill that contained no such provision, and even many conservative Republicans backed it. Representative Dan Burton (R-Ind.), pointing out that his wife's breast cancer drug costs $360 a month in this country and only $60 in Germany, told *The New York Times,* "Every woman in America ought to be angry as hell at the pharmaceutical industry, and you can quote me on that."[17] But the bill didn't make it through the Senate.

The industry is also being hit with a tidal wave of government investigations and civil and criminal lawsuits. The litany of charges includes illegally overcharging Medicaid and Medicare, paying kickbacks to doctors, engaging in anticompetitive practices, colluding with generic companies to keep generic drugs off the market, illegally promoting drugs for unapproved uses, engaging in misleading direct-to-consumer advertising, and, of course, covering up evidence. Some of the settlements have been huge. TAP Pharmaceuticals, for instance, paid $875 million to settle civil and criminal charges of Medicaid and Medicare fraud in the marketing of its prostate cancer drug, Lupron.[18] As of this writing, litigation in this case continues. All of these efforts could be summed up as increasingly desperate marketing and patent games, activities that always skirted the edge of legality but now are sometimes well on the other side.

How is the pharmaceutical industry responding to its difficulties? One could hope drug companies would decide to pull up their socks—trim their prices, or at least make them more equitable, and put more of their money into trying to discover genuinely innovative drugs, instead of just talking about it. But that is not what is happening. Instead, drug companies are doing more of what got them into this situation. They are marketing their me-too drugs even more relentlessly. They are pushing even harder to extend their monopolies on top-selling drugs. And they are pouring more money into lobbying and political campaigns. As for innovation, they are still waiting for Godot and hoping desperately he will come.

The news is not all bad for the industry. The Medicare prescription drug benefit enacted in 2003, and scheduled to go into effect in 2006, promises a windfall for big pharma since it prohibits the government from negotiating prices. The immediate jump in pharmaceutical stock prices after the bill passed indicated that the industry and investors were well aware of the windfall. But at best, this legislation will be only a temporary boost for the industry. As costs rise, Congress will have to reconsider its industry-friendly decision to allow drug companies to set their own prices, no questions asked. More about that later.

This is an industry that in some ways is like the Wizard of Oz—still full of bluster but now being exposed as something far different from its image. Instead of being an engine of innovation, it is a vast marketing machine. Instead of being a free market success story, it lives off government-funded research and monopoly rights. Yet this industry occupies an essential role in the American health care system, and it performs a valuable function, if not in discovering important new drugs at least in developing them and bringing them to market. But big pharma is extravagantly rewarded for these relatively modest contributions. We get nowhere near our money's worth. The United States can no longer afford the pharmaceutical industry in its present form. The question is, Will the industry realize this and agree to real reforms that will curb its appetites but preserve its strengths? One thing is sure. It cannot continue on its present course.

2

The Creation of a New Drug

BRINGING A NEW DRUG TO MARKET IS A long haul. The industry is right about that, but wrong about its role in the process. Drug companies do not play anywhere near as large a part in research and development (R & D) as they would have us believe. It is not my intention to describe pharmaceutical R & D in any detail here, because that is not the focus of this book. But to help show how drug companies are selling us a bill of goods, I need to sketch the highlights. Most of what I will describe applies just to the few innovative drugs that come to market each year. For the many more "me-too" drugs—minor variations of drugs already on the market—the R & D process is much faster, since a great deal of it has already been done.

R & D Lite

You can't just randomly test chemicals to see if one will turn up that might be helpful in treating a disease. That would take an infinitely long time and be dangerous as well. Instead, most of the time you first have to understand the nature of the disease you want to treat—what has gone wrong in the body to cause it. That understanding needs to be fairly detailed, usually at the molecular level, if there is to be any hope of finding a drug that will safely and effectively interfere with the chain of events responsible for the disease. What researchers hope to find is some specific link in the chain that a drug will target.

So learning about the disease or condition is usually the beginning of the "research" part of R & D, and it can take a very long time—sometimes decades. There is no question that this is the most creative, and the least certain, part of the R & D process. Contrary to industry propaganda, it is almost always carried out at universities or government research labs, either in this country or abroad. In the United States, most of it is supported by the National Institutes of Health (NIH).[1]

Once the basic research has reached a critical point—that is, the disease is fairly well understood and so are the possible means to cure or ameliorate it—the search is on to discover or synthesize a molecule that will do the job and be safe to use.

That is the "development" part of R & D, and it is here that drug companies usually get involved—sometimes early, sometimes not until very late.

The development part of R & D is itself divided into two stages—preclinical and clinical. The preclinical stage has to do with finding promising drug candidates and then studying their properties in animals and cell cultures. Companies keep vast libraries of drug candidates—molecules that can now be screened very rapidly by computerized methods to see if they will target the Achilles' heel found by the basic research. In addition, new molecules can be synthesized or extracted from animal, plant, or mineral sources. Only the small fraction of drug candidates that make it through preclinical development go on to be tested in humans—the all-important clinical stage (more on that later).

According to the pharmaceutical industry, only one in five thousand candidate drugs make it to market[2]—one in one thousand survive preclinical testing, and of those, one in five make it through clinical testing. Paradoxically, although it is the least creative part of the process, clinical testing is the most expensive. The great majority of drug candidates are thus weeded out very early on, before there has been a great deal of money invested in them.

Research and development in biotechnology companies is similar in many ways to R & D in big drug companies. But instead of producing small molecules by chemical means, biotech companies focus primarily on making or modifying very large molecules, like proteins or hormones, by using living biological systems—often with recombinant DNA technology. Moreover, there is as yet no industry that makes generic biotech products, so monopoly rights are essentially unlimited. The distinctions between pharmaceutical and biotechnology companies are blurring, however, and the largest biotechnology companies are now members of the industry trade group Pharmaceutical Research and Manufacturers of America (PhRMA).

This is a bare-bones outline of R & D, and as in all bare-bones stories, things are rarely so clear-cut and there are many variations and exceptions. But the general point is that the longest, most difficult part of R & D is the front end—the research part—where the basic discoveries are made that identify how and where a disease or condition can be successfully attacked by a new pharmacological agent. Big drug companies usually contribute very little to that effort. Where they are important in the R & D for most drugs is at the development end, particularly in clinical testing.

An Example—The AZT Story

A good illustration of the R & D process for an innovative drug is the story of AZT (also called zidovudine), the first drug on the market to treat HIV/AIDS. Sold under the brand name Retrovir, it was originally manufactured by the drug company Burroughs Wellcome, which was later swallowed up by the much larger British firm GlaxoSmithKline. Despite the fact that the profits went at first to Burroughs Wellcome and now to

GlaxoSmithKline, the research and most of the development was done in government and university laboratories. This is a story worth recounting in some detail.[3]

Acquired immunodeficiency syndrome, or AIDS, burst on the scene in 1981, with the publication of three papers in *The New England Journal of Medicine* about a handful of gay men in Los Angeles and New York City who had died of overwhelming infections. Their immune systems were virtually obliterated, but no one could say why. The mysterious outbreak spread quickly and gave rise to intense worldwide efforts to find its cause. Speculation ranged widely, from contaminants in illegal drugs to a strange toxin picked up in Haiti to an unknown fungus. Within two short years, however, researchers at the NIH and the Pasteur Institute in Paris had pinpointed the culprit—a type of virus called a retrovirus.

A long time before that, in 1964, the AZT molecule had been synthesized at the Michigan Cancer Foundation as a possible treatment for cancer, and it was studied in many laboratories for that purpose. It did not prove effective against cancer, but in 1974, workers in a German laboratory found it to be effective against viral infections in mice. Burroughs Wellcome later acquired the molecule for possible use against the herpes virus.

Soon after the discovery of the cause of AIDS in 1983, Samuel Broder, head of the National Cancer Institute (NCI)—a part of the NIH—set up a team to screen antiviral agents from around the world as possible treatments for AIDS. Among the many he tested was Burroughs Wellcome's AZT. In 1985, his team, along with colleagues at Duke University, found that AZT was effective against the AIDS virus in test tubes and then in early clinical trials. Burroughs Wellcome immediately patented the drug to treat AIDS and carried out later trials that enabled it to receive Food and Drug Administration (FDA) approval in 1987, after a review of only a few months.

This was an extraordinary achievement. It took a mere six years from the first reports of a new disease for the cause to be found and an effective drug brought to market. But except for the speed, the story is not so different from countless other stories of how innovative drugs are discovered. It required bringing together many threads from many government, university, and other nonprofit sources, and only late in the process—in this case, very late—handing the drug off to a private company for further development, manufacture, and distribution.

As is also typical, the company claimed far more credit than it deserved, probably the better to justify its exorbitant prices—originally about $10,000 per year. After a self-congratulatory letter to *The New York Times* by the company's CEO, Broder and four colleagues from the NCI and Duke University responded angrily, reciting the seminal contributions Burroughs Wellcome did *not* make:

> The company specifically did not develop or provide the first application of the technology for determining whether a drug like AZT can suppress live AIDS virus in human cells,

nor did it develop the technology to determine at what concentration such an effect might be achieved in humans. Moreover, it was not first to administer AZT to a human being with AIDS, nor did it perform the first clinical pharmacology studies in patients. It also did not perform the immunological and virological studies necessary to infer that the drug might work, and was therefore worth pursuing in further studies. All of these were accomplished by the staff of the National Cancer Institute working with the staff of Duke University.

And they added, "Indeed one of the key obstacles to the development of AZT was that Burroughs Wellcome did not work with live AIDS virus nor wish to receive samples from AIDS patients."[4]

Testing Drugs on People—and Finding Volunteers

The clinical stage of drug development is regulated by the FDA.[5] By law, before a company can sell a new drug, it must prove to this agency that the drug is reasonably safe and effective. That proof usually requires a series of clinical trials, which are divided into three phases. Phase I entails giving the drug to a small number of usually normal volunteers to establish safe dosage levels and study its metabolism and side effects. (The exceptions are cancer and AIDS drugs, which are tested on people with the disease even in Phase I.) If the drug looks promising, it moves into Phase II, which involves as many as a few hundred patients with the relevant disease or medical condition. The drug is given at various doses, and the effects are usually compared with those in a similar group of patients not given the drug. Finally, if all goes well, Phase III clinical trials are undertaken. These evaluate the safety and effectiveness of the drug in much larger numbers of patients (hundreds to tens of thousands), and they nearly always involve a comparison group of patients. But not all drugs go through all phases. Sometimes the process is greatly truncated—to one or two trials. If the trials are successful, FDA approval follows.

Drug companies usually obtain a patent on a new drug before clinical testing begins, because it is difficult to keep information about the drug secret after this point. Patents protect companies against competition during the testing period. But clinical trials usually take a few years, and during that time the drug cannot be sold. That means clinical testing eats into a drug's twenty-year patent life—the time it can be sold without competition. For that reason, drug companies are in a terrific rush to get the trials out of the way so they can start to market the drug. And that means they need to find human subjects in a hurry.

Drug companies don't have direct access to human subjects, nor do they employ their own physicians to conduct clinical trials. They need to rely on doctors in teaching hospitals and private offices to do the studies, using either their own patients or volunteers recruited through various kinds of solicitations. At one time, most trials were done at medical schools and teaching hospitals. Companies would give grants to faculty researchers to carry out clinical trials under institutional auspices. That is no longer the case. Because there are so many more trials nowadays, and because drug companies are so eager to get them done quickly, they have shifted much of their business to new, for-profit companies set up exclusively to organize and carry out trials for the industry. These are called contract research organizations (CROs). In 2001, there were about a thousand of them operating around the world, with revenues from their drug company clients of some $7 billion. They establish networks of physicians who, working under the organizations' supervision, are paid to administer the study drugs and collect information on their effects.

The number of clinical trials under way in any given year is staggering.[6] In 2001, an estimated 80,000 of them were ongoing in the United States alone. That year, about 2.3 million Americans served as human subjects. These numbers are only approximate. Exact figures are hard to come by, since not all trials are registered with the FDA or NIH. The point is that the numbers are far larger than most people realize. In fact, it's quite likely that nearly everyone knows someone who has participated in a clinical trial.

Only some of the trials are to test new drugs to get FDA approval. Many are of drugs already on the market—called "post-marketing" or "Phase IV" studies. Often these are to find new uses for old drugs to expand their markets. A few are required by the FDA to look for unknown side effects. And a great many—perhaps most—are really, in the view of many critics, just excuses to pay doctors to put patients on a company's already-approved drug.

Even though the NIH spends nearly as much money on research as does the industry, it concentrates on basic research. Only about 10 percent of clinical trials are sponsored by the NIH, usually in academic medical centers.

All clinical trials cut into the limited supply of human volunteers. In fact, the scarcity of human subjects—not FDA roadblocks, as is often claimed by the pharmaceutical industry—is the biggest cause of delay in getting new drugs to market.[7] Large drug companies have centralized patient recruitment offices, which outsource many of the tasks to a growing number of independent recruitment firms, as well as to CROs. Potential subjects are solicited in a variety of ways—postings on health-related Internet sites; television, radio, and newspaper ads; individual mailings; and posters and flyers distributed throughout communities. Solicitations are often disguised as public service announcements. Drug companies also set up patient advocacy groups as magnets for people with specific diseases. These are rich sources of patients for clinical trials. Most human subjects are now recruited through these kinds of efforts, not referred by their doctors. They are usually paid from a few hundred to a few thousand dollars for participation in a trial.

Whatever they are paid, it is dwarfed by payments to doctors. To get human subjects, drug companies or contract research organizations routinely offer doctors large bounties (averaging about $7000 per patient in 2001) and sometimes bonuses for rapid enrollment. For example, according to a 2000 Department of Health and Human Services inspector general's report, physicians in one trial were paid $12,000 for each patient enrolled, plus another $30,000 on the enrollment of the sixth patient.[8] One risk of this bounty and bonus system is that it can induce doctors to enroll patients who are not really eligible. For instance, if it means an extra $30,000 to you to enroll a patient in an asthma study, you might very well be tempted to decide your next patient has asthma, whether he does or not ("Sounds like a little wheeze you have there. . . ."). Obviously, if the wrong patients are enrolled, the results of a trial are unreliable, and that is probably often the case. (More about biased research in Chapter 6.)

The FDA—Regulation and Reaction

As mentioned, the FDA's involvement with a drug begins at the clinical trials stage. Before trials can begin, a drug company must file an investigational new drug application with the FDA. It describes the proposed research in detail, including measures to protect the rights and welfare of human subjects. After all the trials are completed, which usually takes a few years, the company must file a new drug application to get FDA approval to go to market. With the help of eighteen advisory committees of outside experts, the agency reviews the application, which includes results of the clinical trials, along with other supporting evidence. Only if the drug passes this scrutiny is it allowed on the market. Companies are permitted to promote drugs only for the uses and at the doses for which they were approved, although once they are on the market, doctors may prescribe them for any use and at any dose they deem appropriate.

Generic drugs, you will remember, are copies of brand-name drugs whose exclusive marketing rights have expired. They, too, need FDA approval, but their manufacturers have to demonstrate only that they are equivalent to the brand-name drugs they copy. Since the passage of Hatch-Waxman in 1984, generic companies don't have to do clinical trials to show safety and effectiveness, because the brand-name companies have already done that.

Before leaving the subject of generic drugs, I should mention a new hybrid called "branded generics." Their active ingredients are similar but not identical to those of the brand-name drugs they mimic, so they supposedly do not infringe on patents, but they are said to be similar enough that they don't have to undergo clinical testing. Neither big pharma nor traditional generic companies are happy about the competition from branded generics, and both are mounting legal challenges. Branded generics are priced somewhere between brand-name drugs and true generics, and their market share is growing rapidly. They are likely to become very important in the biotech industry, where there are no traditional generics because it is difficult to show they are equivalent to the originals.

The FDA is also supposed to review drug labeling for accuracy, as well as advertisements for accuracy and balance. Even the most casual observer would have to conclude the agency fails at the latter. For one thing, it just doesn't have the resources to do the job. In 2001, the agency had only thirty people to review 34,000 advertisements.[9] Additionally, the FDA is charged with ensuring safe manufacturing standards, but here again, it is woefully understaffed for that task.[10]

The first regulatory agency in the country, the FDA was an outgrowth of the 1906 Food and Drug Act, which prohibited interstate commerce in falsely labeled and adulterated foods, drinks, and drugs.[11] That act, in turn, was a response to a series of magazine exposés of widespread filth in meatpacking plants, the use of poisonous preservatives and dyes in foods, and cure-all claims for worthless and dangerous patent medicines. Upton Sinclair's sensational portrayal of the meatpacking industry in his 1906 book *The Jungle* was an added impetus. The FDA now consists of 9,000 people (still a fairly small agency by Washington standards), with the awesome responsibility of overseeing three gigantic industries—food; drugs, vaccines, blood products, and medical devices (such as artificial heart valves); and cosmetics. These industries consist of some 95,000 different businesses with more than a trillion dollars' worth of sales annually.

In 1938, in the wake of a cluster of deaths from the use of a poisonous solvent in a new sulfa drug, Congress decided that the FDA should take more systematic steps to protect the public. Accordingly, the agency was given the specific task of requiring drug companies to prove that their products were safe before they could be sold. It wasn't until 1951, however, that prescriptions were required. In that year, Congress decided that doctors' prescriptions would be necessary to purchase drugs that could not be used safely without medical expertise. In 1962, another requirement was added. Drug companies had to prove their products were not just safe but also effective. That mandate soon gave rise to rules for carrying out clinical trials—the only way to show safety and effectiveness unequivocally.

The FDA is the pharmaceutical industry's favorite whipping boy. Drug companies and their acolytes in the media and Congress relentlessly berate the agency for putting bureaucratic obstacles in the way of getting "lifesaving drugs" to market. In particular, *The Wall Street Journal* and an organization called the Washington Legal Foundation hammer away at the agency incessantly. You would think, from reading their material, that the FDA is filled with capricious bureaucrats who spend all their days dreaming up ways to prevent Americans from getting vital medicines—with what motive, they're not clear. In one editorial, for example, *The Wall Street Journal* urged the FDA to "reform its slow and blinkered approach to potentially lifesaving therapies" and "view itself not as a gatekeeper but as a facilitator."[12] The Washington Legal Foundation warned in one of its advertisements in *The New York Times,* "Make no mistake, unnecessary approval delays have human costs. Rigid procedures, endless data requests, and the pursuit of absolutely risk-free products keep new treatments bottled up at FDA while radically ill patients wait, suffer, and often die."[13]

Sounds bad, but it just isn't true. The total time from the beginning of preclinical testing of a candidate drug to its coming on the market ranges from about six to ten years. But the time for FDA review accounts for only a small fraction of that—about sixteen months in 2002 and getting shorter. In fact, under pressure from the industry, the agency in the past decade has moved from being the slowest regulatory drug agency in the developed world to being the fastest. In special cases, approval time can be cut to weeks. Of course, the drug companies would like to cut the whole thing—testing and approval—down to virtually nothing, because the time comes out of the drug's patent life.

But except for libertarian extremists and *The Wall Street Journal,* who could possibly want that? Which of us would pretend that the free market can decide whether drugs and medical devices are safe and effective? Do you really want your doctor to rely on the word of drug companies that the antibiotic prescribed for your pneumonia will work? Doctors are not wizards, and they have no way to know whether drugs will work well unless they can rely on an impartial agency like the FDA to review the scientific data. Deciding simply on the basis of whether individual patients seem to respond is a notoriously unreliable and dangerous method. To be sure, doctors might be able to judge for themselves by assiduously keeping up with medical journals and textbooks, but the truth is most don't have the time to do that. Furthermore, without the pressure of the FDA to make companies do clinical trials, there would be far fewer informative reports published in the medical journals.

Discovering innovative drugs and bringing them to market is a long and difficult process, and there are no shortcuts. It is crucial that new drugs be shown to be safe and effective, as judged by an impartial agency responsible for the public health and not a corporation responsible for the value of its shareholders' stock. The alternative is to go back to 1906, when anything and everything could be sold as a miracle cure and the watchword was caveat emptor. As for all the "me-too" drugs that now constitute the major output of the pharmaceutical industry, it's very hard to make the case that the world should be in any hurry for the next one.

3

How Much Does the Pharmaceutical Industry *Really* Spend on R & D?

DRUG COMPANIES CLAIM DRUGS ARE so expensive because they need to cover their very high research and development (R & D) costs. In 2001, they put these costs at $802 million (in 2000 dollars) for each new drug they bring to market. (Later, the consulting firm Bain & Company upped that to $1.7 billion per drug, but they included marketing expenditures.) Implicit in this claim is a kind of blackmail: If you want drug companies to keep turning out life-saving drugs, you will gratefully pay whatever they charge. Otherwise, you may wake up one morning and find there are no more new drugs.

As Alan F. Holmer, president of the industry's trade association, Pharmaceutical Research and Manufacturers of America (PhRMA), said in a radio interview, "Believe me, if we impose price controls on the pharmaceutical industry, and if you reduce the R & D that this industry is able to provide, it's going to harm my kids and it's going to harm those millions of other Americans who have life-threatening conditions."[1]

The industry admits that it charges Americans, particularly those without insurance, far more than it does people in other countries, but it insists it needs to do so in order to make up for the fact that other countries regulate prices. Americans must bear a disproportionate share of R & D costs, they say, because nobody else will or can. This argument is trotted out whenever there is the faintest whiff in the air that anyone is considering price controls in the United States. William Safire used it in a *New York Times* column where he warned, "The price of most new prescription drugs is high in the U.S. mainly because it includes the producers' huge investment in scientific research."[2]

The Black Box

Given that argument, it is crucial to ask how much it costs the industry to bring a new drug to market. Is it really $802 million? Getting an answer to that question is not as easy as it sounds, because the industry will not supply the necessary data. Individual companies report total R & D expenditures in their Securities and Exchange Commission (SEC) filings, and PhRMA's annual report gives industrywide averages for total R & D, as well as average figures for the breakdown of expenses by general R & D functions (where one of the biggest categories is "other"). But the companies do not make available the really important details, such as what each company spends, and for what purposes, on the development of each drug. They claim that that information is proprietary. As Representative Henry Waxman (D-Calif.) commented, "The basic problem is that all pharmaceutical costs, including research, are in a black box, hidden from view. There is no transparency."[3] This secrecy is odd for an industry that justifies its high prices by its high R & D costs.

We also don't know what activities are included under the heading "R & D." Much of it may really be marketing, which is counted as R & D because it looks better to have a large R & D budget than to have a large marketing budget. One clue that this may be the case is the fact that a growing fraction of clinical trials are Phase IV studies. You will remember from Chapter 2 that these are studies of drugs already on the market—supposedly for the purpose of learning more about long-term effects and possible additional uses. But many Phase IV studies are mainly ways to introduce doctors and patients to a company's drug by paying clinicians to use it and then report some minimal information back to the company. In other words, they can be seen as promotional gimmicks.

Despite the fact that R & D is a black box, you can crudely calculate costs per drug simply by dividing the industry's own figure for total R & D by the number of new drugs. That assumes, of course, a steady state—that about the same number of drugs enter the market each year and total R & D costs stay fairly constant. That is not quite the case. Nevertheless, this simple calculation is a way of making a very rough estimate. If you look at the year 2000, when the industry claims to have spent $26 billion on R & D and ninety-eight drugs entered the market, the average pretax cost for each drug was, under those assumptions, no greater than $265 million, and the after-tax cost about $175 million. (Research and development costs are tax deductible, and the corporate tax rate is now about 34 percent.) That would be the maximum, since it is likely that PhRMA's total R & D figure is inflated by activities that many would regard as promotional, and the industry receives generous tax credits as well as deductions. If you take the next year, when the industry claimed it spent $30 billion and only sixty-six drugs entered the market, the pretax cost per drug would be higher— $455 million—and the after-tax cost $300 million.[4] As you can see, any attempt to determine the cost per drug is highly dependent on the number of drugs—a subject I'll come back to later.

The consumer advocacy group Public Citizen performed a much more sophisticated analysis using the same approach.[5] They looked at all the drugs that entered the market between 1994 and 2000 (thus smoothing out the yearly variations), and made appropriate allowances for the long lag time between R & D expenditures and the dates the drugs came on the market. They found that after-tax costs were probably less than $100 million for each drug approved during that period. Other independent analysts have reached similar conclusions. Even using PhRMA's own figures for total R & D costs for the decade of the 1990s, it can be calculated that the cost per drug came to around $100 million after taxes. That is a lot, but it's a far cry from the much-vaunted $802 million.

The Imaginary Number

So where did the $802 million figure come from? And why has it been uncritically accepted? The number was the finding of a group of economists, headed by Joseph DiMasi of the Tufts Center for the Study of Drug Development, and it was announced with much fanfare at a press conference in Philadelphia on November 30, 2001.[6] The Tufts Center is largely supported by the pharmaceutical industry, and this was an updating of an analysis done by the same group over a decade ago. The results this time were about twice as high. Ever since the press conference, PhRMA and leaders and defenders of the industry have trumpeted the findings as a justification for high drug prices. Kenneth I. Kaitlin, the director of the Tufts Center, said, "Bringing new drugs to market has always been an expensive, high-risk proposition, and our latest analysis indicates that costs have continued to skyrocket." The president of PhRMA, Alan F. Holmer, welcomed the study as confirmation that "drug development is staggeringly expensive."[7] The media seemed to accept it pretty much at face value. Under the heading "Research Cost for New Drugs Said to Soar," for instance, *The New York Times* reported

41

the next day, "A new round in the national debate over prescription drugs opened today with a study from researchers at Tufts University estimating that the average cost of developing a new drug has more than doubled since 1987, to $802 million."[8] The rest of the media carried similar stories.

It was not until a year and a half later that the Tufts group actually published their analysis and it became possible to see how it was done.[9] What they did was to look at sixty-eight drugs developed at ten drug companies over about a decade. But the names of the companies and the names of the drugs were never revealed. Furthermore, all the data on the costs of those drugs were supplied by the companies to the Tufts group confidentially, and as far as I can tell, the authors were not able to verify the information. They were supposed to take the companies' word, and we were supposed to take theirs. That situation is extremely unusual in scientific publishing, where it is understood that the salient data will be made available to readers so they can evaluate the analysis for themselves.

But one thing *is* clear from the paper. The $802 million figure has nothing to do with the "average cost of developing a new drug," in the words of *The New York Times*.[10] It refers only to the cost of developing a tiny handful of the very most expensive drugs. Let's look at this misunderstanding more closely, because it is crucial.

Every year the Food and Drug Administration (FDA) approves a number of new drug applications, which means that those drugs can enter the market. That is what most people mean when they say "new" drugs. In 2002, for instance, the number was seventy-eight, as I mentioned in Chapter 1. But of the new drugs, only a minority are newly discovered or synthesized molecules. The FDA classifies these as new molecular entities (NMEs). The others are just new versions of drugs already on the market. In 2002, only seventeen of the seventy-eight newly approved drugs were NMEs.[11] And of the NMEs, only a fraction are developed entirely by the drug companies themselves. Most of the rest are simply licensed or otherwise acquired from university or government laboratories or biotechnology companies.

The Tufts analysis was restricted to NMEs developed entirely within drug companies—what the authors called "self-originated NCEs" (the old term for NMEs). But these constitute only a tiny percentage of all new drugs. As you might expect, this handful of drugs cost companies more to develop than the others. It is cheaper to license a drug from someone else or make a new version of an old drug. In fact, the Tufts authors state that the drug companies they surveyed spent 75 percent of their R & D money (including the costs of Phase IV studies) on these few self-originated NMEs.[12] I find this an almost unbelievably high percentage, and there is no way to verify it, but the point is the companies agree that they spend much more on self-originated NMEs than on other drugs.

Why didn't the media catch on to the fact that the $802 million figure applied only to a sample of highly selected and very costly drugs? One possible answer is that the industry didn't want them to. In their public relations, PhRMA and the drug companies strongly imply that $802 million is the average for *all* new drugs. Even the Tufts authors seemed to suggest that in the short summary of their paper, where they wrote, "The research and development costs of sixty-eight randomly selected new drugs were obtained from a survey of ten pharmaceutical firms. These data were used to estimate the average pre-tax cost of new drug development."[13] Nothing about *which* new drugs.

. . . And Doubling It

There is a second problem with the Tufts estimate. It is not the actual out-of-pocket cost at all, even for the special group of drugs considered. That cost was $403 million per drug. The $802 million is what the authors call the "capitalized" cost—that is, it includes the estimated revenue that might have been generated if the money spent on R & D had instead been invested in the equity market. It's as though drug companies don't *have* to spend any money at all on R & D; they could invest it instead. Or, in the author's technical jargon, "the expenditures must be capitalized at an appropriate discount rate, [which is] the expected return that investors forego during development when they invest in pharmaceutical R & D instead of an equally risky portfolio of financial securities."[14] This theoretically lost revenue is known as the "opportunity cost," and the Tufts consultants simply tacked it on to the industry's out-of-pocket costs. That accounting maneuver nearly doubled the $403 million to $802 million.

The authors justified the maneuver on the grounds that, from the perspective of investors, a pharmaceutical company is really just one kind of investment, which they choose among other possible options. But while this may be true for investors, surely it is not true for the companies themselves. The latter have no choice but to spend money on R & D if they wish to be in the pharmaceutical business. They are not investment houses. So you can hardly look at the money spent on R & D as money that could have been spent on something else. The Tufts authors say adding opportunity costs is standard accounting practice, and that may be so, but in the context of pharmaceutical R & D, it simply makes no sense.

And there is a third problem with the estimate. It is in pre-tax dollars. But R & D expenses are fully tax deductible. On top of that, drug companies enjoy a number of tax credits worth billions of dollars, including a 50 percent credit for the costs of testing "orphan drugs"—those with an expected market of fewer than 200,000 people. As of the year 2000, the FDA had listed 231 orphan drugs since the tax credit was instituted in 1983. One of those is Retrovir, the first drug for HIV/AIDS, discussed in the last chapter. With the worldwide HIV/AIDS epidemic, the market for Retrovir is far greater than 200,000, but it was considered an orphan drug nonetheless. In addition, the tax credit extends to other drugs if companies can make a case that they are unlikely to be profitable.[15] (What other business gets such a deal?) Presumably, drug companies claiming these tax credits would have to share with the Internal Revenue Service information they are unwilling to share with anyone else—the R & D costs of individual drugs. One wonders whether and how often this information is audited.

In any case, when all the tax benefits are taken together, big pharma pays relatively little in taxes. Between 1993 and 1996, drug companies were taxed at a 16.2 percent rate, compared with an average tax rate of 27.3 percent for all other major industries.[16] Many experts believe that the R & D cost estimate should therefore be lowered by the amount of corporate tax avoided. These tax savings would reduce the net cost of R & D by a percentage at least equal to the 34 percent corporate tax rate (not considering tax credits). You could argue about whether this adjustment is reasonable, but if one accepts that it is, it would reduce the Tufts estimate of $403 million (before adding "opportunity costs") to an after-tax net of less than $266 million per drug.

But remember, that would be the average out-of-pocket, after-tax R & D costs for only the new molecular entities developed entirely in-house, not the average cost of all the drugs approved. Most approved drugs entering the market are not really new, or they are acquired from other sources, or both. I would guess that the real cost per drug is well under $100 million. Were it anywhere near the claimed $802 million, the industry would not be so secretive about the data.

High R & D, Higher Profits

The general industry excitement about the $802 million announcement was partly predicated on the notion that R & D costs can be equated with value. But that is not necessarily true. In fact, they could instead be an indication of inefficiency. Ray Gilmartin, president and CEO of the pharmaceutical giant Merck, sounded the one cautionary note from industry: "If there is any concern, it should be on the part of pharmaceutical companies that are less efficient and that aren't delivering drugs of value to patients."[17] Right. In fact, rising R & D costs per drug can simply mean there are not many new drugs coming to market. To take the extreme, what would the R & D cost per drug be if the entire industry turned out only one new drug? In 2001, it would have been $30 billion. Would that have been an indication of value? Could it in any way be construed as an indication that the industry was productive? Of course not.

Although that extreme case is absurd, something like it is actually happening. Over the past few years, the number of new drugs has been declining, and so has their quality. Yet R & D expenditures have been getting higher. The point is that large R & D expenditures ought to raise the question of whether we are getting our money's worth. How much is too much to spend on developing new drugs, and who should decide? Is the entire industry, in Mr. Gilmartin's words, growing "less efficient"— spending way too much for too little? This matters, not only because we need good drugs but also because the industry expects to be paid back for its R & D expenses.

Let's return to big pharma's essential argument that curbing prices would cut into its R & D spending. Would that really be necessary? Whatever the cost of bringing each new drug to market, total R & D expenditures of the pharmaceutical industry—according to PhRMA, now over $30 billion for all its members in the United States and abroad—are indeed large. But they should be compared with reported expenditures on marketing and administration, which are more than twice as much as R & D expenditures. Furthermore, the most important financial fact about the major drug companies is that, despite their expenses, they are enormously profitable.

In 2002, when the ten U.S. drug companies in the Fortune 500 list had combined worldwide sales of about $217 billion and spent just over 14 percent of that on R & D (about $31 billion), they had a profit margin of 17 percent ($36 billion). Thus, profits were substantially more than R & D costs. Even more startling is the fact that they spent a walloping 31 percent of sales (about $67 billion) on marketing and administration.[18]

Given these figures, it is very hard to make a case that lower prices would reduce R & D spending. In fact, whether price regulation would cut into R & D would depend entirely on whether the industry wanted it to. They could, for example, cut administrative or marketing costs instead, or they could accept lower but still very good profits. Most likely they would *choose* to cut their R & D budgets to maintain profits and marketing, but they wouldn't *have* to. As long as profits are consistently higher than R & D costs, drug companies cannot make a case that reduced prices would necessarily cripple research and development.

The drug companies would protest that there is no way they could voluntarily accept lower profit margins, or reduce their marketing, upon which they believe their profits depend. They would say Wall Street demands that they maximize the value of their shareholders' stock, which means doing everything they can to increase profits. It is their fiduciary responsibility to do so. But that should tell us something about the wisdom of entrusting the development of medicines to an industry that is entirely accountable to investors, and not to the public (except in the limited sense that drugs are supposed to be safe and effective).

It is also worth asking why this extraordinarily profitable industry needs so much equity capital. It could easily finance its R & D out of its sales. One possible explanation is that drug company executives are paid partly in stock options. Families USA, a nonprofit foundation, looked into the 2001 value of the unexercised stock options held by the top executives in each of ten large drug companies. They found the average to be $52 million.[19] But stock options are valuable only when the market price of the company's stock exceeds the exercise price of the option. That creates a powerful incentive for executives to keep stock prices rising any way they can. Enron executives tried to do it illegally, but the incentive is the same in other investor-owned corporations that pay executives in stock options.

Drug Pricing—What Does R & D Have to Do with It?

Big pharma would like us to believe that prices of their top-selling drugs have to be high to cover their costs, including the costs of all the drugs that never make it to market. The implication is that drug companies are just eking out a living—something we know is a long way from the truth. Furthermore, without any information about how they spend their R & D dollars, it's impossible to evaluate the extent to which profitable drugs subsidize ones that never make it. Nor is it possible to decide whether the R & D is worth it. If patients must pay thousands of dollars a year for a vital drug, doesn't the public have a right to know what the markup is and where the money goes? We know that much of it goes to profits and marketing, but we also need to know what companies spend on which drugs and for what purposes. An industry so beholden to taxpayers for research, patent protection, and tax breaks—in short, for taking most of the risks out of the business—ought to do more than just report total R & D expenditures. It should open the black box.

Despite all the rhetoric to the contrary, this is not a high-risk industry in any normal sense of the term. In fact, drug companies are not willing to take any chances at all. As one indication, the law mentioned earlier that provides tax credits equal to 50 percent of the cost of testing orphan drugs extends the credits to other drugs if "there is no reasonable expectation that the cost of developing and making available in the United States a drug for disease or condition will be recovered from sales in the

United States of such drug." In other words, if you can't make a profit, the government will help you out. This is an industry well protected against losses. Risky businesses have variable returns, but the pharmaceutical industry has been, year after year, the most profitable in the United States. As Alan Sager, codirector of the Health Reform Program at Boston University, put it, "If you went to Las Vegas with $1000 and routinely came back with $1400, could your family accuse you of gambling?"[20] What these companies are, in fact, claiming is an entitlement not only to recoup anything they wish to spend on R & D but to make an exorbitant profit margin as well.

The truth is that there is no particular reason to think that R & D costs, no matter what they are, have anything to do with drug pricing. The irrepressibly candid Mr. Gilmartin, president and CEO of Merck, seemed to acknowledge that. Referring to the $802 million per drug estimate, he remarked, "The price of medicines isn't determined by their research costs. Instead, it is determined by their value in preventing and treating disease. Whether Merck spends $500 million or $1 billion developing a medicine, it is the doctor, the patient, and those paying for our medicines who will determine its true value."[21] That sounds to me like an admission that the industry will charge whatever the traffic will bear, and it has little to do with R & D costs. And that is about right. Unfortunately, contrary to Mr. Gilmartin, it doesn't have much to do with medical value either, as I will show.

4

Just How Innovative
Is This Industry?

AS AMERICANS GROW INCREASINGLY
skeptical about the claim that drug prices need to
be high to cover research and development costs,
the pharmaceutical industry falls back on Plan B
—the claim that high prices are necessary to reward innovation. Yes, the industry confesses,
profits are indeed high. But remember, extra high
profits stimulate us to be extra creative. Look at
all the wonderful new drugs you get in return.
Once again, Alan F. Holmer, president of the
Pharmaceutical Research and Manufacturers of
America (PhRMA), sounds the theme. In his tire-
less crusade against any form of price regulation,

he put it this way, "Voters do not want to jeopardize the miracle of life-saving innovation in modern medicines."[1] The contention that we need to treat this industry with kid gloves to preserve "life-saving innovation" calls for a close look at big pharma's drugs. Are they truly innovative? And if so, who deserves the credit?

The Output of Innovative Drugs

Even a glance at the industry's output shows that miracles are few and far between. The evidence is on the U.S. Food and Drug Administration (FDA) website (www.fda.gov/cder/rdmt/pstable.htm). As I explained in Chapter 2, before a drug can be marketed, a company must file a new drug application with the FDA. The FDA then classifies the drug in two ways. First, it looks at the compound itself, what the agency calls the "chemical type." Is it a molecule that is already on the market in some form? Or is it brand new—what the FDA calls a "new molecular entity (NME)"? If it's a new molecule, then it's classified as a number 1 drug. Otherwise, it is classified as a chemical derivative, or new formulation or combination of an old drug. Or it might just be an old drug with a new manufacturer.

The second way the drug is classified is according to whether it is likely to offer any benefit above drugs already on the market to treat the same condition. If so, then the FDA gives it more rapid attention. This is called a "priority review," which is for drugs likely to represent a "significant improvement compared to marketed products, in the treatment, diagnosis, or prevention of a disease." The agency lists these drugs with the abbreviation "P." All other drugs receive a standard—or "S"—review. A "standard review" drug, in the FDA's words, "appears to have therapeutic qualities similar to those of one or more already marketed drugs."

New molecular entities aren't necessarily classified as priority review drugs. Even brand-new molecules may not be any better than an older drug for the same condition. And likewise, priority review drugs are not necessarily new molecular entities. It's possible for an old drug to be modified in such a way that it offers a definite treatment advantage over the earlier form. But as a general rule, a drug that can be called innovative in any usual meaning of the word is both a new molecular entity and a priority review drug. In other words, the drug is a new molecule that will probably be a significant improvement over drugs already on the market. (The industry often uses the word *innovative* to mean just a new molecular entity, but that leaves aside the all-important question of whether the drug offers any clinical advantages over old drugs.)

So let's look at the yield over the five years 1998 through 2002—the most recent five years for which I have complete data on both the numbers and the properties of the drugs. Altogether, 415 new drugs were approved—an average of 83 per year. Of those, 133 (32 percent) were new molecular entities. The others were variations of old drugs. And of those 133, only 58 were priority review drugs. That averages out to no more than 12 innovative drugs per year, or 14 percent of the total. Not only is the yield very low, but over those five years, it got worse. In both 2001 and 2002, only 7 innovative drugs (that is, new molecular entities with priority review) were approved each year, as compared with 9 in 2000, 19 in 1999, and 16 in 1998. *And that's it—the five-year grand total of innovative drugs from this mighty industry.*

Now, just to get a sense of what kinds of drugs are being produced and which companies are producing them, let's look closely at the fourteen innovative drugs for those last two years. Were they miracles from big pharma, as suggested by Mr. Holmer? At the time, there were some thirty-five members of PhRMA, consisting of the world's major pharmaceutical companies and a few of the larger biotechnology companies.[2] Of the seven innovative drugs approved in 2001, five came from companies that were PhRMA members—two from the Swiss company Novartis and one each from the American companies Merck, Allergan, and Gilead Sciences (a biotechnology company).[3] The Novartis drugs were the orphan drug Gleevec, for a rare form of leukemia (I'll come back to this drug in a bit), and Zometa, an injection to treat a complication of widespread cancer. The Merck drug was Cancidas, an injection to treat a rare fungus infection when other treatments have failed; the Allergan drug was Lumigan, an ophthalmic solution for glaucoma not responsive to other treatment; and the Gilead drug was Viread, a drug similar to AZT to treat HIV/AIDS.

Of the seven innovative drugs approved in 2002, only three

came from members of PhRMA: Zelnorm, a Novartis drug for irritable bowel syndrome with constipation; Eloxatin, an injection made by the French company Sanofi-Synthelabo, to treat (although rarely, if ever, to cure) widespread colon cancer when other treatments have failed; and Hepsera, a treatment for hepatitis B made by Gilead Sciences. Nothing from any major American drug company.

That output hardly seems to warrant Mr. Holmer's high-flown rhetoric. To be sure, we do occasionally get important new drugs. Gleevec, for example, may mean the difference between life and death for people with a certain type of leukemia. But in recent years truly innovative drugs like that have come along very infrequently. Most of the drugs mentioned here, even though innovative, were last-ditch treatments—rarely cures—to be used when older drugs hadn't worked. And given the trend, we have to ask whether the $30-plus billion big pharma ostensibly puts into its R & D is well spent. We also have to conclude that, if high prices and profits in excess of any other industry are indeed a stimulus for innovation, drug companies have not kept their part of the bargain.

The Real Source of Innovation

The meager output is bad enough. But the real scandal is the fact that the few innovative drugs that *do* come to market nearly always stem from publicly supported research. In this country, almost all of that is sponsored by the National Institutes of Health

(NIH) and carried out at universities, small biotechnology companies, or the NIH itself. (About 90 percent of NIH-sponsored research is "extramural," which means it is done mainly at medical schools and teaching hospitals. The remainder is "intramural," carried out by institute scientists on their campus outside Washington, D.C.) Big pharma began to rely on publicly funded research in 1980, with passage of the Bayh-Dole Act and a related piece of legislation, the Stevenson-Wydler Act. Bayh-Dole applies mainly to extramural research and Stevenson-Wydler to intramural research. This legislation, which I mentioned in Chapter 1, permitted NIH-funded work to be patented and licensed exclusively to drug companies in exchange for royalties. And increasingly, that is exactly what big pharma depends on—licensed drugs, which the drug companies then market and often patent for additional uses. Sometimes the drugs are completely developed before they are licensed. We saw, for example, in Chapter 2 how AZT, the first drug to treat HIV/AIDS, was developed and clinically tested by researchers at the National Cancer Institute (a part of the NIH) and Duke University before being licensed to what is now GlaxoSmithKline. In other cases, the drugs are acquired just before they are ready to enter large-scale clinical trials.

At least a third of big pharma's drugs are now licensed or otherwise acquired from outside sources—including smaller companies all over the world.[4] You would think the companies might be embarrassed by that fact, and no doubt they are reluctant to be very public about it, but they are certainly not embarrassed enough to change their way of operating. Bob

Ingram, chief operating officer of GlaxoSmithKline, candidly explained to *The Wall Street Journal,* "We're not going to put our money in-house if there's a better investment vehicle outside."[5] Lamenting that Glaxo got only 17 percent of its revenues from licensed products, compared with 30 percent for Pfizer and 35 percent for Merck, he said his company "is keen to reach similar levels." The big drug companies are competing not so much to find new drugs but for the limited number of drugs to license. "I don't see a respite for at least three to five years," said one spokesman. "We're all going to be chasing the same compounds. We see them at the same airport; they're coming in when we're going out."[6] Let's look at a few of the many important drugs *not* discovered by big pharma.

Taxol

Take the case of Taxol (the brand name for paclitaxel), the bestselling cancer drug in history.[7] Now used to treat cancers of the ovary, breast, and lung, it was derived from the bark of the Pacific yew tree in the 1960s. All of the research on the drug was conducted at, or supported by, the National Cancer Institute over nearly thirty years, at a cost to taxpayers of $183 million. In 1991, Bristol-Myers Squibb signed a cooperative research and development agreement with the NCI—a deal made possible by the Stevenson-Wydler Act and a 1986 amendment called the Federal Technology Transfer Act. The company's part of the bargain was mainly to supply the NCI with seventeen kilograms of paclitaxel (which it obtained from a chemical company). No ingenuity there. In 1992, after Taxol was approved by the FDA for treatment of cancer of the ovary, entirely on the basis of NIH-supported research, Bristol-Myers Squibb was given five years of exclusive marketing rights.

The only remaining problem for Bristol-Myers Squibb was the fact that the Pacific yew tree was in short supply. That problem was solved in 1994 by NIH-funded scientists at Florida State University. They devised a method to synthesize Taxol, which they promptly licensed to Bristol-Myers Squibb in return for royalties. No company ingenuity there, either.

The worldwide use of Taxol (for cancers of the ovary, breast, and lung) generated between $1 and $2 billion a year for Bristol-Myers Squibb and tens of millions in annual royalties for Florida State University. The company spent very little on R & D in getting initial FDA approval to treat cancer of the ovary, although it has undoubtedly spent substantial sums since then for testing the drug for other cancers. But that takes no ingenuity, either. The story of Taxol is a prime example of tax-payer-supported research discovering a valuable and lucrative drug that was virtually given as a gift to a large drug company for marketing, commercial exploitation, and further development.[8] The public pays again when it buys Taxol at the exorbitant price Bristol-Myers Squibb charges for a drug it neither discovered nor developed.

Epogen

Or take the case of Epogen, an innovative drug to treat anemia in patients with kidney failure.[9] Technically, Epogen is a biological and not a drug, because it was originally a natural substance made in the body—a hormone produced by the kidneys that stimulates the production of red blood cells. This hormone, called erythropoietin, was discovered in 1976 by Eugene Goldwasser at the University of Chicago, after much basic work done in several other academic laboratories had shown that the kidney must produce such a substance. Neither Goldwasser nor the University of Chicago patented the hormone or tried to synthesize it. But another NIH-funded researcher at Columbia University invented a technique for synthesizing biologicals, which the university patented soon after passage of Bayh-Dole. A small start-up biotechnology company named Amgen then licensed the technique from Columbia to develop a method for the large-scale commercial synthesis of the erythropoietin molecule. Amgen, now a giant in the industry, makes over $2 billion a year selling Epogen to the Medicare program to treat patients with kidney failure. So, as in the case of Taxol, the public gets to pay for Epogen twice—first by having supported the research that discovered it, and second, by paying for it through Medicare. Goldwasser never received a penny of royalties for his seminal discovery.

The identical molecule is marketed under the name Procrit (as though it were a different substance) by the huge firm Johnson & Johnson (J & J). This unnecessary duplication was the result of a deal between Amgen and J & J. As it happens, a similar type of anemia occurs in many conditions, not just kidney failure. In particular, it can be a debilitating side effect of cancer treatment. Before Amgen began reaping its huge profits from Epogen, it needed to come up with a way to stay afloat. So it licensed to J & J its rights to sell Epogen in the United States for conditions other than kidney failure (mainly cancer) and for all uses in Europe. J & J paid Amgen a lump sum of several million dollars plus the promise of future royalties. Ortho, a division of J & J, markets the drug as Procrit. Procrit's worldwide sales are estimated at nearly $3 billion annually, of which a small percentage goes to Amgen. Amgen, for its part, pays Columbia one percent of all its sales of Epogen. Not to be outdone by J & J, Amgen has now gotten approval for another, longer-acting form of the same agent, called Aranesp, which it hopes will compete with Procrit without violating the original deal. But they're all essentially the same substance under different names.

Here again, a truly important new therapeutic agent was discovered and identified through basic research outside the drug industry. Unlike Taxol, which had been tested in clinical trials before Bristol-Myers Squibb acquired rights to it, erythropoietin had to be biosynthesized by Amgen before it could undergo preclinical and clinical testing. I learned from sources at Amgen that J & J made essentially no contribution to the original development of erythropoietin. It simply paid Amgen for the right to market the substance and develop it for other uses.

Clearly, there was ingenuity aplenty on the part of both Amgen and J & J in exploiting commercial opportunities, but not much of that had to do with the initial discovery of the hormone and its role in the treatment of anemia.

Gleevec

The story of Gleevec (the brand name of imatinib mesylate) is a little different.[10] Here the drug company—in this case Novartis—had patented the molecule and had it on the shelf, but its usefulness was discovered mainly by an NIH-funded university researcher. One of the seven innovative drugs approved in 2001, Gleevec halts a rare type of leukemia, called chronic myeloid leukemia, dead in its tracks, with relatively few side effects. (How long it works is not yet clear, because the drug is still very new.) Leukemia is really a kind of cancer of the blood, and before Gleevec came on the market, this type of leukemia was universally fatal unless the patient underwent a dangerous bone marrow transplantation (assuming there was a suitable donor). So Gleevec is one of the few "breakthroughs" that really is a breakthrough. Novartis uses it as the poster child for drug company innovation. One of its ads, for instance, shows a smiling young woman saying, "Not long ago, my cancer was all I could think about. Now I feel so good I have to remind myself I'm a cancer patient." And in the body of the text is the statement "Novartis put her deadly cancer into remission quickly and completely."[11]

Well, not really. Novartis had more than a little help. The story begins in 1960, with the discovery under the microscope of a peculiar-looking chromosome in patients with chronic myeloid leukemia. That discovery was made at the University of Pennsylvania, and for that reason the new chromosome was called "the Philadelphia chromosome." Later work from many laboratories showed that the Philadelphia chromosome carries a gene that directs the production of an abnormal enzyme. That enzyme causes white blood cells to become cancerous. Similar types of enzymes were thought to be involved in other cancers. As a result of these studies, chemists in Israel and at Novartis set about synthesizing molecules that would inhibit the action of this family of enzymes. Novartis patented several such inhibitors in 1994 and added them to its collection of potentially useful drug candidates.

There was apparently no immediate interest by the management at Novartis in determining whether any of them might be useful in treating chronic myeloid leukemia until Brian J. Druker, a researcher at the Oregon Health & Sciences University in Portland, became interested in the problem. Working with a scientist at Novartis, Nicholas Lydon, he obtained a small supply of several of the company's most promising inhibitors. He found that imatinib mesylate was the most potent in suppressing the growth of the cancer cells in culture and, furthermore, that it had no effect on normal blood cells. Such specific action is almost unheard of in cancer treatment, and Druker urged Novartis to explore this exciting lead.

But, according to Druker, the company showed little enthusiasm for undertaking further clinical work on imatinib mesylate. Whether the reluctance was because of the small potential market or the finding that the drug was toxic to dogs at high doses is not clear. Druker nevertheless persisted, and Novartis finally agreed to support cautious, limited tests in his clinic and at two other sites. By 1999, Druker was able to report spectacularly successful preliminary results before a national meeting of American hematologists. The news spread quickly, and the company then decided to proceed with large-scale clinical trials. In only two years, the trials were completed and the FDA had approved the drug. Thus, most of Novartis's R & D investment in Gleevec was made several years *after* there was good scientific evidence to suggest that the drug would be useful.

These kinds of stories could be multiplied many times over. A recent study published in the journal *Health Affairs* reported that, in 1998, only about 15 percent of the scientific articles cited in patent applications for clinical medicine came from industry research, while 54 percent came from academic centers, 13 percent from government, and the rest from various other public and nonprofit institutions.[12] Remember that these are patent applications for *all* new drugs and medical innovations, not simply for those ultimately judged to be clinically important. Had the data been limited to major breakthrough drugs, the industry's role would undoubtedly have been even smaller.

An unpublished internal document produced by the NIH in February 2000, which was obtained by Public Citizen through the Freedom of Information Act, revealed similar percentages. The NIH had selected the five top-selling drugs in 1995 (Zantac, Zovirax, Capoten, Vasotec, and Prozac) and found that sixteen of the seventeen key scientific papers leading to their discovery and development came from outside the industry. (Eli Lilly had sponsored one of the four key studies leading to the development of Prozac.) Looking at all the relevant published research, not just at the key studies, only 15 percent came from industry, whereas 55 percent came from NIH-funded laboratories and 30 percent from foreign academic institutions.[13]

A 1997 report by the National Bureau of Economic Research found that of the twenty-one most effective drugs approved between 1965 and 1992, public research was responsible for fifteen.[14] A *Boston Globe* review of the bestselling fifty drugs approved from 1992 to 1997 found that forty-five of them had received government funding.[15] And so on and so on. There is no question that publicly funded medical research—not the industry itself—is by far the major source of innovative drugs. That is particularly true of drugs for cancer and HIV/AIDS. Merrill Goozner, in his book *The $800 Million Pill*, recounts in detail the discovery and development of drugs for these diseases, and clearly shows that the driving force was publicly funded researchers.[16]

Paying Twice

Given the contributions of taxpayers to big pharma's products, you might think the drug companies would give us a break in pricing. But you would be wrong. Let's look at the pricing of Taxol and Gleevec.

When it came on the market, Taxol sold for $10,000 to $20,000 for a year's treatment—reportedly a twentyfold markup over manufacturing costs. Bristol-Myers Squibb, you will remember, put next to nothing into the initial R & D, although it has since sponsored clinical trials aimed at expanding the uses of the drug. In a blazing act of hubris, the company fought tooth and nail to extend its exclusive rights on Taxol beyond the original five-year term, and managed to win another three years by suing the generic manufacturers who wanted to enter the market. As of 2003, the company had paid royalties to the NIH of only $35 million on its $9 billion in sales of Taxol (the agreement was 0.5 percent in royalties). Going in the other direction, the government paid Bristol-Myers Squibb hundreds of millions of dollars for Taxol through the Medicare program.

Novartis priced Gleevec at about $27,000 for a year's supply. In a recent book, Daniel Vasella, the chairman and CEO of Novartis, acknowledged that the drug is already profitable.[17] I would think so, given that its development was so rapid and that it qualified for the orphan drug tax credit. He also acknowledged that the price was based partly on the price of interferon, the drug that Gleevec replaced as the recommended treatment for chronic myeloid leukemia. In other words, the price was what the market would bear. In response to the outcry over the staggering price to treat this lethal disease, Novartis announced a discounting policy for patients of limited means. But according to a 2003 article in *The New York Times,* the plan had not worked very well so far, particularly in poor countries, where only a handful of patients have received the drug free. At a meeting I attended, someone in the audience complained to Vasella that a friend with chronic myeloid leukemia had had difficulty obtaining the discount for which he was said to be qualified. Somehow, I was not surprised.[18]

Perhaps the most extreme example of this sort of price gouging is the story of Cerezyme, a synthetic enzyme made by the biotechnology company Genzyme. This drug treats a rare abnormality, called Gaucher's disease, which affects only about 5,000 people worldwide. The research and early development was done entirely by NIH-funded scientists, two of whom later left their university to start the company and exploit their work. (The major contributor to the early effort, Roscoe Brady, who discovered the cause of Gaucher's disease, remained at the NIH.) Genzyme charges patients on the order of $200,000 to $300,000 for a year's supply. According to the author and reporter Merrill Goozner, at least one patient is not grateful to the company. "This is government-developed technology," said the boy's father. "This isn't Genzyme working late at night to help sick people. The NIH did it. But as soon as the government transferred that intellectual property to the company, they lost all control over the pricing."[19]

A more recent example is the story of Roche's new HIV/AIDS drug, Fuzeon.[20] Approved by the FDA in 2003, this drug is an important advance in AIDS treatment. According to a detailed story by the *Wall Street Journal* reporter Vanessa Fuhrmans, Fuzeon was discovered at Duke University, developed by a local biotechnology company, and only then acquired by Roche. Despite its minimal contribution to early research and development, Roche charges $20,000 a year for the drug—three times the price of most AIDS drugs. About a fifth of AIDS drugs are purchased by the federal-state AIDS Drug Assistance Programs. These programs simply can't afford to buy Fuzeon for all the patients who need it, so they are restricting access to it, setting up waiting lists, or tightening income eligibility criteria. In thirteen states, the program has simply stopped providing Fuzeon to new patients. Although Roche is reported to have a patient assistance program, the company declined to tell *The Wall Street Journal* how many people are in it, and it refuses to provide assistance in states where the drug assistance program restricts access to Fuzeon. We are used to hearing about patients with AIDS in the Third World going without lifesaving treatment, but now it may be happening in the United States. High prices have real, sometimes deadly, consequences.

There Oughta Be a Law—And There Is

This sort of exploitation is not supposed to happen. The Bayh-Dole and Stevenson-Wydler Acts, with subsequent amendments, contained a number of stipulations that would prevent it.[21] First, under "exceptional circumstances," which are vaguely defined in terms of serving the public interest, the

NIH may require that work it supports in medical schools, teaching hospitals, and small biotechnology companies not be patented but remain in the public domain. The same is true of its intramural research. Thus, the right to patent or license NIH-funded work is not automatically assured. Second, Bayh-Dole requires that work licensed to drug companies be made "available to the public on reasonable terms." That could certainly be interpreted as meaning that it should be priced reasonably. And until 1995, the NIH explicitly required reasonable pricing for drugs stemming from collaborations like the one that led to Taxol. Third, work patented and licensed under the terms of Bayh-Dole must be reported to the NIH, so that the institute can keep track of which drugs originate in that way. If profits are very large, there is a requirement that some part of the royalties be returned to the government. The same is true of intramural research. Fourth, the government retains the right to "march in" and use a licensed drug itself or issue compulsory licenses to other companies if the original company is not fulfilling its obligations. All of these provisions have been pretty much ignored by both industry and academia.

The NIH, too, has been supercasual about fulfilling the terms of the legislation. The fact is that while the NIH represents, and is supported by, the public, it behaves more as if its constituency were the academic medical centers. And there is indeed a revolving door between them. Researchers at medical schools often receive part of their training at the NIH, and of course, NIH scientists and leaders emerge from, and frequently return to, academia. It's a very tight community, with much in-breeding and a strong common culture. When there was talk of redirecting a small fraction of the royalties received by medical centers back to the government, the NIH actually argued against it.

The NIH has been friendly to big pharma as well. (As we will see, some senior scientists at the NIH have had extensive financial dealings with drug companies.) Under considerable pressure from industry, in 1995, the agency completely abandoned its 1989 policy requiring "a reasonable relationship between the pricing of a licensed product, the public investment in that product, and the health and safety needs of the public." According to an NIH report, "Shortly after the policy of 'reasonable pricing' was introduced, industry objected to it, considering it a form of price control."[22] And so it was! A well-intended but doomed effort to hold the industry accountable. As a result, companies like Bristol-Myers Squibb could charge whatever they liked for drugs like Taxol.

In 2001, at the behest of Senator Ron Wyden (D-Ore.), the NIH attempted to account for its contributions to a list of the top forty-seven drugs on the market. The fact that four of them (Taxol, Epogen, Procrit, and Neupogen) were developed largely with public funding was widely publicized. What was not publicized was the fact that the NIH did not seem to know one way or another about many of the other forty-three drugs. According to its report, "NIH encountered difficulty in being able to cross-reference NIH grants and contracts that gave rise to inventions with any patents or licenses covering the final product, as well as an inability to identify other federal and/or nonfederal sources of funds that contribute to an inventive technology." The drug companies claim that this lack of information shows the drugs were developed by *them* (they often state that "only four" of the forty-seven drugs were developed outside the industry), but there is no reason to assume that. What the facts really show is that the NIH, in violation of the Bayh-Dole Act, failed to keep proper records of patenting and licensing arrangements.

The drug companies are not the only ones to ignore the provisions of Bayh-Dole that have to do with "reasonable terms" and recouping some of the public's investment. Universities are just as resistant. There is no question that they benefit by high pricing of the fruits of their research. Columbia University, which patented the technology used in the manufacture of Epogen and Cerezyme, collected nearly $300 million in royalties from more than thirty biotechnology companies over the seventeen-year life of the patent. The patent was based on NIH-funded research during the 1970s. Because it is in their interest, universities seldom criticize the exorbitant pricing of drugs that stem from their research.

A Fruitful Public-Private Collaboration?

You might argue that, yes, the ideas for innovative drugs come from outside the industry, but ultimately it is the industry that actually brings drugs to market. Universities can't put pills in bottles and sell them. Isn't that just the kind of fruitful public-private collaboration that we should want (and that Bayh-Dole intended)? Publicly funded scientists come up with the ideas and early development, and drug companies put that to practical use. The companies sponsor clinical trials, they convert the drugs to forms that can be safely and readily administered, and they produce and distribute the final products. And sometimes, although rarely, they actually discover an innovative drug on their own. What's wrong with that?

What's wrong with it is that the industry is not satisfied to be that sort of "partner." Instead, it claims far more for itself. It claims to be the innovator, as well as the developer and manufacturer of new drugs. It takes credit for the whole shebang. And on that basis it makes the case that it is more than entitled to its gargantuan profits and all the other special favors it receives—the long periods of exclusive marketing rights, freedom from any price regulation, and huge tax breaks. If the much more modest role big pharma really plays were widely known, if the public knew where the miracles really come from, people would demand that the industry's rewards be more commensurate with its contributions and that there be some form of public accountability.

The drug companies are now beginning to acknowledge that they are in a dry spell. But they contend that advances in genetic research will shortly open limitless possibilities for the development of important new drugs. And that may be true, although it will probably not happen in the next few years. But note what that claim implies: that the industry is just waiting to feed on research done on the outside. It is treading water, hoping universities and biotechnology companies will turn out a wealth of new ideas. It is waiting for Godot. That is hardly the image a dynamic industry that claims to be the source of innovative research should want to project, but it is the true state of affairs. And it explains why major drug companies are now setting up their R & D operations near important research universities and medical centers, and trolling small companies all over the world for drugs to license.

The industry obscures not only the origin of its innovative drugs but also the fact that those drugs constitute only a small proportion of its total output. Big pharma likes to refer to itself as a "research-based industry," but it is hardly that. It could best be described as an idea-licensing, pharmaceutical formulating and manufacturing, clinical testing, patenting, and marketing industry. All that takes a lot of money, but the majority of its products are drugs that, in the words of the FDA, "have therapeutic qualities similar to those of one or more already marketed drugs"—in other words, me-too drugs. How me-too drugs came to dominate the market is one of the more shameless chapters in the larger story of the pharmaceutical industry—the one that I'll address next.

5

"Me-Too" Drugs—
The Main Business of the
Pharmaceutical Industry

MY MOTHER HAD MANY FINE QUALITIES, but good cooking was not one of them. Every meal consisted of leftovers. It wasn't just that leftovers were a supplement. They seemed to be the entire meal. My brother and I often marveled at how she managed this. We eventually settled on what we came to call the big bang theory of Mom's cooking. Sometime in the distant past, we decided, before we were born, our mother had cooked a single stupendous meal, and the family had been living on it ever since. We were only sorry we had missed that meal.

So it is with big pharma. Every now and then,

drug companies bring an innovative drug to market, but mainly they turn out a seemingly inexhaustible supply of leftovers— "me-too" drugs that are versions of drugs in the distant past. But unlike my mother's mythical first meal, the drug companies seldom do their own cooking. Researchers supported by the National Institutes of Health (NIH) usually do the initial work of drug discovery. Then the drug companies keep stringing out and exploiting those discoveries.[1]

As we saw in the last chapter, in the five years 1998 through 2002, 415 new drugs were approved by the Food and Drug Administration (FDA), of which only 14 percent were truly innovative. A further 9 percent were old drugs that had been changed in some way that made them, in the FDA's view, significant improvements. And the remaining 77 percent? Incredibly, they were all me-too drugs—classified by the agency as being no better than drugs already on the market to treat the same condition. Some of these had different chemical compositions from the originals; most did not. But none were considered improvements. So there you have it. Seventy-seven percent of the pharmaceutical industry's output consisted of leftovers.[2]

This travesty is made possible by one crucial weakness in the law—namely, drug companies have to show the FDA only that new drugs are "effective." They do not have to show that they are *more effective than* (or even as effective as) what is already being used for the same condition. They just have to show they are better than nothing.[3] And that is exactly what the companies do. In clinical trials, they compare their new drugs with placebos (sugar pills) instead of with the best current treatment. That is a very low hurdle indeed. In fact, on the basis of placebo-controlled trials, drugs can be approved that are actually *worse* than drugs already on the market. The last thing drug companies want is a head-to-head comparison. Only when it would be clearly dangerous to human subjects to deprive them of treatment by using a placebo are drug companies likely to compare a new treatment with an old one. That doesn't happen very often.

This defect in the law is critical in understanding the modern pharmaceutical industry. Almost alone, it has enabled the industry to transform itself into a giant me-too business. If companies had to show their drugs were better than older treatments, there would be far fewer me-too drugs, because not many of them would pass that test. The companies would have no choice but to look for important new drugs, instead of taking the easier and cheaper route of spinning out old ones. But spinning out old ones is what they do. Let's look at some of the ways they do it.

Patent Extenders

Sometimes it's simply a matter of extending the life of a blockbuster drug that is going off patent by making a virtually identical drug and shifting users to the new one. The drug just has to be different enough to qualify for a new patent. Take the case of Nexium. Nexium is a heartburn drug of the proton pump inhibitor type made by the British company AstraZeneca. It came on the market in 2001, just as the company's block-buster drug for heartburn, Prilosec, was scheduled to go off patent. That was no coincidence. Unless there was a replacement, the loss of the Prilosec patent would have been a devastating blow to AstraZeneca. At $6 billion in annual sales, Prilosec was once the top-selling drug in the world. When the patent expired, it would face competition from generic manufacturers, and its sales would plummet.

So as part of a multifaceted strategy to prevent this loss of revenue (involving, among other things, lawsuits against potential generic manufacturers), AstraZeneca developed an audacious plan. Prilosec is a mixture of an active and a possibly inactive form (called isomers) of the omeprazole molecule. The company would take out a new patent on the active form of the Prilosec molecule, name it Nexium (it wouldn't have done to call it "Half-o'-Prilosec," but that is what it was), and promote it as an improvement over Prilosec just in time to switch people over before the Prilosec patent expired. The plan worked.[4]

Shortly before the patent on Prilosec was set to expire, the company got FDA approval for the newly patented Nexium. Then it launched a massive advertising campaign to persuade Prilosec users and their doctors that Nexium was somehow better. Very quickly, Nexium became the most heavily advertised drug in the United States. The media was blanketed with Nexium ads—"Today's purple pill is Nexium, from the makers of Prilosec." To help with the switch, AstraZeneca priced Nexium slightly below Prilosec, gave discounts to managed care plans and hospitals, barraged doctors with free samples, and even offered coupons in newspapers. The campaign reportedly cost the company a half billion dollars in 2001. Virtually overnight, Nexium—the new purple pill—began to replace Prilosec. Soon the company dropped all references to the older drug in its advertisements. Now they just refer to "the purple pill called Nexium." It is as though Prilosec never happened. (In fact, Prilosec is now sold over the counter for a fraction of the cost of Nexium.)

Many people know this much of the story, or at least the outlines of it, and they know that such corporate shenanigans are one reason drug prices are so high. But what you may not appreciate is the role of clinical trials. To get FDA approval for Nexium, AstraZeneca had to test it in several clinical trials. Some of these trials merely compared Nexium with placebos to show that it worked better than nothing, since that is all the FDA requires. But four trials compared Nexium head to head with Prilosec (for esophageal erosions), and these were crucial to the marketing strategy. The company wanted to show that Nexium was better than Prilosec—an advance over the older drug.

But note what AstraZeneca did. Instead of comparing likely equivalent doses (which would have been no more than 20 and possibly as little as 10 milligrams of Nexium, versus the standard 20-milligram dose of Prilosec), the company used higher doses of Nexium. It compared 20 milligrams and 40 milligrams of Nexium with 20 milligrams of Prilosec. With the dice loaded in that way, Nexium looked like an improvement—but still only marginally so and in just two of the four trials.[5] In fact, the only surprise is that at the high doses chosen for comparison, Nexium didn't do better than it did. The logical conclusion might have been simply to double the standard dose of Prilosec, allow generic competition, and forget about Nexium—but that would not have been of help to Astra-Zeneca, only to people with heartburn who object to paying $4 a pill (which in itself might produce heartburn). Tom Scully, the former head of the Centers for Medicare & Medicaid Services, told a group of doctors, "You should be embarrassed if you prescribe Nexium."[6]

The story of Clarinex is similar. This is Schering-Plough's replacement for its blockbuster allergy drug, Claritin, which went off patent at the end of 2002.[7] The potential loss to the company could hardly be exaggerated. Claritin had sales of $2.7 billion in 2001 and accounted for about a third of Schering-Plough's revenues. Back in 1987, the company had patented the active metabolite of Claritin—that is, the molecule into which the body converts Claritin, which is entirely responsible for the action of the drug. Late in 2001, it received FDA approval to market the Claritin metabolite under the name Clarinex and began a massive promotional campaign to switch Claritin users to the new drug before Claritin lost its exclusive marketing rights. To that end, it also priced Clarinex slightly below Claritin. Clarinex was approved for the treatment of year-round indoor allergies as well as seasonal outdoor allergies. That means Schering-Plough can market Clarinex as an improvement, even though it is simply what Claritin turns into after it is swallowed. But there is no reason to think Clarinex is an improvement. It was approved for the additional use only because the company decided to test it for that use. If they had tested Claritin for indoor allergies, it would undoubtedly have been the same as Clarinex—because it *is* the same.

Competing Me-Too Drugs

More often, me-too drugs are made by competing companies, who create their own versions of blockbuster drugs to cut into a market that has already proved both lucrative and expandable. In addition to Prilosec and Nexium, there are three proton pump inhibitors on the market, made by other companies. There are also two competing antihistamines of the Claritin and Clarinex type.

Perhaps the best-known family of me-too drugs is the statins—drugs to lower blood cholesterol levels.[8] In the summer of 2003, the FDA approved the latest of them, AstraZeneca's Crestor. The original statin drug, Merck's Mevacor, came on the market in 1987. It was a truly innovative drug, based on research in many university and government laboratories throughout the world. The potential market was huge, since the theory that high cholesterol contributes to heart disease was gaining ground and the "normal" level of cholesterol was being revised downward. Other companies were quick to produce their own statins. Mevacor was joined by the same company's me-too drug, Zocor, Pfizer's Lipitor, Bristol-Myers Squibb's Pravachol, Novartis's Lescol, and now Crestor. (Bayer's Baycol had to be removed from the market because, at the approved dose, it caused a deadly side effect.)[9]

There is little reason to think one is any better than another at comparable doses. But to get a toehold in the market, me-too statins were sometimes tested for slightly different outcomes in slightly different kinds of patients, then promoted as especially effective for those uses. For instance, a statin might be tested for how well it prevented future heart attacks in patients who had already had one and then promoted as the only statin approved for that use, even though the other statins, if tested in the same kinds of patients, would likely have shown the same effects.

Or a new statin could be compared with an older one in strengths not likely to be equivalent. That is an extremely common way of breaking into the me-too market—not just for statins but for other families of me-too drugs. The FDA approves a drug not just for a particular use but for a specific dose—and that is the dose the company selects for testing in clinical trials. Choosing that dose is something of an art form, then. Recently, for instance, much was made of a trial showing that Pfizer's Lipitor was more effective in some ways than Bristol-Myers Squibb's Pravachol. But the study, which began in 1998, compared 80 milligrams of Lipitor with only 40 milligrams of Pravachol. These were the approved doses at the time, but since then an 80-milligram dose of Pravachol has also been approved.[10] Would Lipitor be better than the higher dose of Pravachol? No one can say. Crestor is now promoted as the strongest statin, but that may be because the dose approved by the FDA was relatively high. A larger dose of one of the other statins might be just as good.[11] So whenever a drug company claims its me-too drug is better than another, it is important to ask whether the difference is in the dosing. We also need to remember that higher doses carry greater risks. Some experts worry that Crestor, like Baycol, might prove too dangerous when it comes into widespread use.

Mevacor is now sold as generic lovastatin and is therefore cheaper than the others. But the me-too business relies heavily on marketing, and as a tribute to the fact that nearly anything can be marketed and people persuaded to pay more for it, both Lipitor and Zocor, which are more expensive than lovastatin, were among the top ten drugs in the world in 2002—but not lovastatin.[12] Like Prilosec, Mevacor is no longer mentioned.

Prozac, made by Eli Lilly, was the first of a new type of antidepressant called selective serotonin reuptake inhibitors (SSRIs). It was developed mainly on the basis of research done outside the company. In 1987, the FDA approved Prozac for the treatment of depression; in 1994, for the treatment of obsessive-compulsive disorder; in 1996, for bulimia; and in 1999, for geriatric depression. It rapidly replaced other types of antidepressants because of its milder side effects. Prozac soon accounted for one-quarter of Lilly's revenues, with annual sales reaching $2.6 billion. Seeing the size of the market and its potential for expansion, other companies began turning out SSRIs.

GlaxoSmithKline's Paxil came on the market in 1997, followed by Pfizer's Zoloft in 1999. The upstart Forest Laboratories put itself on the map with its SSRI Celexa, then created a me-too of its me-too, called Lexapro. Prozac lost its patent protection in August 2001 and is now sold as generic fluoxetine at about 80 percent less than it used to cost. Nevertheless, the much more expensive Paxil and Zoloft are in the top ten drugs—but not fluoxetine. Like Prilosec and Mevacor, the original Prozac is forgotten.

But that doesn't mean Eli Lilly just gave up. It tried to stay in the SSRI business by patenting a weekly dosage form of Prozac. And in a move even more audacious than the switches from Prilosec to Nexium or from Claritin to Clarinex, it renamed Prozac Sarafem, colored it pink and lavender, and got FDA approval to market it for "premenstrual dysphoric disorder," its term for severe premenstrual symptoms. Same drug, same dose, but priced three and a half times higher than generic Prozac at my local pharmacy.[13]

Making It in the Me-Too Business

Success in the me-too market depends on several conditions. First, the market has to be large to accommodate all the competing drugs. For that reason, me-too drugs usually target very common, lifelong conditions—like arthritis or depression or high blood pressure or elevated cholesterol. The conditions are not so serious that they are imminently lethal, but they don't go away, either. Sometimes they are little more than annoyances, like hay fever. Consequently, large numbers of people may take these drugs for years, producing a huge and steady volume of sales. People with uncommon diseases are not of much interest to drug companies, because the market is small. (Witness the initial reluctance of Novartis to undertake development of Gleevec.) Nor are people with transient conditions, like most acute infections. Antibiotics, for example, seldom generate huge revenues (there are exceptions here), because while infections are common, they usually do not last very long. Lethal diseases kill the customer, so drugs to treat them are not usually blockbusters, either.

Second, the market has to consist of *paying* customers. It doesn't help the bottom line to turn out drugs for nonpaying customers. That is why the pharmaceutical industry is supremely uninterested in finding drugs to treat tropical diseases, like malaria or sleeping sickness or schistosomiasis (an extremely common Third World disease caused by parasitic worms). Although these diseases are widespread, they are not important to the industry, since those who suffer from them are in countries too poor to buy drugs. Of all the drugs approved in the past two decades, only a tiny fraction were for tropical diseases. The contrast with the cornucopia of drugs to lower cholesterol or treat mood disorders or hay fever or heartburn is dismaying. Even some diseases that strike people in rich countries as well as poor ones, like tuberculosis, are not of great interest to big pharma, since they occur mainly in pockets of poverty.

Third, the market has to be not only large but highly elastic, so it can expand. Recently, for instance, the market for blood pressure medication was increased when an expert panel changed the definition of high blood pressure (hypertension). For many years, it was defined as a blood pressure above 140 over 90. But this panel decided to recognize something it called prehypertension.[14] This, they said, is a blood pressure between 120 over 80 and 140 over 90. Overnight, people with blood pressures in this range found they had a medical condition. Although the panel recommended that prehypertension generally be treated first with diet and exercise, human nature being what it is, many people will almost certainly prefer to be treated with drugs. That expansion in the definition will add millions of customers for blood pressure drugs—despite the absence of convincing evidence of their benefit in this group.

Similarly, the cutoff for high cholesterol has been lowered over the years. Once it was reserved for blood cholesterol levels over 280 milligrams per deciliter. Then it was lowered to 240, and now most doctors try to knock cholesterol down to below 200. As with prehypertension, many doctors will recommend diet and exercise to achieve that level, but people find that advice very difficult to put into practice, and the next step is to reach for a statin. That's why Lipitor was the top-selling drug in the world in 2002, and its competitor Zocor was second. I am not arguing that cholesterol levels *shouldn't* be lowered, only that this market is easily expanded and therefore rich territory for me-too drugs.

Markets can be created, as well as enlarged. Some of the normal accompaniments of aging are now treated as diseases. Over the past few decades, hundreds of millions of women have taken hormones for postmenopausal symptoms. Now many older men are being treated with testosterone patches for "testosterone deficiency," and sometimes with growth hormone, as a sort of all-purpose tonic.

Once upon a time, drug companies promoted drugs to treat diseases. Now it is often the opposite. They promote diseases to fit their drugs. Nearly everyone experiences heartburn from time to time. The remedy used to be a glass of milk or an over-the-counter antacid to relieve the symptoms. But now heartburn is called "acid reflux disease" or "gastroesophageal reflux disease (GERD)" and marketed, along with the drugs to treat it, as a harbinger of serious esophageal disease—which it usually is not. As a result, in 2002, Prilosec was the third best selling drug in the world (Nexium had not yet had a chance to replace it), and its competitor Prevacid was seventh.

Similarly, most young women experience at least some premenstrual tension from time to time. Lilly's launch of Sarafem made premenstrual symptoms a disease—now called "premenstrual dysphoric disorder (PMDD)." It is not yet officially recognized in the psychiatric diagnostic manual, but given the influence of the industry, I would not be surprised if it is in the next edition. While the company defines PMDD as particularly severe premenstrual symptoms, the message is clear—there is a pill for it, so why not buy it? Some women feel duped when they learn Sarafem is just Prozac in another color at a higher price, but Lilly, understandably, does not advertise that fact. Zoloft, one of the SSRI me-too drugs, quickly got into the act and was also approved for PMDD.

As the whole world knows, there is now a condition recently christened "erectile dysfunction," and a drug, Viagra, and two me-toos, Levitra and Cialis, to treat it. Advertisements for these drugs feature not decrepit old men but young athletes. The implication is obvious. Any episode of impotence, no matter how rare and how mild, is "erectile dysfunction," there is a pill for it, and if this macho quarterback is not too embarrassed to ask for it, you don't have to be, either.[15]

Me-too drugs often worm their way into lucrative markets and then expand those markets by coming up with slightly different uses. As I mentioned earlier, the FDA doesn't just approve a new drug. It approves it for a particular use and at a particular dose. If a company tests a drug for a use slightly different from those of other drugs in the class, no other company can promote it for that purpose. It doesn't matter how obvious the new use is, or how closely related to the use for which the original drug was approved. The aim is simply to find some basis for marketing your me-too drug as an improvement. Clarinex was tested for indoor allergies to differentiate it from its parent drug, Claritin. Even after initial FDA approval, companies continue to do Phase IV trials to look for new uses, get new patents, and extend marketing rights.

All of these dubious techniques have seen their apogee in the marketing of SSRI antidepressants. Prozac, you will remember, was approved not only for depression but also for a series of related disorders. The me-too manufacturers simply expanded the list of psychiatric disorders. GlaxoSmithKline's Paxil, for instance, was approved to treat something called "social anxiety disorder"—said to be a debilitating form of shyness. But what shy person has not from time to time found this trait debilitating? As the bioethicist Carl Elliott put it, "The way to sell drugs is to sell psychiatric illness. If you are Paxil and you are the only manufacturer who has the drug for social anxiety disorder, it's in your interest to broaden the category as far as possible and make the borders as fuzzy as possible."[16] The fact that few psychiatric disorders have objective criteria for diagnosis makes these disorders easier to expand than most physical illnesses. According to *The Washington Post,* Barry Brand, Paxil's product director, told the journal *Advertising Age,* "Every marketer's dream is to find an unidentified or unknown market and develop it. That's what we were able to do with social anxiety disorder."[17]

Paxil was also approved for "*generalized* [my italics] anxiety disorder," and shortly after September 11, 2001, the company launched an ambitious campaign promoting the drug for this use. Commercials showed images of the World Trade Center towers collapsing. And who didn't feel anxious about that?

But the implication was that even this perfectly appropriate (and, for most people, temporary) anxiety should be treated with drugs. The *New York Times* columnist Maureen Dowd summed it up best: "The more anxious the companies feel about profits, the more generalized the generalized anxiety disorders get."[18]

Justifying Me-Too Drugs

How do drug companies justify all the me-too drugs? They use two arguments. First, they say the competition keeps prices down. And second, they say that it is good to have more than one drug to treat a condition, because if the first one doesn't work for a particular individual, the second one might. Does either of these arguments have merit?

The first certainly doesn't. There is almost no evidence of price competition in the me-too business. When the first me-too comes on the market, the price of the original drug does not drop. That is because me-too drugs are not promoted on the basis of price. Have you ever heard Lipitor being advertised as cheaper than Zocor, or vice versa? Instead, they are marketed as being especially effective or safe—usually in total disregard of the fact that since clinical trials almost never compare me-too drugs with one another for the same condition at equivalent doses, no one can say which is more effective. Or they are promoted as the only drug to treat some particular aspect of the general condition—also in total disregard of the fact that the other drugs were not tested for that wrinkle but *probably* would be just as good. The me-too market operates more like an oligopoly than like a competitive market; it is simply expanded and shared. I can't think of any other industry in which price is almost never mentioned in advertising.

The second argument is based on the quite reasonable-sounding assumption that in drugs, as in socks, one size does *not* fit all. Big pharma argues that very similar drugs may vary in their effects from patient to patient, so it is important to have choices. But while that sounds reasonable, there is little evidence to support the notion that if a particular drug doesn't work for a patient, a virtually identical one will. Or if one drug causes side effects, another one won't. The companies could easily test that proposition. They could test their me-too drugs in patients who have not done well on the first one. But they don't do that, probably because they don't really want to know the results—if Prilosec doesn't work, Nexium probably won't, either. They simply compare their me-too drugs with placebos. But unless the proposition is tested in proper clinical trials, there is no way to know whether it is true. Anecdotes about individual patients are no substitute.

So the idea that patients respond differently to me-too drugs is merely an untested—and self-serving—hypothesis. But let's assume for the moment that it is true. That would still not justify having four or more me-too drugs, as is now the case for many conditions. One or two would do. I know of no rationale for, say, the seven brand-name angiotensin-converting-enzyme

(ACE) inhibitors that are sold to treat high blood pressure and heart failure. No less an authority than Dr. Robert Temple, the FDA's associate director of medical policy, said of me-too drugs, "I generally assume these drugs are all the same unless somebody goes out and proves differently. I don't think you lose much if you just always use the cheapest drugs."[19]

Scarcity amid Plenty

While me-too drugs flood the market, there are growing shortages of some important, even lifesaving drugs.[20] If companies find drugs unprofitable, they just stop making them. Sometimes companies decide to stop making important drugs to free up production capacity for drugs with bigger market potential—often me-too drugs. The FDA requires six months' notice if the sole manufacturer of a "medically necessary" drug decides to stop making it, but that requirement is often honored in the breach. According to Mark Goldberger, an FDA official, "We have to give approval for companies to make the drugs, but companies can leave the market anytime they wish."[21] In 2001, there were serious shortages of many important drugs, including certain anesthetics, antivenins for poisonous snakebites, steroids for premature infants, antidotes for certain drug overdoses, an anticlotting drug for hemophilia, an injectable drug used in cardiac resuscitation, an antibiotic for gonorrhea, a drug to induce labor in childbirth, and vaccines against flu and pneumonia in adults.

Perhaps the worst shortages are of childhood vaccines. In 2000, the supply of the combined vaccine against diphtheria, tetanus, and whooping cough was so short that the U.S. Centers for Disease Control (CDC) recommended that infants receive only the first three of the five recommended doses. Booster shots were eliminated. The agency also suggested deferral of the second dose of the measles, mumps, and German measles vaccine and of the chickenpox vaccine. While those shortages have eased somewhat, so that the CDC recommended resumption of the usual schedule in late 2002, the situation remains precarious because fewer drug companies are bothering to make vaccines. There are now just four such companies, compared with about four times that many twenty years ago.

In 1994, the CDC capped prices of childhood vaccines the agency purchased for use in public health centers throughout the country—the source for most children in the United States. Some companies then stopped selling vaccines to the government, although they continued to supply private doctors and health plans at much higher prices. There is no doubt that drug companies could not make as much on childhood vaccines as they could on remedies for high cholesterol or erectile dysfunction, but were they taking a loss? Drug company profits are so large that one would hope the companies would be willing to make less profitable but vital drugs as a social service—and a thank-you to the public that subsidizes them so handsomely. But that is not the way this industry works. It all comes down to dollars and cents. As a spokesman for American Home Products (now Wyeth) explained when his company stopped making iso-proterenol, a drug used in cardiac resuscitation, "It was strictly a business decision."[22] If you get bitten by a rattlesnake, you may not be able to get antivenin, but you can certainly get something for your cholesterol.

You might ask why the FDA doesn't do something about all the machinations that make the me-too business not only possible but the order of the day. Isn't there some way big pharma can be reined in? You might also ask why doctors continue to write prescriptions for expensive me-too drugs, even when the originals have gone off patent and are much cheaper. These are key questions I'll discuss in later chapters. Suffice it to say here that neither the FDA nor the medical profession seems much inclined to exercise the authority they have. In short, there does not seem to be much hope in the near term that the pharmaceutical industry will stop flooding the market with me-too drugs, and trying to persuade us that one is different from another. So get ready for the next new Crestor and the next new Lexapro and, of course, the next new Cialis.

6

How Good Are New Drugs?

HOW DO WE KNOW PRESCRIPTION drugs are any good? You might answer that doctors wouldn't use them if they weren't. Doctors, you might say, know what works by experience, and so do their patients. But experience can be highly misleading. The assumption that a drug works if a patient gets better does not allow for natural variations in the illness, for the placebo effect (the tendency of both doctors and patients to imagine a drug is working), for all the other times when the drug might fail, or for the possibility that another drug might have worked better. That is why clinical trials are required by the

Food and Drug Administration (FDA). Only by testing drugs in large numbers of people under rigorously controlled conditions can we really know what works and how well it works.

Okay, you might say, I'll buy that. Still, we know drugs work because otherwise the FDA would not approve them. After all, drug companies can't bring new drugs to market until they have carried out clinical trials to show they're safe and effective. But that raises another problem. Can we believe those trials? After all, that crucial last stage of research and development is usually sponsored by the company that makes the drug, even if the early research was done elsewhere. Is there some way companies can rig clinical trials to make their drugs look better than they are? Unfortunately, the answer is yes. Trials can be rigged in a dozen ways, and it happens all the time.

A Wake-Up Call

Let's start by looking at one of the few recent drug trials *not* sponsored by a drug company. Called ALLHAT (short for Antihypertensive and Lipid-Lowering Treatment to Prevent Heart Attack Trial), this was a mammoth trial of the treatment of high blood pressure (hypertension).[1] Although it received some support from Pfizer, it was mainly supported and organized by the National Heart, Lung, and Blood Institute—a part of the National Institutes of Health (NIH). The ALLHAT study was eight years long and involved over 42,000 people at more than six hundred clinics, the largest clinical trial of the treatment of high blood pressure ever done. It compared four types of drugs: (1) a calcium channel blocker—sold by Pfizer as Norvasc, the fifth-best-selling drug in the world in 2002;[2] (2) an alpha-adrenergic blocker—sold by Pfizer as Cardura, and also sold generically as doxazosin; (3) an angiotensin-converting-enzyme (ACE) inhibitor—sold by AstraZeneca as Zestril and by Merck as Prinivil, and also sold generically as lisinopril; and (4) a generic diuretic ("water pill") of a type that has been on the market for over fifty years.

The results, reported in 2002 in *The Journal of the American Medical Association,* were startling. To nearly everyone's surprise, the old-time diuretic turned out to be just as good for lowering blood pressure, and actually better for preventing some of the devastating complications of high blood pressure— mainly heart disease and strokes. Participants treated with the diuretic were much less likely to develop heart failure than those treated with Norvasc. And they were less likely to develop heart failure, strokes, and a number of other complications than those treated with the ACE inhibitor. As for Cardura, that part of the trial had to be stopped early, because so many people who received that drug developed heart failure. The director of the National Heart, Lung, and Blood Institute was unequivocal in his conclusion: "ALLHAT shows that diuretics are the best choice to treat hypertension, both medically and economically."[3]

Yet over the years the newer drugs had largely supplanted diuretics as treatment for high blood pressure. Diuretics were not promoted because generic manufacturers don't usually spend money on marketing. In contrast, when the new drugs came on the market, they were promoted incessantly. In 1996, for example, Norvasc was the most heavily advertised drug in *The New England Journal of Medicine,* but there was not a single ad for diuretics.[4] As you might guess, the use of diuretics plummeted. Whereas in 1982 they accounted for 56 percent of prescriptions written for high blood pressure, ten years later, after ACE inhibitors and calcium channel blockers hit the market, they accounted for only 27 percent. In general, the newer the drug, the better it sells. If you look at the top fifty drugs used by senior citizens in 2001, Norvasc was number two. Three brand-name ACE inhibitors were also in the top fifty. But diuretics like the one that proved superior in ALL-HAT appeared nowhere on that list.[5]

And look at the costs. Diuretics were priced at about $37 a year in 2002 (among the cheapest drugs on the market), compared with $715 for Norvasc and $230 for a generic ACE inhibitor.[6] So people with high blood pressure who use Norvasc get to pay nineteen times more for the privilege of taking a drug that is no better, and probably worse, than a diuretic. The cost in health may be worse. High blood pressure is extremely common—about 24 million Americans are now being treated for it. If the ALLHAT findings are correct, a great many people may have suffered serious complications that could have been avoided if they had been treated with diuretics. As Dr. Curt

Furberg, the principal author of ALLHAT, put it, "We find out now that we've wasted a lot of money. In addition, [the current practice] has probably caused harm to patients."[7]

Why didn't we learn a long time ago that the new drugs were not as good as the old ones? Well, to begin with, no one tried to find out. The last thing drug companies want is a head-to-head comparison with older drugs. So the new drugs were approved mainly because—in accord with the minimal FDA requirements—they were shown to be better than placebos. With few exceptions, no one wanted to know how they compared with a diuretic—or with one another, for that matter. New drugs came to market because they were better than nothing, then were promoted as though they were great advances in medicine. Since ALLHAT, industry apologists have protested that most people with high blood pressure need more than one drug, so new agents are indeed important. That is true but disingenuous. Drug companies tested and promoted their blood pressure drugs not as supplements but as first-line treatments.

Studies like ALLHAT are rare. The NIH does not ordinarily conduct clinical trials of drugs. It focuses on basic research into the underlying mechanisms of disease and leaves drug testing to the companies that manufacture the drugs. But sometimes it makes exceptions. The ALLHAT study was begun in 1994 because people were increasingly unhappy with the fact that no one knew which of the one hundred blood pressure drugs belonging to seven drug classes was best for the first-line treatment of hypertension. Of course, no single study can be considered the last word on this question. In fact, a subsequent, smaller Australian study comparing Merck's Prinivil with a diuretic indicated that Prinivil was slightly better.[8] But the ALLHAT study was a wake-up call. It raised the possibility that the "miracles" big pharma is so proud of really aren't miracles at all. Maybe many new drugs are actually worse than old ones. Unless we test the new against the old, head to head, there is simply no way to know.

The Research Enterprise

How do doctors decide which drugs to use for their patients? Some of them, unfortunately, depend on drug company marketing—the subject of the next chapter. But most doctors depend, at least in part, on a number of supposedly unbiased sources of information. They read medical journals to find out about new research and how to interpret it; they use textbooks to see what conclusions the expert authors draw from the overall body of scientific evidence; and they go to meetings and continuing medical education courses to hear from these experts (called "thought leaders") firsthand. These last two sources are, in fact, derivatives of the first. Textbooks and the thoughts of thought leaders are no better than the evidence on which they are based. And that evidence comes from research reports in medical journals. So it is crucial that those reports be unbiased. Are they?

Increasingly, the answer is no. As I have said, most clinical research on drugs is sponsored by the companies that make them. By itself, industry sponsorship does not mean the research is biased. But in addition, drug companies now have considerable control over the way the research is carried out and reported. That is new. Until the 1980s, researchers were largely independent of the companies that sponsored their work. Drug companies would give a grant to an academic medical center, then step back and wait for faculty researchers to produce the results. They *hoped* their product would look good, but they had no way of knowing for sure. They certainly did not attempt to tell the researchers how to run their clinical trials. Now, however, companies are involved in every detail of the research— from design of the study through analysis of the data to the decision whether to publish the results. That involvement has made bias not only possible but extremely likely. Researchers don't control clinical trials anymore; sponsors do.

Why the change? It comes down to the immense growth in industry wealth and influence since the watershed year of 1980. As they became richer, more powerful, and more profit-driven, drug companies became less willing to sit back and wait for academic researchers to produce their results. For one thing, the trials ate into the patent life of drugs, and for another, just waiting was too uncertain. The research findings could go against them. So instead of relying on academic centers to test their drugs, drug companies turned to the new for-profit research industry that grew up to serve them—the contract research organizations I described in Chapter 2. As you will remember, these companies contract with private doctors to collect data on patients in their offices according to company instructions. The doctors are not themselves trained researchers, so they simply do what they are told—or risk losing their lucrative deals with the contractors. The contract research organizations, in turn, answer only to big pharma. That means the drug companies have nearly total control over these trials.

The academic medical centers were unhappy to lose drug company contracts—even though they were a small fraction of their research income. Whereas in 1990, about 80 percent of industry-sponsored trials were done at academic institutions, within a decade that share had dropped to less than 40 percent. The loss came at a time when many medical schools and teaching hospitals were in financial trouble because of shrinking reimbursements from patient care and reduced support for medical education. So they began to compete with contract research organizations the only way they could—by becoming more accommodating to pharmaceutical sponsors. When companies insisted on controlling the way clinical trials were done, they met remarkably little resistance.

Furthermore, the whole context of academic-industry relations had changed. With the 1980 Bayh-Dole legislation, the traditional boundaries between academia and industry were blurred. Academic medical centers now saw themselves as "partners" of the pharmaceutical industry in common endeavors—and junior partners, at that. Consider some of the academic-industrial arrangements at Harvard University.[9] The

Dana-Farber Cancer Institute, a Harvard hospital, has a deal that gives Novartis rights to discoveries that lead to new cancer drugs. The Japanese cosmetic maker Shiseido gave Harvard's Massachusetts General Hospital $180 million over ten years for first rights to discoveries by faculty dermatologists. Merck is building a twelve-story research facility next door to Harvard Medical School. Both sides expect a close, multifaceted collaboration, although the terms have not yet been announced. Partners HealthCare, a pair of Harvard teaching hospitals, issued a request for faculty applications to be part of a "Partners Faculty Exchange Program" with Millennium Pharmaceuticals. It promised that, as part of Partners' collaboration with Millennium, "interested faculty will be integrated into Millennium project teams." Harvard is not unique. One recent survey showed that two-thirds of academic medical centers hold equity in start-up companies that sponsor some of their research.[10] The drug companies, for their part, are generous to the medical schools. In Harvard Medical School's Dean's Report for 2003–4, for instance, the list of benefactors included about a dozen of the largest drug companies. So it was just part of the new climate to do clinical trials pretty much the way the pharmaceutical industry wanted them done.

As a result, drug companies now design clinical trials to be carried out by researchers who are little more than hired hands— whether the trials are in academic centers or in physicians' offices. Sponsoring companies keep the data, and in multicenter trials, they may not even let the researchers themselves see all of it. They also analyze and interpret the results, and decide what, if anything, should be published. The authors of a recent survey of academic policies on the matter concluded, "We found that academic institutions rarely ensure that their investigators have full participation in the design of the trials, unimpeded access to trial data, and the right to publish their findings."[11] All of this makes a mockery of the traditional role of researchers as independent and impartial scientists. Academic institutions and their faculties vary in how much control they are willing to cede to sponsors, but in general, they cede much more than they should. Contract research organizations and their networks of private doctors cede most of it.

If faculty researchers have lost much of their independence, they've gained in other ways. Many of them have lucrative financial arrangements with drug company sponsors that would have been impossible twenty years ago. Researchers serve as consultants to companies whose products they are studying, become paid members of advisory boards and speakers' bureaus, enter into patent and royalty arrangements together with their institutions, promote drugs and devices at company-sponsored symposiums, and allow themselves to be plied with expensive gifts and trips to luxurious settings. Many also have equity interest in the companies. These kinds of deals can add significantly to their salaries. The head of the Department of Psychiatry at Brown University Medical School, for instance, was reported by *The Boston Globe* to have made over $500,000 in consulting fees in 1998.[12] It's hard to believe that close and remunerative personal ties with drug companies do not add to the strong pro-industry bias in medical research and education. Big pharma not only controls the details of the way clinical trials are performed, but as backup, it also seeks to win the hearts and minds of researchers.

One of the more sobering indications of the extent to which big pharma has compromised the research community is its extensive inroads into the NIH itself. This agency funds the lion's share of basic medical research throughout the country, using taxpayer dollars. It is supposed to award grants entirely on the basis of scientific merit, and conduct its own research, including the selection of industry collaborators, entirely in the public interest—free from commercial considerations. But a 2003 piece of investigative reporting by David Willman in the *Los Angeles Times* called that picture into serious question.[13] Willman found that senior NIH scientists (who are among the highest paid employees in the government) routinely supplement their income by accepting large consulting fees and stock options from drug companies that have dealings with the institutes. At one time, most of these kinds of connections would have been prohibited, but in 1995, the then director of the institutes, Harold Varmus, with a stroke of the pen, lifted the restrictions. After that, the NIH placed no limits on the amount of money its scientists could earn from outside work or the time they could devote to it.

According to Willman, senior scientists with financial ties to industry included the director of the National Institute of Arthritis and Musculoskeletal and Skin Diseases, the director of the NIH Clinical Center (the main site for human subjects research), the former director of the division of diabetes, endocrine, and metabolic diseases at the National Institute of Diabetes and Digestive and Kidney Diseases, and the former director of the National Human Genome Research Institute. Some NIH scientists made hundreds of thousands of dollars in consulting fees. The deputy director of the Laboratory of Immunology, for instance, whose salary was $179,000 in 2003, was reported to have collected more than $1.4 million in consulting fees over eleven years and received stock options valued at $865,000.

It is impossible to know to what extent these financial deals influenced NIH judgments about grants, research priorities, or the interpretation of results, but they certainly are cause for concern. Outside activities were said to be approved by supervisors, and scientists supposedly excused themselves from direct involvement in decisions that affected their outside clients, but Willman reported instances in which even those minimal restrictions seem to have been ignored. Moreover, the NIH did not even require most senior scientists to file public disclosures of their outside income. (That was accomplished by jiggering the pay scale in such a way that highly paid scientists were included with those with lower salaries, who were not required to disclose conflicts of interest.) The result was that, as of 2003, more than 94 percent of the agency's 2259 top scientists did not have to reveal their outside consulting income.

In an editorial in the *Los Angeles Times* that accompanied

the Willman revelations, the paper got it exactly right: "The pharmaceutical industry is everywhere in Washington, all but writing the Medicare prescription drug bill, fielding more lobbyists than there are members of Congress, flinging gifts and trips at doctors and trying to prevent double-blind drug trials that pit one drug against another, instead of against a placebo." It concluded, "Willman's story, shocking as it is, is just one piece of an unwholesome picture. Congress helped make this system and can help unmake it. Start with high-level hearings. Repeal the most destructive portions of the Bayh-Dole Act. Above all, restore the integrity of the National Institutes of Health."[14] In January 2004, the Senate Appropriations Subcommittee on Labor, Health and Human Services, and Education had begun to hold hearings on the matter, and the Department of Health and Human Services inspector general and the U.S. General Accounting Office launched their own inquiries. As might be anticipated under these circumstances, the NIH director appointed a Blue Ribbon Panel on Conflict of Interest Policies.

Bias—And Lots of It

Not surprisingly, bias is now rampant in drug trials.[15] A recent survey found that industry-sponsored research was nearly four times as likely to be favorable to the company's product as NIH-sponsored research (despite the Willman revelations).[16] That is in accord with a large body of evidence showing that researchers with industry connections are far more likely to

favor company products. In the case of calcium channel blockers like Norvasc, for instance, one survey of seventy articles
about their safety found that 96 percent of authors who were
supportive of the drugs had financial ties to the companies that
made them, whereas only 37 percent of authors who were critical had such ties.[17]

I will not detail all the ways research can be biased.[18] But a
few are worth mentioning. Sometimes, bias is just a matter of
spin—researchers extol a drug even though the results do not
support their enthusiasm. One recent survey showed that authors of industry-funded studies were more than five times as
likely to recommend the company drug as authors of studies
funded by nonprofit organizations—regardless of the actual results.[19] But often, bias is built into the study design, as is the case
with placebo-controlled clinical trials. Almost inevitably new
me-too drugs seem to be effective. But in fact, as shown by
ALLHAT, if they were compared with drugs already on the market, they might be revealed to be less effective. Researchers even
in the most prestigious medical centers go along with loading
the dice this way, because sponsors insist on it. The information
from such trials may be of very little use to practicing doctors,
who usually are not interested in whether a new drug is better
than nothing. They want to know whether it is better than what
they are already using.

Another way to load the dice is to enroll only young subjects
in trials, even if the drugs being tested are meant to be used
mainly in older people. Because young people generally experi-

ence fewer side effects, drugs will look safer in these trials than they would in practice. Another is to compare the new drug not just with a placebo but with an old drug given at too low a dose. In the last chapter, I described how this was done with the statins. This bias was also present in many trials of nonsteroidal anti-inflammatory drugs (NSAIDS). (These are drugs like Naprosyn that are taken mainly for arthritis.) The new NSAIDS looked better because the comparison drugs were given at lower doses. Or the old drug can be administered incorrectly. That was true of trials comparing fluconazole with an older drug, amphotericin B, to treat fungus infections in patients with AIDS. Amphotericin B was administered orally, which dramatically cuts down on its effectiveness. Not surprisingly, the trials were sponsored by the makers of fluconazole. Or trials can be designed to be too brief to be meaningful. That is true of many trials of drugs that need to be taken long term. Blood pressure trials usually last for just a few months, and antidepressant trials for a few weeks, yet patients may have to take these kinds of drugs for years. Some treatments look pretty good for a short time but are not effective and may even be harmful for long-term use.

One of the most common ways to bias trials is to present only part of the data—the part that makes the product look good—and ignore the rest. That happened in a clinical trial of the arthritis drug Celebrex. A study sponsored by the drug company that makes it, Pharmacia (since acquired by Pfizer), ostensibly showed that Celebrex caused fewer side effects than two older arthritis drugs. These results were published, along with a favorable editorial, in *The Journal of the American Medical Association*. Not until after publication did the editors learn that the results were based on only the first six months of a yearlong trial. When the entire trial was analyzed, there was no advantage to Celebrex. The editorialist was understandably outraged. *The Washington Post* quoted him as saying, "I am furious. . . . I wrote the editorial. I looked like a fool. But . . . all I had available to me was the data presented in the article." And the editor of the journal said, "I am disheartened to hear that they had those data [the second six months] at the time that they submitted [the manuscript] to us. We are functioning on a level of trust that was, perhaps, broken."[20]

Suppressing Things You Don't Like

The most dramatic form of bias is out-and-out suppression of negative results. That is easily done in privately run trials, but it also occurs in trials done at academic centers. There have been several widely publicized cases. It's instructive to look at one of them.[21] In 1996, a biotechnology company called Immune Response Corporation contracted with Dr. James O. Kahn of the University of California at San Francisco and Dr. Stephen W. Lagakos of the Harvard School of Public Health to conduct a multicenter trial of its drug Remune. This drug was supposed to slow the progression of AIDS by boosting the immune system, and the company was seeking FDA approval to market it as a "therapeutic vaccine." Kahn and Lagakos undertook the trial, which was carried out in 2500 HIV-infected patients at seventy-seven medical centers. But the company held the data.

After three years, it became clear that Remune was not effective. But the company objected to Kahn and Lagakos presenting the results as negative (meaning that the vaccine had no effect). It wanted them to include in their paper an analysis of a subgroup of patients that it said showed positive effects. Kahn and Lagakos refused, saying that the company's analysis was not in accord with scientific standards. Immune Response then threatened to withhold the final 5 to 10 percent of data if the investigators did not agree to include the company's analysis. Finally, after much pulling and tugging, the company agreed to turn over the remaining data, but only on condition that it be given the right to approve the paper. Kahn and Lagakos again refused. On the basis of the data they already had (which was enough), they published a negative report in *The Journal of the American Medical Association.* Immune Response filed a multi-million-dollar claim against Kahn and his university, alleging harm to its business. (The company eventually lost.)

It is interesting to look behind the scenes in this dispute. The contract between the company and the researchers contained the seeds of the problems that developed. While it did not give Immune Response veto power over publication, it did involve the company in every detail of the work. It set up a five-person committee that included the company's medical director to write the paper; it stipulated that Kahn would keep the company abreast of the progress of the trial; and it provided for the company to see the final paper before submission for publication. When it became clear that the trial was negative, the company asserted the right to do the analysis. The president and CEO of Immune Response later complained, "Just put yourself in my position. I spent over $30 million. I would think I have certain rights."[22] He really seemed to think he had a "right" to favorable results.

Kahn and Lagakos showed courage and integrity in sticking to their guns. It is essential that clinical research be conducted with impartiality, which means sponsors must be kept at arm's length. Many researchers simply accept the will of sponsors or cave in under pressure. But the conditions of the contract were in a sense the camel's nose under the tent. By involving the company in all aspects of the trial, even including the medical director as a coauthor, Kahn and Lagakos were virtually inviting the camel inside. The company had a clear conflict of interest. Yet by today's standards, the contract gave Kahn and Lagakos an unusual amount of independence. Many current contracts give companies far more control.

So What Do We *Really* Know?

When a drug company applies to the FDA for approval of a new drug, it is required to submit results from every one of the clinical trials it has sponsored. But it is not required to publish them. The FDA may approve the drug on the basis of minimal evidence. For example, the agency usually requires simply that the drug work better than a placebo in two clinical trials, even if it doesn't in other trials. But companies publish only the positive results, not the negative ones. Often, in fact, they publish positive results more than once, in slightly different forms in different journals. The FDA has no control over this selective publishing. The practice leads doctors to believe that drugs are much better than they are, and the public comes to share this belief, on the basis of media reports. There is a general inflation in the notion of the good that drugs can do (and a deflation in concern about side effects).

Take the case of antidepressants. Among the top ten drugs in 2002 were two antidepressants of the SSRI type—Zoloft and Paxil. It is generally accepted that SSRIs are highly effective drugs. Millions of Americans take them, and many psychiatrists and primary care doctors swear by them. But a recent study throws doubt on the general enthusiasm. Using the Freedom of Information Act (a law that allows citizens to obtain government documents), the authors obtained FDA reviews of every placebo-controlled clinical trial submitted for initial approval of the six most widely used antidepressant drugs approved between 1987 and 1999—Prozac, Paxil, Zoloft, Celexa, Serzone, and Effexor (all but the last two are SSRIs).[23] As is typical, most of the forty-two clinical trials lasted for just six weeks.

Their findings were sobering. On average, placebos were 80 percent as effective as the drugs. And the difference between drug and placebo was only about two points on the sixty-two-point Hamilton Depression Scale (a measure of the severity of depression). While that is statistically significant, it is very unlikely to be of any clinical importance. The results were much the same for all six drugs. These figures, of course, are averages, and it is possible that certain types of patients have much better (or worse) responses. But the point is that, based on all the evidence, not just what the drug companies published, the new antidepressants certainly do not look like the miracle drugs we have been led to believe they are. More recently, there have been serious charges that manufacturers of SSRIs have suppressed data indicating that the drugs are not only ineffective but sometimes dangerous in children.[24]

Another recent NIH study is also instructive. For decades, women have been taking estrogen and progesterone hormone replacement therapy, not just to treat the symptoms of menopause but also in the belief that it will prevent heart disease. That belief was based mainly on industry-sponsored studies. But now a large NIH clinical trial indicates that, instead of preventing heart disease, combination hormone replacement actually increases it. This trial underscores the fact that we need to question how reliable publications from industry-sponsored research really are.

I do not want to sound like a nihilist or a Luddite. I know

very well that as a result of innovative research and development—in both academia and industry—we have available to us many drugs of immense importance. No one would want to be without, say, insulin for diabetes, antimicrobial agents to fight infections, vaccines to prevent a host of serious diseases, anticlotting agents to treat heart attacks, chemotherapy for cancer, a panoply of effective painkillers and anesthetics, and many others. Gleevec is a major advance, as are Epogen and Taxol. Prilosec is important, too, as are statins and ACE inhibitors and many other drugs. All of these agents have extended and greatly improved our lives. I would not have spent my professional life at *The New England Journal of Medicine* if I did not deeply believe in the value of medical research and innovative treatments.

So I do not mean to suggest that prescription drugs are generally useless or dangerous or some sort of hoax. What I do mean to suggest is that many of them *may* be, particularly new me-too drugs that have been tested by companies and researchers with financial interests in the outcomes. Are new drugs any better than old ones? Are they worse? The worrying answer is that frequently we just don't know. Too often, all we have is bias and hype.

7

The Hard Sell . . . Lures, Bribes, and Kickbacks

IN 2001, DRUG COMPANIES GAVE DOC-
tors nearly $11 billion worth of "free samples."
These were almost always the newest, most expensive me-too drugs. The companies knew that
when the free samples ran out, you and your doctor would be hooked on them. The drugs weren't
really free, of course. The costs were simply added
on to drug prices (these firms are not charities).

The same year, drug companies sent some
88,000 sales representatives around to doctors'
offices to hand out the free samples, plus lots of
personal gifts, and talk up company products.[1]
The industry claims it spent another $5.5 billion

on this activity, an amount that seems much too low to me, since it is unlikely to have cost only $62,500—$5.5 billion divided by 88,000—for each sales representative's salary, benefits, travel costs, and gift giving.[2] But whatever the amount, you paid for it. And you continue to pay for it.

You also pay for a nearly infinite variety of promotions directed at you, not your doctor. Here the expectation is that you will ask your doctor to prescribe the drugs for you. For instance, GlaxoSmithKline and its co-marketer Bayer signed a deal with the National Football League to promote their me-too drug Levitra to compete with Viagra for the huge "erectile dysfunction" market. Reportedly the deal cost the companies $20 million. In addition to exclusive league sponsorship, they made individual deals with some of the teams. The agreement with the New England Patriots, for instance, called for Levitra's burning flame logo to appear on signs ringing Gillette Stadium. Mike Ditka, former coach of the Chicago Bears, would make a thirty-second pitch on a large screen.[3] In fact, to watch the 2004 Super Bowl was to wonder whether football *causes* erectile dysfunction.

Not to be outdone, Pfizer, the maker of Viagra, phased out its former promoter, Bob Dole (too old, too tired), in favor of the baseball star Rafael Palmeiro. Pfizer also sponsors a Viagra car on the NASCAR circuit. And an ad for Eli Lilly's Cialis, the latest impotence drug, was emblazoned on a yacht in the America's Cup race. As a Pfizer spokesperson put it, "Sports is really a great way to reach men with this condition of erection problems. Men feel passionate about their sports, and it's a nice way to educate people while they are feeling comfortable."[4] You pay for this, too, whether you use any of these drugs or not.

Some ads are far less visible. In fact, they're stealth ads. Morley Safer, of CBS's *60 Minutes,* made hundreds of videos that resembled newscasts but were really promotional spots for drug companies. They were given to local public television stations to show between regular programs. Safer was hired by a marketing company called WJMK, on behalf of its pharmaceutical clients. The drug companies reportedly were allowed to edit and approve the videos, and Safer was paid six figures for one day in the studio. When he decided the "news breaks" (as WJMK called them) did not meet the standards of CBS News, the company decided to hire the retired CBS News anchor Walter Cronkite and CNN's Aaron Brown to replace him.[5] Cronkite later pulled out of the deal and was sued by WJMK. His lawyer argued that he was defrauded into believing the advertising was journalism.

A new type of stealth ad consists of celebrities apparently spontaneously talking about health ailments on news or entertainment shows in the course of an ordinary interview.[6] Lauren Bacall, for instance, in conversation with Matt Lauer on the *Today* show, spoke about a friend who had become blind from macular degeneration. She urged the audience to get tested for it and mentioned the Novartis drug Visudyne. What she did not reveal is that she was paid by Novartis. It was all just part of a celebrity interview. You also paid for this.

As we learned in Chapter 5, AstraZeneca spent a half billion dollars in 2001 to convince consumers to switch from Prilosec to Nexium. The company is still heavily promoting its me-too purple pill—now with ads showing improbable crowds of despairing people strewn around on barren cliffs surrounding pits of something that looks like boiling lava. (Ulcers of the earth?) Deliverance comes in the form of a giant purple capsule. This, too, you pay for.

Another Black Box

These are just a few examples of the pharmaceutical marketing that permeates our existence. No one knows how much of it there really is, because drug companies are even more secretive about their marketing expenditures than they are about their research and development costs. And well they might be. Those expenditures are so immense they simply can't be defended. Instead, the industry tries to obfuscate them or define them away by accounting for only a fraction of them and maintaining that is the whole. The major method of obfuscation is to pretend marketing is really education. Walter Cronkite's lawyer, for instance, told *The New York Times* that he was assured the videos would be educational instead of promotional. To accept a whopper like that requires a good deal of innocence or willingness to feign it. As for the local stations that aired the videos, a spokesperson for KSMQ in Austin, Texas, explained, "They offer them to us for free, so I don't go digging around for any other information."[7]

According to Securities and Exchange Commission (SEC) and shareholder reports for 2001, the biggest drug companies spent on average about 35 percent of their revenues on "marketing and administration" (called by slightly different names in different companies). That percentage was probably about the same for members of the Pharmaceutical Research and Manufacturers of America (PhRMA) generally, and it had not changed much over the past decade.[8] It is the largest single item in big pharma's budget, larger than manufacturing costs and much larger than R & D. In 2002, for the top ten U.S. companies, that percentage dropped slightly, to about 31 percent of revenues. That's a heap of "marketing and administration." Many countries would love to have a gross domestic product as big as that.

How much of this amount is "marketing" and how much is "administration"? That is hard to determine, because nearly all the big drug companies combine marketing and administration in their SEC reports (for no apparent reason except concealment). However, one major company, Novartis, does separate marketing from administration in a way that helps to answer the question. In 2001, Novartis assigned 36 percent of total revenues to "marketing and distribution" and 5 percent to "administration and general overhead," which suggests that 5 percent is probably a reasonable estimate of the "administration" component of the "marketing and administration" budget item.[9] Another way to get at the question is to look at the distribution of personnel in the industry, as reported by PhRMA. In 2000, 35 percent of drug company employees were in "marketing" and 12 percent in "administration."[10] We don't know precisely how employee numbers translate into expenditures. A reasonable conclusion would be that of the 35 percent "marketing and administration" budget for the industry in 2001, not much more than 5 percent went to administration, and the rest, close to 30 percent, went to marketing. According to PhRMA, total revenues for its members that year (excluding some overseas sales) were $179 billion, so that would mean they spent about $9 billion for administration and nearly $54 billion for marketing.

What is included in "administration"? First, of course, are the rewards executives give to themselves. Top officers of major drug companies make from a few million to tens of millions of dollars in salaries, bonuses, and other compensation, plus at least that much again in stock options. Then there are the general costs of running any big corporation—accounting, financial, and human resources. Finally, there are legal costs—and they have to be enormous.[11] As we will see in Chapter 10, drug companies are constantly in litigation (or threatening it) to extend marketing rights on their blockbuster drugs. Manipulating the law to extend marketing rights more than pays for itself, of course. In fact, it is one of the most lucrative things big pharma can do. But lawyers don't come cheap, and this industry employs a lot of them. Increasingly, they are also necessary to fend off charges of illegal activity, as we will see.

So now let's look at "marketing." The companies throw sand in our eyes by using different terms for the same thing. Some call it "selling," some "marketing," and Pfizer adds the term "informational expenses"—evidently for the benefit of Walter Cronkite's lawyer, among others. Bristol-Myers Squibb even breaks it down into two budgetary items—"marketing, selling, and administrative" and "advertising and product promotion." But once administration is taken out, what is left is really all marketing in one form or another. It doesn't matter whether it is called selling, promotion, or advertising.

Now You See It, Now You Don't

But look at what the industry does. In 2001, even while admitting that it spent about 35 percent of revenues on marketing and administration, it defined marketing so narrowly that it added up to far less than that. It insisted that marketing has just four components: (1) direct-to-consumer (DTC) advertising (mainly TV ads), (2) sales pitches to doctors in their offices, (3) free samples for doctors, and (4) advertising in medical journals. So defined, PhRMA reported that the sum total of its members' promotional spending in 2001 came to "only" $19.1 billion—$2.7 billion for DTC ads, $5.5 billion for visits to doctors, $10.5 billion for the retail value of free samples, and about $380 million for medical journal advertising.[12] The trade association told everyone who would listen that this was much less than the $30.3 billion they spent on R & D that year.

The U.S. General Accounting Office (GAO) and the media, unfortunately, repeated this assertion as though it were true. In a 2002 report on DTC advertising, the GAO said, "Pharmaceutical companies spend more on research and development than on all drug promotional activities, including DTC advertising," and cited the figures given in the PhRMA report.[13] And *The New York Times,* in its story on the GAO report, relayed those figures uncritically, although it did point out that the data came from the drug companies.[14]

In view of its record, it's amazing to me that anyone would accept a self-serving pronouncement from this industry without verification—particularly when it is as inconsistent and unbelievable as this one. The fact is that big pharma spent much more on marketing that year than on R & D. The $19.1 billion was just a piece of it. And that should have been obvious from the companies' own SEC filings and the fact that many more employees worked in marketing than in R & D. As I explained, a reasonable estimate is that marketing expenditures in that year were actually close to $54 billion—that is, 30 percent of the $179 billion in revenues disclosed in PhRMA's annual report. That is a very long way from $19.1 billion. It leaves some $35 billion unaccounted for—a lot of money to overlook.

What happened to it? A clue is provided by a tiny footnote in the GAO report: "These figures do not include educational meetings arranged by pharmaceutical companies for physicians, which are not generally considered to be promotional activities." They're not? I'll get to that crucial matter in the next chapter.

Direct-to-Consumer Advertising

First, let's look at the marketing the industry *is* willing to acknowledge—direct-to-consumer advertising, sales visits to doctors, free samples, and medical journal advertising. Since the last is less than 1 percent of the total, I won't discuss it further, except to say that, like sales visits, it is meant to influence doctors' prescribing habits. Because most medical journals are dependent on drug ads for their survival, it probably also influences what they publish.

Direct-to-consumer advertising, while still relatively small in terms of expenditures, seems to be the fastest growing part of the marketing budget (as far as anyone can tell). Until 1997, drug companies didn't advertise much on television, because the Food and Drug Administration (FDA), which has jurisdiction over all prescription drug advertising, required them to include full information about side effects in their ads. That made thirty-second spots difficult—and even counterproductive. A drug could sound pretty scary with a rapid-fire listing of side effects. But in 1997, the FDA announced it would change the rules for broadcast ads. Instead of including a complete rundown of risks, companies would merely have to mention the major ones and refer viewers to a source of additional information (for example, a toll-free phone number). After the rule change, drug companies began to flood the airwaves with commercials about their latest drugs. Expenditures on DTC ads nearly tripled between 1997 and 2001, and the percentage accounted for by television increased from 25 to 64 percent. In terms of numbers, there are still many more print ads, but they are far less expensive.[15]

The great majority of DTC ads are for very expensive me-too drugs that require a lot of pushing because there is no good reason to think they are any better than drugs already on the market. There is overwhelming evidence that the ads work.[16] People go to their doctors and ask for the new drugs, and very often get them. Furthermore, the ads not only increase the sales of the particular drug advertised but also increase sales for the class of drugs as a whole. In other words, an ad for Paxil increases sales for Zoloft and Celexa as well as for Paxil.

Drug companies are required by law to send their DTC ads to the FDA when they launch a new ad campaign, and the agency is supposed to check that the ads present a "fair balance" between risks and benefits. If an ad is misleading, the FDA is supposed to notify the company in an official letter, and the company must fix the ad or stop it. Obviously, given the nature of the ads we're subjected to, the agency fails at this job. For one thing, it is not staffed to do it. It had only thirty reviewers to cull through the 34,000 DTC ads submitted to it in 2001.[17] Nor can the agency verify whether it receives all the ads it is supposed to.

In addition, the FDA under the Bush administration has deliberately adopted a go-slow policy. It is sending far fewer letters about misleading ads than it used to, and those it does send sometimes go out so late that the offending campaign has already run its course. Review by the FDA's legal office is now required before a letter is dispatched.[18] Even when letters are sent promptly, they don't seem to be taken seriously. The particular ad campaign may be stopped, only to be replaced by another just as bad. Some companies have received several letters about successive campaigns for the same drug. Pfizer, for instance, has received four letters in four years about misleading ads for Lipitor.[19]

There is no doubt in my mind that DTC ads mislead consumers far more than they inform them, and they pressure doctors to prescribe new, expensive, and often marginally helpful drugs, even when a more conservative option (including no drug) might be better and safer. Doctors don't want to alienate their patients, and too many of them find it faster and easier to write a prescription than to explain why it isn't necessary. That is why DTC ads are prohibited in every other developed country (except New Zealand).

The industry claims the ads are beneficial, because they stimulate people to go to their doctors for symptoms they had not previously recognized or thought could not be treated.[20] But there are no properly controlled studies of the health effects of ads. Just about everyone is now exposed to the flood of drug ads on television, so it is impossible to compare their behavior with that of people not exposed to ads. Furthermore, most ads do not introduce drugs for rare or previously untreatable conditions but rather promote drugs for well-known conditions for which there are plenty of treatments already at hand. Finally, whether the public benefits from taking more and more medicines for increasingly broadly defined diseases is open to serious question. One could make a strong argument that Americans with minor ailments suffer more from overmedication, and all the side effects and drug interactions that go with it, than from undermedication.

The Big Target—Doctors

As saturated as we are by DTC advertising, the main target of the industry's marketing efforts is not the public but doctors. After all, they are the ones who write the prescriptions. If the drug companies can get to doctors directly, it is even better than getting to them indirectly through their patients. Katharine Greider, in her book *The Big Fix,* describes in vivid detail how drug marketing permeates the medical profession.[21] I mentioned that in 2001 the industry employed some 88,000 sales representatives to visit doctors in their offices and hospitals to promote their products. That comes to something like one for every five or six practicing physicians, depending on whether you count interns and residents.[22] These drug reps or detailers, as they are known, are ubiquitous in the medical world. Usually young, attractive, and extremely ingratiating, they roam the halls of almost every sizable hospital in the country looking for chances to talk with the medical staff and paving the way with gifts (such as books, golf balls, and tickets to sporting events). In many teaching hospitals, drug reps regularly provide lunches for interns and residents while standing by to chat about their drugs. This "food, flattery, and friendship," as it has been called, creates a sense of reciprocity in young doctors with long prescribing lives ahead of them. They naturally feel indebted to congenial people who keep giving them gifts. Some teaching hospitals have begun to curb these practices, but not nearly enough of them.

Drug reps are allowed to attend medical conferences, may be invited into operating and procedure rooms, and sometimes are even present when physicians examine patients in clinics or at the bedside. Patients are often allowed to assume the reps are doctors—an assumption that is strengthened when drug reps offer advice about treatment. Take the case of Azucena Sanchez-Scott, reported in *The Boston Globe*.[23] After finishing chemotherapy for breast cancer, she went to see her doctor and found another man in the examining room. The doctor said that the stranger was "observing my work."

Only later did she learn he was a drug rep from a Johnson & Johnson subsidiary. She sued the company, which settled out of court. But her experience is not unusual. Drug companies pay doctors several hundred dollars a day to allow sales reps to shadow them as they see patients, a practice called a "preceptorship." One Schering-Plough rep explained that "it's another way to build a relationship with the doctor and hopefully build business." That was very candid of her. But patients should not be used for that purpose.

Meetings with doctors in their offices are extremely valuable to drug companies, and they've become valuable to doctors as well. It's a symbiotic relationship. There is no way to exaggerate how much a part of some doctors' daily lives drug reps have become. A typical doctor is visited by several every week (if you remember the ratio of one drug rep to every five or six practicing doctors, that is not as surprising as it seems), and doctors in high-prescribing specialties may be visited by a dozen in one day. The reps make friends not only with the doctors but with their entire staffs, and often announce their arrival by distributing goodies to everyone. Sometimes they provide lunch. Doctors, for their part, look to drug reps for information about the latest drugs, as well as the inevitable sack full of free samples.

Gifts to doctors are often lavish. Doctors can pretty much count on being taken to dinner in fine restaurants whenever they want; there company-selected experts sometimes give talks. But there are also other expensive gifts. An editorial in *USA Today* painted a vivid but all too accurate picture: "Christmas trees. Free tickets to a Washington Redskins game, with a champagne reception thrown in. A family vacation in Hawaii. And wads of cash. Such gifts would trigger a big red 'bribery' alert in the mind of just about any public official or government contractor. But not, it seems, in the minds of many doctors. They have been raking in jaw-dropping gifts from pharmaceutical firms battling to give their products an edge in an increasingly competitive market."[24]

In 2000, the American Medical Association issued guidelines to curb these practices, and the pharmaceutical industry followed suit in 2002 (more about that shortly). In 2003, the Office of the Inspector General of the U.S. Department of Health and Human Services warned that excessive gift giving to doctors could be prosecuted under antikickback laws. These guidelines and the inspector general's warning may have discouraged the most extreme practices, but the guidelines are voluntary and even the warning is filled with loopholes.[25]

Free samples are the most important gifts. They are an effective way to get doctors and patients familiar with an expensive, newly approved drug when an older, cheaper one might be better or just as good. For the same reason, companies often give hospitals and HMOs steep discounts on their new drugs. I was told, for instance, that two of Harvard's teaching hospitals include Nexium on their formularies because AstraZeneca gave them a good deal. It is a form of bait and switch, although what is switched is the price, not the product. When patients are discharged from the hospital with a prescription for Nexium, they pay market price.

As doctors have become busier and busier under the pressures of managed care, drug reps are starting to find it tough to get enough face time with them. Increasingly, they are being put off, or their visits squeezed down to a minute or two—"Just leave the goodies at the door." The intense competition for doctors' time and attention has given rise to new businesses that specialize in helping drug reps deliver an effective pitch quickly. Prescription-tracking companies buy information from big pharmacy chains about doctors' prescribing habits and sell it to drug companies. Using these physician profiles, drug reps know exactly what a doctor prescribes before each visit, so they can tailor their sales pitch and make every minute count. If they know that a doctor is using a competitor's drug, for instance, they can spend their time undermining that drug without acknowledging that they know the doctor uses it. And they can tell whether the visit paid off by seeing what the doctor does afterward. This monitoring enables drug companies to focus their attentions on the most promising doctors.[26]

A Lesson

Many promotional practices can only be described as bribes and kickbacks. Although it is illegal to pay doctors to prescribe drugs, very few cases have been prosecuted. One of those is the case of TAP Pharmaceuticals and its cancer drug, Lupron. That is a story worth recounting in some detail, not because it is unique but because it is only an extreme example of the more general phenomenon.[27]

Lupron is a hormone treatment for prostate cancer. Most patients with this cancer are over the age of sixty-five, and therefore eligible for Medicare. Because the drug is given by injection in doctors' offices, usually every month or so, 80 percent of the charges are paid by Medicare—unlike the case for outpatient drugs. Doctors buy the drug directly from the company, then bill Medicare for reimbursement based on the average wholesale price (see p. xiii) listed by the company. In the mid-

1990s, Lupron began to face competition from a cheaper drug of the same type, Zoladex. To get doctors to stick with Lupron, TAP Pharmaceuticals reportedly inflated its average wholesale price to about $500 a dose, then sold it to doctors for as little as $350. Medicare reimbursement would then be based on the $500 price, and the doctors could keep the difference—known as the "spread." That was, of course, a real incentive for doctors to stick with Lupron. According to government prosecutors, the company was essentially using taxpayer money to bribe doctors to prescribe its drug instead of a cheaper one.

And TAP didn't stop there. In 1996, the company also tried to persuade a large Massachusetts HMO, Tufts Health Plan, to stay with Lupron by offering its medical director of pharmacy programs a $25,000 "educational" grant that he could use for anything he wanted. The company couldn't have chosen a worse target: The medical director of pharmacy programs, Joseph Gerstein, is someone I know to be among the least likely people to take a bribe. When Gerstein refused, the company upped the offer to $65,000. But this time Gerstein, who with the support of Tufts had alerted federal authorities, taped the conversation, and that led to the unraveling of the company's illegal activities.

Eventually, after a long delay, during which Gerstein and another whistle-blower from within the company sued under the federal False Claims Act, TAP Pharmaceuticals agreed to plead guilty to health care fraud and settled the criminal and civil charges for a record $875 million. In addition, eleven TAP employees and a Massachusetts doctor were indicted for their part in the fraud. The indictment alleged, among other things, that TAP drug reps bribed doctors with trips to resorts, debt forgiveness, TVs and VCRs, and cash in the form of "educational grants," as well as free drug samples (for which they could bill Medicare). This was a huge settlement in a high-profile case, but the practices of TAP Pharmaceuticals and the doctors involved were not so very different from what goes on every day. In fact, one irony is that AstraZeneca, the maker of the rival drug Zoladex, later had to pay $355 million to settle similar charges.

The year after the TAP case became public, PhRMA issued voluntary guidelines similar to the AMA guidelines. They would limit the value of gifts to less than one hundred dollars, and require that the gifts be relevant to patient care—like textbooks. But the guidelines don't specify how often such gifts may be given. Once a week? Once a day? Nor do they bother to tell us why drug companies should be giving gifts to doctors in the first place, when the costs will just be added on to drug prices. The guidelines also permit more extravagant gifts and junkets if they can be construed as furthering an educational or research purpose.

The 30 Percent Markup

Since drug companies try to justify their prices by pointing to their large R & D costs, what can they possibly say about their much higher marketing expenditures? Would they argue that these also justify the high prices? Not likely. Instead, they do whatever they can to obscure the fact that in 2001 consumers paid something like a 30 percent markup for sales promotion (roughly the marketing portion of their approximately 35 percent "marketing and administration" budget that year). That is the name of the game here, and it is even harder to justify than the industry's secrecy about R & D costs. Since there is no proprietary reason to keep marketing costs hidden (as there could conceivably be for some R & D costs), the only possible rationale is to avoid a public backlash. But the industry owes the public a full accounting of exactly how it uses the tremendous revenues it garners. It needs to open this black box too.

The huge amount of marketing also raises the question: If prescription drugs are so good, why do they need to be pushed so hard? Wouldn't the world beat a path to the door of a company that produced, say, a cure for cancer? The answer is that truly good drugs don't have to be promoted very much. A genuinely important new drug, such as Gleevec, sells itself. Cancer doctors treating patients with the kind of leukemia that responds to Gleevec know about the drug from professional meetings and journal articles. And they use it. No sales pitch is needed. (Novartis does, however, use the Gleevec story to promote *itself*—implying that all of its drugs are that good.) Important new drugs require very little marketing. Me-too drugs, by contrast, require relentless flogging, because companies need to persuade doctors and the public that there is some reason to prescribe one instead of another. So it is no surprise that the drugs most heavily promoted are me-too drugs, like Nexium and Lipitor and Paxil.

We've accounted for the $19.1 billion the pharmaceutical industry admits it spent on marketing in 2001, but we still need to account for the mysterious $35 billion the industry doesn't acknowledge—the elephant in the living room. Some of that probably goes to gifts and a variety of promotional activities not acknowledged by the industry. But in addition, a great masquerade takes place. The industry has somehow persuaded both the government and the medical profession that it is in the education business—big time. Education, it contends, is different from marketing, even though it comes out of the marketing budget and is perforce hardly impartial. How the pharmaceutical industry gets away with that masquerade is the subject of the next chapter.

8

Marketing Masquerading as Education

NO ONE SHOULD RELY ON A BUSINESS for impartial evaluation of a product it sells. Yet the pharmaceutical industry contends it educates the medical profession and the public about its drugs and the conditions they treat, and many doctors and medical institutions—all recipients of the industry's largesse—pretend to believe it. So does the government. But "education" comes out of the drug companies' marketing budgets. That should tell you what is really going on. As in all other businesses, there is an inherent conflict of interest between selling products and assessing them. Pfizer, for instance, is hardly likely to provide impartial information about how its Zoloft compares with GlaxoSmithKline's Paxil to treat depression, or indeed, about whether either one of them is any good. Nor can it be relied on to teach us about depression itself.

In the last chapter, we learned that in 2001 the pharmaceutical industry acknowledged it spent over $19 billion on marketing (leaving about $35 billion unaccounted for). Like all businesses, drug companies claim their advertising is also educational. They claim, for instance, that people learn about diseases they didn't even know they had by watching direct-to-consumer television ads. ("Omigosh, this Clarinex ad makes me realize I have hay fever!") But drug companies at least admit direct-to-consumer ads are primarily promotional. That is not what I will be talking about in this chapter.

At issue in this chapter is the probably much larger amount spent on what drug companies contend are purely educational activities. Most of those are directed toward doctors. Although no outsider knows for sure, they probably account for the lion's share of the missing $35 billion of the marketing budget. It is crucial for big pharma to maintain the fiction that these expenditures are for education, not promotion, because by doing so it can evade legal constraints on its marketing activities. It is also good public relations.

Let's start by looking at two of these constraints. First, it is illegal for drug companies to market drugs for unapproved uses. When the Food and Drug Administration (FDA) approves a new drug, it approves it for a particular use. And that makes sense. If a drug is shown to be useful for treating a certain kind of infection, it may not work against another kind of infection. To stop drug companies from broadening their claims without evidence, they are not allowed to market drugs for "off-label" uses—that is, uses not approved by the FDA. Doctors, however, are not constrained by this law. They are permitted to prescribe drugs for whatever uses they want. So if drug companies can somehow convince doctors to prescribe drugs for off-label uses, sales go up. The problem is how to get around the law prohibiting marketing for those uses.

That is where "education" comes in. If drug companies pretend they are merely informing doctors about other potential uses, they can circumvent the law. And that is what they do. They sponsor make-believe education, and often buttress it by references to flimsy research studies they sponsor.

Second, it is illegal to offer doctors kickbacks (essentially bribes) to prescribe drugs. In the last chapter, we saw how TAP Pharmaceuticals got into trouble for that. In the wake of the TAP case, there has been increasing scrutiny of big pharma's lavish gift giving to doctors and medical facilities. The American Medical Association and the Pharmaceutical Research and Manufacturers of America (PhRMA) issued voluntary guidelines suggesting limitations on outright gifts, and the Department of Health and Human Services Office of the Inspector General warned that even adhering to those guidelines would not necessarily protect against prosecution for violating anti-kickback laws.

But what the guidelines and warnings have in common is an exemption for educational or research activities. If drug companies can plausibly construe their blandishments as having an educational or research purpose, they can get away with almost unlimited gifts to promote sales. Furthermore, it is largely left to them to decide what is education or research and what is marketing. As the inspector general's office said in its 2003 warning notice, "The manufacturer should determine whether the funding is for bona fide educational or research purposes."[1] The greater the scrutiny of outright gifts, the more the industry shifts to educational and research support as a substitute.

Continuing Medical Education

Luckily for the industry, the demand for physician education is enormous. That is because in most states doctors are required to receive continuing medical education (CME) throughout their professional lives to maintain their licenses. The requirements are substantial, and the education must be provided through accredited institutions. Most doctors earn the necessary credits by attending meetings and lectures—as many as a hundred a year. That means CME meetings are an integral part of doctors' lives. Every day, all across the country, hundreds, maybe thousands, of them take place. Doctors stream into hospital auditoriums, as well as convention centers and vacation spots, to hear about the latest in medical advances. A professional organization called the Accreditation Council of Continuing Medical Education

(ACCME) is responsible for accrediting the organizations that provide the educational programs. They include medical schools, hospitals, and various professional societies.

But who pays for these programs? You might assume doctors pay for their own postgraduate education, just as other professionals do, but you would be wrong. In 2001, drug companies paid over 60 percent of the costs of continuing medical education, and that fraction has increased since then.[2] Formerly, they directly supported the accredited professional organizations, but now they usually contract with private medical education and communication companies (MECCs) to plan the meetings, prepare teaching materials, and procure speakers. Oddly enough, the ACCME has accredited about a hundred of these new firms to offer continuing medical education programs themselves—even though they are for-profit firms hired by the drug companies. So here we have firms working for big pharma who are supposed to be providing impartial instruction about their clients' drugs. People pretend not to notice this flagrant conflict of interest. But the way MECCs advertise themselves to drug companies tells the real story. One pitched its services by observing, "Medical education is a powerful tool that can deliver your message to key audiences, and get those audiences to take action that benefits your product."[3] In other words, hire us, and we will get doctors to prescribe your drug. Some MECCs are even owned by large advertising agencies, making the connection between continuing medical education and drug marketing still more obvious.

Now why should MECCs, which are paid by drug companies, be accredited by the ACCME? Well, the answer may have something to do with the makeup of the Task Force on Industry-Professional Collaboration in Continuing Medical Education, which was created to help the ACCME formulate policies on conflicts of interest. About half the members of the task force are representatives of educational institutions and professional organizations, but the other half are from the pharmaceutical industry or MECCs themselves. So it should come as no surprise that the ACCME has accredited not only MECCs but even one of the large pharmaceutical companies—Eli Lilly. The task force evidently never even considered requiring that drug companies have *no* role in the preparation or presentation of educational programs.

There is a certain amount of obligatory hand waving to make it appear that continuing medical education is not influenced by drug company sponsors. For instance, support by the pharmaceutical industry is nearly always stated to be "an unrestricted educational grant," which implies that drug companies don't influence the content of the programs. And speakers, who are often paid consultants for the companies, are usually required to disclose their financial ties—and that disclosure is supposed to make it acceptable that they have them. But drug companies or their agents, the MECCs, often suggest the topic and speaker and put together the graphics and other educational materials. That medical schools and hospitals have the final say does not change the fact that if they want to continue to get the support, they will go along with the sponsors. Continuing medical education gives drug companies an unparalleled opportunity to influence doctors' prescribing habits, and it seems to work. It's been shown that doctors prescribe more of the sponsors' drugs after these meetings. If it were otherwise, the industry would not spend the huge sums it does on these programs. The adage is right. He who pays the piper usually does call the tune, regardless of efforts to make it appear otherwise.

Bribing Doctors—or Nurturing Consultants?

Drug companies are extremely generous to doctors in their "educational" activities. The education is often said to go in both directions. The companies provide information to doctors, and the doctors provide feedback to the companies. But the money goes in only one direction—from industry to doctors. Doctors are invited to dinners in expensive restaurants or on junkets to luxurious settings to act as "consultants" or "advisers." The doctors listen to speakers and provide some minimal response about how they like the company drugs or what they think of a new advertising campaign. That enables drug companies to pay doctors just for showing up. As one doctor told *The Boston Globe*, "The companies used to call it coming to dinner. Now it's called consulting."[4]

Participants may also receive training to serve on speakers' bureaus, so that they, too, can become company shills.[5] The work on junkets is not too onerous. Lectures usually occupy just a few hours in the morning, with plenty of time left for golf or skiing in the afternoon and elegant meals and entertainment in the evenings. By calling it education or consulting or market research or some combination of those things, but *not* marketing, companies needn't worry about antikickback laws. But doctors are no less beholden to the companies that lavish such attention on them, and they are no more immune to the sales pitches. It's been estimated that the industry hosted over 300,000 pseudo-educational events in 2000, about a quarter of which offered continuing medical education credits.[6]

Drug companies pay particular attention to wooing so-called thought leaders. These are prominent experts, usually on medical school faculties and teaching hospital staffs, who write papers, contribute to textbooks, and give talks at medical meetings—all of which greatly affect the use of drugs in their fields. Thought leaders have influence far beyond their numbers. Companies shower special favors on these doctors, offer them honoraria as consultants and speakers, and often pay for them to attend conferences in posh resorts, ostensibly to seek their advice. In many drug-intensive medical specialties, it is virtually impossible to find an expert who is not receiving payments from one or more drug companies. As I said in Chapter 7, drug companies sway doctors with "food, flattery, and friendship."[7] In the case of thought leaders, flattery is key. They are told their expertise is invaluable in helping companies to develop new drugs. But in fact, thought leaders are usually clinicians, who study drugs after they are developed. What they really have to offer drug companies is the ability to sway large numbers of other doctors.

I mentioned in Chapter 6 that the head of Brown University's Department of Psychiatry reportedly made over $500,000 in one year consulting for drug companies that make antidepressants. When *The New England Journal of Medicine,* under my editorship, published a study by him and his colleagues of an antidepressant agent, there wasn't enough room to print all the authors' conflict-of-interest disclosures. The full list had to be put on the website. In a footnote, I wrote, "Our policy requires authors of Original Articles to disclose all financial ties with companies that make the products under study or competing products. In this case, the large number of authors and their varied and extensive financial associations with relevant companies make a detailed listing here impractical. Readers should know, however, that all but one (B.A.) of the twelve principal authors have had financial associations with Bristol-Myers Squibb—which also sponsored the study—and, in most cases, with many other companies producing psychoactive pharmaceutical agents. The associations include consultancies, receipt of research grants and honorariums, and participation on advisory boards." I also wrote an accompanying editorial, titled "Is Academic Medicine for Sale?" in which I expressed my concern about the merging of commercial and academic interests. In response, a reader sent a letter to the editor asking rhetorically, "Is academic medicine for sale? No. The current owner is very happy with it."[8]

Professional Meetings

The meetings of professional societies, like the American College of Cardiology or the American Society of Hematology, are now partly supported by drug companies. This is where much of the ongoing education of doctors takes place. At annual meetings, which may be attended by thousands of doctors, drug companies present their own satellite symposia—with free lunches and dinners. A few years ago, I attended one such symposium. It took place over a four-course meal at a hotel near the main meeting, and about two hundred doctors were there. The topic was osteoporosis—thinning of the bones. At first, I did not know which of the several types of drugs to treat osteoporosis the sponsor made, but I soon guessed. In slide after slide, this was the drug at the top of the list of drugs to consider, even though it is probably the least effective. And in most of the hypothetical patients discussed, there was some reason not to give one of the more effective drugs. For example, one patient was said to have an ulcer as well as osteoporosis. That would have been a reason not to use the most effective treatment, but it would also have been an unusual situation. In short, the whole symposium was slanted to promote a third-choice treatment. The main speaker was a distinguished endocrinologist from a major medical school. He later told me that the company had given a grant of $10,000 to his department, as well as paid his expenses and an honorarium. The company had also made his slides.

Many big professional meetings resemble bazaars, dominated by garish drug company exhibits and friendly salespeople eager to ply doctors with gifts while they pitch their companies' drugs. Doctors wander the vast exhibit halls carrying canvas bags displaying drug company logos and brimming with goodies, munching on free food, and partaking of all sorts of free services, such as cholesterol screening and putting green practice. Instead of sober professionalism, the atmosphere of these meetings is now trade-show hucksterism.

In a vivid article on the subject, a reporter from *The Boston Globe* described her encounter with one psychiatrist at the annual meeting of the American Psychiatric Association (APA):

> Ivonne Munez Velazquez, a psychiatrist from Mexico, rooted through her goody bag like a child on Halloween. As a reward for attending the APA's annual meeting, she had received a small egg-shaped clock from the makers of the antidepressant Prozac; a sleek thermos from Paxil, also an antidepressant; and an engraved silver business card holder courtesy of Depakote, an anticonvulsant [often prescribed off label for a variety of psychiatric disorders]. She got a neat little CD carrying case from Risperdol [*sic*], an antipsychotic; a passport holder from Celexa, an antipsychotic [actually, an antidepressant]; a neat green paperweight from Remeron, an antidepressant; and a letter opener, representing what drug she could not remember. For the duration of the weekend, though, Velazquez's loyalty belonged to Pfizer, which had

paid her airfare from Mexico City (along with thirty of her colleagues and her eighteen-year-old nephew) and put them all up in hotels near the APA meeting. That night, also courtesy of Pfizer, she would attend a glittering banquet at the Philadelphia Academy of Fine Arts.[9]

(The new PhRMA guidelines would prohibit this, but they are voluntary, and even if followed could probably be evaded by calling her a consultant.)

Membership dues for the APA are dropping. And well they might. According to the *Boston Globe* story, drug companies spent between $200,000 and $400,000—plus a $60,000 direct payment to the association—for each of fifty-plus "industry-sponsored symposia." Without the drug company money, officials said, the annual meeting would lose educational benefits along with amenities. "How much are you willing to pay for that, if we don't accept drug company money?" asked Anand Pandya, an APA official. "Are you willing to pay $3000?" (Dues are now $540.) That is an excellent question. How much *are* these meetings worth? And how many "amenities" are necessary? Perhaps members should pay exactly what the meetings are worth to them. The meetings might then assume a more serious tone and a more modest dimension. By allowing drug companies to foot the bill for carnival-like meetings, doctors are really passing the costs along to people who buy prescription drugs.

Pretending Drug Companies Are Educators

Why do doctors pretend they believe drug companies are interested in education? (Some of them may actually believe it.) The answer is: It pays. Membership dues would be far higher if professional societies were not supported by industry. Doctors would also have to pay for their own continuing medical education. In addition, they would lose the travel and entertainment and other emoluments too many of them have come to believe are entitlements of their profession. Many doctors become indignant when it is suggested that they might be swayed by all this industry largesse. But why else would drug companies put so much money into them? As Stephen Goldfinger, chairman of the APA's Committee on Commercial Support, said, "The pharmaceutical companies are an amoral bunch. They're not a benevolent association. So they are highly unlikely to donate large amounts of money without strings attached. Once one is dancing with the devil, you don't always get to call the steps of the dance."[10]

Big pharma, for its part, insists that it has an educational mission that can be separated from its commercial interests. The 2002 PhRMA Code on Interactions with Healthcare Professionals begins with the statement that "relationships with healthcare professionals . . . should be focused on informing healthcare professionals about products, providing scientific and educational information, and supporting medical research and education."[11] In other words, big pharma insists it is in the education business.

147

Then it goes on to recommend that companies not provide payments or gifts to doctors unless they serve an educational or research purpose. (Precisely how gifts serve such purposes is never explained.) In case there is any confusion, the code presents a series of hypothetical scenarios. Here are a couple:

> Question: Company A invites 300 physicians/consultants to a two-day and one-night speaker-training program at a regional golf resort. All attendees are compensated for their participation and their expenses are reimbursed. . . . Training sessions take both days, and the Company provides for a few hours of golf and meals. Does this program conform to the Code? . . .
>
> Answer: This arrangement appears to comply with the Code. . . . [Spouses, it adds, should pay their own way.]
>
> Question: Company A retains a small group of 15 nationally known physicians regarding a therapeutic area relevant to company A's products to advise on general medical and business issues and provide guidance on product development and research programs for those products. These physicians are paid significant fees, but those fees are typical of the fees paid to thought leaders in this therapeutic area. They normally meet once or twice a year at resort locations to discuss the latest product data, research programs and Company plans for the product(s). Does this comply with the Code? If it does, is it appropriate to pay for the spouse of the healthcare professional to attend, as well?

Answer: This arrangement appears to comply with the Code. . . . It would not be appropriate to pay for the cost of the spouse of the advisor.

You can see from these examples how calling marketing "education" and doctors "consultants" enables drug companies to evade antikickback laws. They can lay on all the boondoggles they want.

The government, too, seems willing to accept the fiction that drug companies are educators. In its 2003 guidelines, the Department of Health and Human Services Office of the Inspector General (OIG) warned against offering incentives to induce health care professionals to prescribe, recommend, or purchase particular drugs or devices. But it also said, "Absent unusual circumstances, grants or support for educational activities sponsored and organized by medical professional organizations raise little risk of fraud or abuse, provided that the grant or support is not restricted or conditioned with respect to content or faculty."[12] "The OIG's main concern about such funding," according to its senior counsel, "is that it not be used as a disguise to channel improper remunerations to physicians or others who may be in a position to generate business."[13]

To erect a firewall between illegal inducements and education, the inspector general advised drug companies "to separate their grant-making functions from their sales and marketing functions." The dubious premise that drug companies can be engaged in both education and promotion at once was not questioned. But it is not really possible for companies to promote their drugs, which means touting only their favorable effects, and to provide impartial information, some of which might be unfavorable. Even less plausible is the idea that by "separating" these activities, say, by locating them down the hall from each other instead of in the same office or by creating two divisions, you can somehow obliterate the reality that they are part of the same company with the same overall goal of selling drugs.

Educating Consumers

Drug companies claim that they also "educate" consumers. In 2002 General Electric, with funding from big pharma, launched The Patient Channel, which shows medical programming interspersed with drug ads to patients in hospitals and waiting rooms across the country. Within a year, some eight hundred hospitals were carrying the network twenty-four hours a day, seven days a week. Supported entirely by its advertisers, The Patient Channel cost hospitals nothing. Patients could choose among half-hour segments, such as "Cancer Related Fatigue" or "Breathe Easy: Allergies and Asthma." Hospitals liked the idea, because they were told it would satisfy accreditation requirements that they educate patients about their illnesses. But the Joint Commission on Accreditation of Healthcare Organizations, the accrediting body, disagreed. In a 2003 letter to General Electric, the president of the commission pointed out that hospitals are supposed to provide education specific to a given patient's needs, not a television program.

The letter added the observation that "the viewer is not sufficiently alerted to the transition between educational programming and marketing programming." Like the Health and Human Services inspector general, the accrediting commission seemed to endorse the notion that drug companies can both market and educate, the only problem being that they need to be clearer about when they are doing which—they need a firewall. But in fact, there can be no firewall, because drug companies are not really in the education business. (If they were, they would *sell* their educational programs, not give them away or pay people to accept them.) The problem with separating the educational programming from the marketing programming is that it is really *all* marketing. The Patient Channel's marketing director, Kelly Peterson, was much closer to the mark when she solicited drug company advertising by saying it would allow companies to "directly associate their products with a particular condition in a hospital setting." You bet it would. It would deliver vulnerable, captive customers right to the companies' doorstep—or more precisely, bring the companies' doorstep to them.[14]

Another form of marketing disguised as education is the sponsorship of patient advocacy groups. Many of these groups are simply fronts for drug companies. People who suffer from a certain disease believe they have found a support network devoted to expanding awareness of the disease, but it is really a way for drug companies to promote their drugs. Some people aren't even aware that a drug company is behind their advocacy group; others believe the companies just want to help educate people.

Take the hepatitis C coalitions. They look like a grassroots movement to draw attention to the dangers of a liver infection called hepatitis C, which affects some 4 million Americans. But in fact, according to *The Washington Post,* the movement was begun by Schering-Plough, which makes Rebetron, the primary treatment for hepatitis C. Rebetron costs $18,000 a year. The advocacy groups are likely to increase sales by making the disease more widely known and putting pressure on insurers to cover treatments. That may be a good thing, but the company apparently kept its sponsorship largely hidden. As Thomas Murray, president of the Hastings Center (a bioethics think tank), put it, "It's ethically problematic when a company creates entities but then tries to pass them off as authentic and spontaneous grass-roots organizations. What bothers me is the deceptiveness."[15]

One of the least savory marketing efforts is Wyeth's campaign to "educate" college students about depression. What is really being marketed is the condition. If students can be convinced they have a treatable depression, selling the company drug Effexor is easy. To that end, Wyeth sponsors a ninety-minute forum on college campuses called "Depression in College: Real World, Real Life, Real Issues." It features doctors, psychologists, and Cara Kahn of the MTV reality show *Real*

World Chicago, who takes Effexor. In 2002, when the campaign was launched, Wyeth told Alex Beam of *The Boston Globe* that four colleges had agreed to host the forum. Harvard declined. Its provost, a psychiatrist who was formerly head of the National Institute of Mental Health, told Beam, "In the case of celebrities speaking, who are actually being paid by the company, there is a risk that inappropriate marketing will go on." That's putting it mildly. Beam himself was more outspoken: "Millions of college students feel lousy, for any number of reasons: they are far from home; college is an unfamiliar and sometimes threatening environment; the object of their affection is inattentive. God knows we all have been there. Do they need a $120-a-month Effexor fix to see them through these tough years? Probably not. But who could be more suggestible, or vulnerable, than a boy or girl making the transition to adulthood?"[16] Well, maybe a patient lying in his hospital bed watching The Patient Channel.

It Takes Two

The pretense that pharmaceutical marketing is education requires the participation of at least two parties—the industry and the medical profession. We know why big pharma fosters that illusion: It helps the bottom line. It increases sales and promotes a highly drug-intensive style of medical practice. Indeed, if it didn't help the bottom line, if all this "education" were just that and had no impact on sales, heads would roll in the executive suites of the drug companies. After all, they are investor-owned businesses, and it is their responsibility to maximize profits, not give away billions of dollars.

It is much harder to excuse the medical profession and its institutions and organizations. Medical education worthy of the name requires an impartial analysis of all the available evidence, led by experts who have no vested interest in the drugs they are discussing. It is the job of medical schools and their faculty, and of professional societies, to educate doctors in that way. To abdicate that responsibility is wrong, and it is doubly wrong to leave it to an industry with an obvious financial interest in the enterprise and then pretend it is otherwise. That a noble profession has been willing to do this is a testament to the power of "food, flattery, and friendship"—and money, lots of it.

No one outside the industry has ever added up the costs of the "educational" activities described in this chapter, because they are not publicly disclosed. But these and similar activities could easily account for most of the unaccounted-for expenditures in big pharma's marketing budgets. It is far too much money to imagine that it represents some sort of public-spirited contribution to education. This masquerade leads to no end of problems—the corruption of the profession, the misuse and overuse of expensive prescription drugs, and, as we will see in Chapter 12, an avalanche of governmental investigations and lawsuits based on the spurious notion that the pharmaceutical industry provides bona fide medical education and it is therefore possible to distinguish lawful educational expenses from illegal marketing. If we acknowledged the fact that the pharmaceutical industry cannot possibly be expected to provide unbiased education about its own products, there would be no need to pursue the hopeless task of trying to differentiate "educational grants" from kickbacks, as the Department of Health and Human Services inspector general tries to do. Neither would be permissible.

9

Marketing Masquerading as Research

SUPPOSE YOU ARE A BIG PHARMACEU-
tical company. You make a drug that is approved
for a very limited use—say, it treats a condition
that affects only 250,000 people. How could you
turn it into a blockbuster? There are essentially
two ways. First, you could test it for other conditions in clinical trials. If the trials showed it was
safe and effective, you could apply for Food and
Drug Administration (FDA) approval to market it
for additional uses. That is what Bristol-Myers
Squibb did with Taxol, for instance. It was originally approved to treat cancer of the ovary, but
the company immediately launched additional tri-

als to see if it also worked for cancer of the breast and cancer of the lung—which it did. That greatly expanded the market.

Alternatively, you could simply market the drug for unapproved ("off-label") uses—despite the fact that doing so is illegal. You do that by carrying out "research" that falls way below the standard required for FDA approval, then "educating" doctors about any favorable results. That way, you could circumvent the law. You could say you were not marketing for unapproved uses; you were merely disseminating the results of research to doctors—who can legally prescribe a drug for *any* use. But it would be bogus education about bogus research. It would really be marketing.

The Neurontin Case

Parke-Davis apparently took the second approach with its epilepsy drug Neurontin. Parke-Davis was a division of Warner-Lambert, which in 2000 was swallowed up by the drug giant Pfizer. In 1996, David P. Franklin, a Parke-Davis sales representative (called a "medical liaison" because of his additional technical training), brought suit against the company for defrauding Medicaid and other government health programs. (As a whistle-blower, he would be entitled to a portion of any fines.) Franklin had thousands of pages of internal documents. He charged that the company had carried out a massive illegal scheme to promote Neurontin for off-label uses—mainly by paying academic experts to put their names on flimsy research papers that purported to show the drug worked for these other conditions.[1]

Eventually, federal prosecutors filed a brief in support of Franklin and launched both criminal and civil investigations of their own. Parallel actions were filed by forty-seven states and the District of Columbia. Court documents were originally sealed at the company's request, but many of them were released in 2002 in response to media petitions. They showed a well-coordinated plan of staggering dimensions. What appears here is drawn from newspaper reports of Franklin's complaint and of the company records released by the court.

Neurontin had been approved by the FDA in 1994 for a very narrow use—to treat epilepsy as an add-on when other drugs failed to control seizures. (Later it was approved to treat shingles as well.) There wasn't much money in that, and the company wanted to expand the drug's market. But there was no time to do proper clinical trials that might allow it to get FDA approval for other uses, because the patent was due to expire in 1998 (later extended to 2000). So the company apparently devised a plan to get doctors to prescribe Neurontin for unapproved uses—mainly common but vague conditions like pain and anxiety of various forms, and also as the sole treatment for epilepsy. If the campaign were successful, huge markets would be opened up.

Parke-Davis reportedly called its plan a "publications strategy." It would sponsor minimal research, prepare journal articles based on it, and pay academic researchers to put their names on those articles. The studies themselves were so small or poorly designed that few valid conclusions could be drawn from them. Some of the articles contained no new data at all, just favorable comments about Neurontin. Medical education and communication companies were hired to prepare the articles and find authors. One of these firms, for instance, was to be paid $12,000 for each of twelve journal articles it prepared.[2] It in turn paid academic "authors" $1000 to sign them. Apparently it wasn't always easy. In a progress report to Parke-Davis, the education company lamented, "Author interested; still playing phone tag." Then in caps, "[OUR COMPANY] HAS DRAFT COMPLETE, WE JUST NEED AN AUTHOR."[3]

The second part of the publications strategy was to see that the articles and the information in them were widely disseminated to practicing doctors, so that they would be persuaded to start prescribing Neurontin for off-label uses. It doesn't do any good to create favorable articles if nobody hears about them. Parke-Davis "medical liaisons," who are purported to have more of an educational mission than ordinary sales representatives, would visit doctors' offices to answer questions about the research. One company manager was said to have been recorded by Franklin haranguing liaisons in what sounded like a pregame pep rally: "When we get out there, we want to kick some ass. We want to sell Neurontin on pain. All right?"[4]

Parke-Davis also sponsored educational meetings and conferences all over the country. At these meetings, the "authors" of the papers and other experts would describe the success of the drug for off-label uses. Dozens of doctors were allegedly paid tens of thousands of dollars each to speak to other physicians about using Neurontin for more than a dozen unapproved uses. Not only were the speakers paid for their services but often the doctors in the audience were also paid. They were called "consultants"—which had the effect of circumventing antikickback laws. Consultant meetings were sometimes little more than vacations for potential high prescribers of Neurontin. The company tracked doctors' prescriptions to see if they prescribed Neurontin more after the meetings or after they were hired to speak about the drug. According to a *New York Times* story, the company found an increase of about 70 percent in prescriptions after dinner meetings.[5]

One thing about this research-education one-two strategy is that the speakers and the audience are essentially interchangeable. In essence, they are all being persuaded to prescribe a drug for off-label uses; it doesn't really matter who is doing the talking and who is doing the listening. As we learned in the last chapter, it is simply a matter of getting a message out to thought leaders and potential high prescribers, while skirting both antikickback laws and laws against off-label marketing.

As a result of these efforts, Neurontin did become a blockbuster, with sales of $2.7 billion in 2003. About 80 percent of prescriptions that year were for unapproved uses—conditions like bipolar disorder, post-traumatic stress disorder, insomnia, restless legs syndrome, hot flashes, migraines, and tension headaches.[6] In fact, Neurontin has become a sort of all-purpose restorative for chronic discomfort of almost any type—yet there is almost no good published evidence that it works for most of these conditions. In May 2004, eight years after the case began, Pfizer pleaded guilty to illegal marketing and agreed to pay $430 million to resolve the criminal and civil charges against it. As whistle-blower, Franklin will receive nearly $27 million of that. That sounds like a lot of money, but it is small potatoes compared with the $2.7 billion in Neurontin sales.[7]

Phase IV Clinical Trials—Real and Bogus

This case may have been unusual in its scope and in the fact that a whistle-blower brought it to court, but I suspect it is a fairly standard way of doing business. The common denominator is the use of flimsy Phase IV clinical research for marketing purposes. As you will recall from Chapter 2, Phase I through III clinical trials are directed toward getting initial FDA approval, and they must meet the agency's scientific standards. Phase IV trials, in contrast, are studies of drugs already on the market, and many of them don't have to meet any standards at all. It was estimated in 2002 that Phase IV studies, sometimes called "post-marketing" studies, accounted for at least 25 percent of all clinical trials, and their number is growing much faster than that of Phase I through III trials.[8]

There are two legitimate reasons for Phase IV studies. The first is to see whether a drug is effective for an additional use and, if so, to get FDA approval to market it for that use—as in the case of Taxol. It is analogous to getting approved in the first place, in the sense that the research must meet the same scientific standards as the original Phase III trials. By getting FDA approval for new uses, companies not only expand the size of a drug's market but can also get an additional three years' exclusive marketing rights.

The second legitimate reason for Phase IV trials is to look for side effects or other properties of the drug that were missed in the earlier clinical trials. Even large, well-designed Phase III trials may not reveal side effects if they are very rare or no one thought to look for them. They may also miss other effects that show up only in patients different from those previously studied. After the drug comes on the market and is used widely in the general population, those properties may be discovered in large Phase IV studies.

These latter sorts of studies are more important than they once were, because until a decade ago, drugs were usually first approved in Europe. That meant serious side effects would probably show up there, before a drug was used in the United States. But now, most drugs are approved first in the United States. Furthermore, an increasing number of them are given accelerated review by the FDA, which means they come to market on the basis of less evidence. Thus, a drug may come into widespread use with very little research to back it up, and no experience in another country.

As a condition of accelerated approval, and sometimes even with regular approval, the FDA requires companies to conduct Phase IV confirmatory studies just to make sure the new drug is safe. In fact, about two-thirds of all new molecular entities approved in 2000 were supposed to undergo Phase IV studies.[9] These are called "commitment studies," because companies have a commitment to do them. But in fact, they don't want to do them. They have nothing to gain, and everything to lose if a serious side effect turns up. So they drag their feet. As of 2003, only half of all drugs that had undergone accelerated approval had been fully investigated in "commitment studies." Thomas Fleming, a biostatistician at the University of Washington and an adviser to the FDA, observed, "Sponsors, particularly industry sponsors, have a keen sense of urgency to develop an agent in a timely fashion, but once the agent is approved, there is almost a reverse motivation—you'll market the product until it's shown not to work."[10] Theoretically, the FDA has the authority to pull a drug from the market if the company reneges on its commitment, but it has never done so.[11]

However, the majority of Phase IV studies fall into neither of these categories. Their purpose is not to get FDA approval for a new use. Nor is it to fulfill a commitment. Instead they are mainly gimmicks to increase sales—as in the Neurontin case.[12] The most common Phase IV trials are so-called surveillance studies. Here sponsors pay doctors to put patients on drugs and answer a few simple questions about how they fared. There is no randomization and no comparison group, so it is usually impossible to draw any reliable conclusions. CenterWatch, a company that serves as a clearinghouse for information about the clinical trials industry, recently ran an article titled "Phase IV

Market Steams Ahead." In it, the aim of surveillance studies was made clear: "The primary purpose of this type of post-marketing research is to familiarize physicians and patients with new drugs." And the article pointed out that such research does indeed influence doctors' drug choices and formulary recommendations.[13] How many Phase IV studies are funded out of drug company research and development budgets and how many out of marketing budgets is impossible to know. Probably both contribute.

A few years ago, a doctor sent me an invitation he received to participate in a study sponsored by Salix Pharmaceuticals. It asked him to start five patients with active ulcerative colitis on the company's drug Colazal. After eight weeks, he would fill out a form and return it to Salix, which would then pay him a $500 "honorarium." The company would also provide free samples for the patients, plus coupons to cover part of the costs of the drug. The clinical summary to be filled out was short and simple. In fact, it was so short and simple it could have no real scientific value. The first question, for instance, asked, "Overall, how was your experience with Colazal?" and you could check one of three boxes: "extremely pleased," "pleased," or "not pleased." It is hard to believe that this was anything but an excuse to pay doctors to prescribe Colazal. But as CenterWatch observed, "Sponsors must sometimes simplify study protocols to meet their marketing needs and thus limit the scientific validity of the studies." Anything to get doctors to prescribe your drug.

A "Sweet Spot"

You may remember that I mentioned in Chapter 2 the growth of a large industry to perform clinical trials for drug companies. It consists mainly of private contract research organizations (CROs). These firms run clinical trials for drug companies, using networks of private doctors in their offices. They concentrate particularly on Phase IV studies. "Phase IV studies are the fastest growing segment of clinical spending," CenterWatch wrote. "This sweet spot in the market is being actively pursued by CRO's and offers unique opportunity for experienced, community-based clinical investigators."[14] It's a "sweet spot" for the doctors, too. They usually make more working for CROs than spending the same time caring for patients. There are now tens of thousands of private doctors doing this work—many of them essentially being paid to prescribe a company drug.

Since the majority of Phase IV studies will never be submitted to the FDA, they may be totally unregulated. Few of them are published. In fact, like all industry-sponsored trials, they are not likely to be published at all unless they show something favorable to the sponsor's drug. If they are published, it is often in marginal journals, because the quality of the research is so poor. CenterWatch described Phase IV studies this way: "Whereas companies generally prefer [phase I through III] studies to be done by experienced research investigators, phase IV programs offer sponsors the opportunity to initiate and develop strategic relationships, especially with high-volume prescribers."[15] In other words, it isn't really research, so don't worry too much about its scientific validity.

Some of the largest advertising agencies in the world have gotten into the pharmaceutical research and education business on behalf of their clients in the drug industry. They include the three Madison Avenue giants—Omnicom, WPP, and Interpublic. To provide their clients with more integrated service, they have purchased or invested in CROs and medical education and communication companies (MECCs). Take Omnicom. It is part owner of SCIREX—a CRO. That relationship enables the marketers to direct research toward drugs they think could be big sellers. One advertising executive said, it is "getting closer to the test tube." Omnicon also owns Proworx—a MECC accused of ghostwriting articles in the Neurontin case.[16]

The ad agency WPP owns Intramed—another MECC apparently in the ghostwriting business. *The New York Times* obtained a transcript of a conference call in which an Intramed vice president reportedly told doctors, "We would like to help draft this manuscript, and then submit it to you for your—for your editing and for approval." According to the account, a representative of WPP's client Novartis was also on the phone. He added that the company wanted "a quick, down and dirty" article. One of the doctors responded, "I think we're quite clear on what you want the next manuscript to look like."[17] The fact that these huge advertising agencies own or employ research and education companies shows clearly just what is subordinate to what in this business. "Clinical research" and "education" are just tools of the marketers.

One of the more convoluted examples of research that at least in part serves marketing purposes is the story of Eli Lilly's drug Xigris.[18] In 2001, Xigris was approved to treat severe sepsis, blood-borne infections that are a common cause of death in intensive care units (ICUs). Its approval was not a sure thing. In the key clinical trial submitted to the FDA, 25 percent of patients taking Xigris died, compared with 31 percent of those on standard treatment. That is not a big difference, although it was statistically significant. The FDA advisory panel split evenly on whether to recommend approval, with some saying another clinical trial was needed. Lilly priced Xigris at $6800 per treatment and expected it to become a blockbuster and make up for the sales the company would lose when Prozac's patent protection ran out that year. But because of the high cost, many hospitals decided that the drug was not worth it. They could get more bang for the buck, they thought, by putting that money to other uses. By the spring of 2002, it was clear that sales of Xigris were not meeting expectations.

So Lilly hired a new advertising firm, Belsito & Co., to handle the Xigris account. The company pitched a campaign it called "The Ethics, the Urgency and the Potential." The idea was not to do more research on the drug's effectiveness but instead to do research on whether ICU patients were generally being deprived of treatments because of cost. That approach could be used to convince people that it was unethical *not* to use

Xigris, because it was tantamount to rationing lifesaving treatment. To that end, Lilly gave a $1.8 million grant for a comprehensive study of rationing in ICUs. Dr. Mitchell Levy, head of the medical ICU at Rhode Island Hospital, who pronounced the data behind Xigris "damn good," was tapped to lead a twenty-person committee called the Values, Ethics & Rationing in Critical Care Task Force. (It has its own website, www.vericc.org.) Other members include prominent ethicists, hospital directors, and ICU specialists from all over the country.

Lilly also managed to get a new federal diagnostic code for severe sepsis, so that the incidence could be tracked. That way they would have a better idea of the size of the potential market and how to promote Xigris better. More important, it got the Centers for Medicare & Medicaid Services to agree to reimburse half the charge for Xigris, up to $3400 a treatment. That kind of deal is unheard of. The standard way Medicare reimburses hospitals is according to the diagnosis—so much for a heart attack, so much for a stroke, so much for pneumonia, and so forth. It does not pay for a specific drug or other treatment. What Lilly got for Xigris is unique. In case you are wondering, Lilly told *The Wall Street Journal* it has no intention of lowering the drug's price. And the profit margin? The company isn't telling.

The Xigris story shows how throwing money at academics can shift the focus from where it should be in this case—the exorbitant price of a drug of uncertain effectiveness—to the ethics of rationing. One clinical trial is usually not enough to prove benefit conclusively. The FDA asked Lilly to conduct Phase IV commitment studies to elucidate further the risks and benefits. One would hope the company is as keen on doing those studies as on demonstrating rationing in ICUs, but somehow I doubt it.

Consequences of the Masquerades

This chapter and the last have been about marketing masquerading as education and research—often coupled together. First, faux research yields a faux answer to a clinical question. Then faux education assures that doctors everywhere hear about it, so they can write millions of prescriptions based on the faux information. Bribes and kickbacks sometimes grease the skids.

Well, you might ask, what is really wrong with that? The process is admittedly deceptive, but if it means that more people get prescription drugs, isn't there a net benefit? After all, the drugs are probably on balance helpful, or the FDA wouldn't have approved them and doctors wouldn't prescribe them. Shouldn't we pay more attention to the outcome and less to the process?

I find it hard to imagine that a system this corrupt can be a good thing, or that it is worth the vast amounts of money spent on it. But in addition, we have to ask whether it really is a net benefit to the public to be taking so many drugs. In my view, we have become an overmedicated society. Doctors have been taught only too well by the pharmaceutical industry, and what they have been taught is to reach for a prescription pad. Add to that the fact that most doctors are under great time pressure because of the demands of managed care, and they reach for that pad very quickly. Patients have also been well taught by the pharmaceutical industry's advertising. They have been taught that if they don't leave the doctor's office with a prescription, the doctor is not doing a good job. The result is that too many people end up taking drugs when there may be better ways to deal with their problems.

This conclusion was underscored by a large trial sponsored by the National Institutes of Health of ways to prevent adult-onset diabetes in people at high risk for the disease.[19] One group in the trial received placebo, and 29 percent of patients in that group developed diabetes over a three-year period. The second group received a drug called metformin (the generic form of Bristol-Myers Squibb's blockbuster Glucophage), and they did somewhat better—22 percent developed diabetes. But the third group did much better than either of the other two. They were placed on a moderate diet and exercise program, and only 14 percent got diabetes. In other words, diet and exercise were better than the drug. But trying diet and exercise instead of a drug is not likely to happen in real life. Drenched as we all are in prescription drug promotions, both doctors and patients are far more likely to go for the Glucophage. Besides, insurers don't usually pay for diet and exercise programs.

More serious is the fact that many of us are taking a lot of drugs at once—often five, maybe ten, or even more. This practice is called "polypharmacy," and it carries real risks. The problem is that very few drugs have just one effect. In addition to the desired effect, there are others. Some are side effects doctors know about, but there may also be ones we are not aware of. When several drugs are taken at once, those other effects may add up. There may also be drug interactions, in which one drug blocks the action of another or delays its metabolism so that its action and side effects are increased. When the function of an organ, for instance the liver or the kidneys, is even slightly impaired, the probability of complications from one or more medications increases. And the more medications taken, the more likely it is that one of them will interfere with the normal function of some organ.

Recently, *The Boston Globe* carried a story about polypharmacy.[20] The case in point was a fifty-year-old woman who was taking eighteen prescription drugs at a cost of nearly $16,000 per year. Nearly all of them were expensive brand-name drugs. They were meant to treat a variety of ailments, including diabetes, depression, anxiety, allergies, migraines, and pain (for which she was taking the ubiquitous Neurontin). Four of the drugs were for psychiatric problems—clonazepam for anxiety, Lexapro for depression, Trileptal for depression (not approved for this use), and Elavil for depression and sleeplessness. Reportedly, she could barely get around, and her roommate said that she was sometimes dizzy or fell or couldn't stand up. No wonder! Most psychiatric drugs cause some degree of drowsiness, and so does Neurontin. I can only imagine what all of them together do. It would be virtually impossible to sort out which of her complaints were caused by illness and which by all the drugs. What she probably needed was less medication and more medical attention. Experienced specialists are familiar with this phenomenon of overmedication and often start their evaluation of a patient who is not doing well on multiple drugs by eliminating most or all of the medications. Frequently, the patient improves.

This is not to gainsay the vital role of good prescription drugs in health care. There is no doubt that many people live longer, better lives because of them. As I said in Chapter 6, we need them. But they should be prescribed carefully and only when necessary, and doctors' judgment about their prescription should be based on real research and education, not on the marketing that passes for it.

10

Patent Games—
Stretching Out Monopolies

NOTHING DRUG COMPANIES DO IS AS profitable as stretching out monopoly rights on their block-busters. For all the talk about free enterprise, the pharmaceutical industry's lifeblood is government-conferred monopolies—in the form of patents granted by the U.S. Patent and Trademark Office (USPTO) and exclusive marketing rights granted by the Food and Drug Administration (FDA). The two forms of exclusivity operate somewhat inde-pendently, as discussed in Chapter 1. Both make it illegal, for a specified time, for competitors to sell the same drug.[1] Extending that privileged time by a variety of stratagems is the most innovative activity of big pharma. For blockbuster drugs, it is certainly the most lucrative.

Once a company loses exclusive rights to a drug, the FDA permits generic versions to come on the market. When that happens, sales of the brand-name drug plummet—partly because brand-name drugs almost never lower their prices in response to competition. When only one generic drug is on the market, its price may not be much lower than that of the brand-name drug, because generic manufacturers engage in something called "shadow pricing"—keeping prices just beneath the brand-name price. But when more generics enter the market, prices fall to as little as 20 percent of that of the brand-name drug.[2] Since pharmacists are permitted to substitute a generic unless doctors specify otherwise in their prescriptions, that competition usually spells the end of the brand-name drug's run. For manufacturers of blockbusters (drugs with annual sales of more than a billion dollars), that means a loss of hundreds of millions of dollars a year.

You can see that keeping generics off the market, even for six months, is worth a lot, and drug company lawyers are amazingly creative at devising ways to do so. "There are anywhere from ten to twenty tactics [drug companies] use to protect their products," observed Roger L. Williams, the FDA director of pharmaceutical science. And the stock analyst Hemant K. Shah explained, "The anti-generic strategy by pharmaceutical companies has probably the highest rate of return of any business activity they do right now."[3] (Note that he didn't mention research and development or innovation.) In short, the legions of lawyers companies employ for this purpose more than earn their keep.

How to Get a Monopoly

Let's look at patents first. I don't propose to, nor can I, make you experts in patent law, but a quick review will help to understand how drug companies abuse it. Patents were provided for in Article I, section 8, of the U.S. Constitution, which reads, "Congress shall have power . . . to promote the progress of science and useful arts, by securing for limited times to authors and inventors the exclusive right to their respective writings and discoveries." You can see that the original idea was to stimulate useful discoveries and inventions, as well as to reward inventors. But over time, patents have come to be seen primarily as rewards, even when they actually obstruct the "progress of science and useful arts." Drug company patents, in particular, are immensely valuable property, but although they encourage companies to bring drugs to market, they have relatively little to do with stimulating innovation, which usually occurs outside the industry, as we saw in Chapter 4. Companies may later get patents on new uses of innovative drugs they acquire.

There are several types of patents, but the one that applies to prescription drugs has a term of twenty years from the date the application is filed with the USPTO. A patent can apply to one of four possible features of a drug: the drug substance itself;

the method of use; the formulation; or the process of making it. Drug substance patents simply cover the chemical composition of the active ingredient. Method of use patents cover the use of a drug to treat a particular condition, such as heart failure or depression. Formulation patents cover the physical form of a drug, such as liquid or capsule, and the method of administration, such as by mouth or injection. And process patents cover manufacturing methods. To be patentable, the "invention" is supposed to be "useful, novel, and non-obvious." *Useful* originally meant what it seems to—that it had some practical benefit. *Novel* meant it was significantly different from earlier inventions. And *non-obvious* meant it was not simply the next step any knowledgeable person in the field would take but rather a conceptual leap.[4]

In Chapter 1, I spoke of 1980 as a watershed year for the pharmaceutical industry—the year it went from being just a very good business to being a stupendous one. Among the changes was a general relaxation in the requirement that patentable inventions had to be useful, novel, and non-obvious.[5] In 1980, the U.S. Supreme Court lowered the standard for usefulness by holding that inventions didn't have to have practical implications but could be useful only for further research (this allowed for the patenting of genes). And in 1982, a new court (called the Court of Appeals for the Federal Circuit) was created to hear appeals of patent denials. It has been generally very lenient, particularly with regard to the non-obviousness standard. Many patents are now granted for highly obvious uses of drugs—for example, Lilly obtained a patent to use Prozac for depression, then another to use it for obesity. Hardly a conceptual leap. Furthermore, the USPTO actually has an incentive to grant patents rather than deny them, because its examiners are paid bonuses that depend in part on the number of patents they process. Since it is faster to grant a patent than to deny it and risk having the decision appealed, granting patents is what the examiners tend to do. The result is that nowadays nearly anything—including new uses, dosage forms, and combinations of old drugs, even the coatings and colors of pills—can be patented.

Exclusivity conferred by the FDA is different from patents.[6] It is granted at the time a drug is approved for marketing, which is usually much later than the primary patent is obtained. The agency essentially says to the company, "Okay, you've shown your drug is safe and effective in clinical trials, so you may market it for a certain period of time, during which we won't approve the same drug made by anyone else." (Technically, what is protected is the clinical trial data, but in practical terms, it amounts to the same thing as exclusivity for the drug itself.) During that time, there can be no generic competition, even if there is no patent in effect. The FDA's standards for granting exclusivity are more stringent than the USPTO's standards for patents, since the FDA standards depend on successful clinical testing. And the period of exclusivity is shorter—usually five years for new molecular entities, seven years for orphan drugs (those with an expected market of fewer than 200,000 people), and three years for changes in already approved drugs.

Even after that time is up, however, the agency is not allowed to approve a generic drug while a relevant patent is still in effect (the trick is deciding whether it is relevant, as we will see shortly). For that reason, companies are supposed to list relevant patents with the FDA in a publication known as the Orange Book (available on the FDA website). These are not *all* patents on the drug, of which there may be many. They are just the patents on the FDA-approved drug substance itself, its formulation, and its approved use. Thus, generic competition can be held off by either a relevant patent or an FDA grant of exclusivity, or both.

. . . And How to Stretch It

As a result of a number of industry-friendly laws and regulations passed in the last two decades, periods of exclusivity have become stretched to an absurd extent. In 1980, exclusivity lasted for the standard seventeen-year patent term (since changed to twenty years), minus the time for clinical testing. Now, given the ingenuity of the industry's patent lawyers, it can be much, much longer. Let's look at the most important of the new laws before we see how drug companies abuse them.

In 1984, Congress passed the Drug Price Competition and Patent Term Restoration Act, commonly known as Hatch-

Waxman after its sponsors, Senator Orrin Hatch (R-Utah) and Representative Henry Waxman (D-Calif.). The original intention was to stimulate the generic drug industry while providing some additional exclusivity for brand-name drugs to make up for long development and FDA approval times. The law was supposed to establish a balance between the generic industry, which was foundering at the time (probably Representative Waxman's main concern), and big pharma (no doubt Senator Hatch's main concern).

Accordingly, the law greatly simplified the FDA approval process for generic companies. No longer did they have to test their drugs in clinical trials. All they had to do was show the FDA that their drugs contained the same active ingredients as the brand-name drugs they copied (called the "pioneer" drugs) and acted in the same way in the body—that is, they were "bioequivalent." That made sense. After all, brand-name drugs have already been tested in clinical trials. Why do it again? That part of Hatch-Waxman has worked well. Generic drugs went from representing less than 20 percent of prescriptions in 1984 to about 50 percent now (even though they account for only about 10 percent of total sales because they are much cheaper).[7]

But let's look at what else Hatch-Waxman did.[8] It provided for up to five years of additional patent life for drugs that experienced long delays in coming to market because of clinical testing and FDA approval. And it contained two other provisions that have led to no end of mischief. It stipulated that if a brand-name company sues a generic company for patent infringement, FDA approval of the generic drug will automatically be delayed for thirty months (unless the case is decided before then, which is unusual)—whatever the merits of the suit. In effect, the FDA will add thirty more months to the brand-name drug's exclusivity.

This is how it works. You'll remember that drug companies are supposed to list relevant patents in the FDA Orange Book. If a generic company seeking FDA approval believes a patent still in effect is *not* relevant (that is, it was improperly listed), it is supposed to notify the brand-name company. Then the brand-name company has the option of suing within forty-five days and triggering the thirty-month delay. The idea was that thirty months would be long enough for the legal issues to be worked out. Furthermore, Hatch-Waxman stipulated that the first generic company to challenge a patent in that way would have six months of exclusivity—free from competition by other generics. That would be its reward for taking on a big drug company.

Hatch-Waxman has been a bonanza for big pharma. While it was meant to stimulate generic competition, it has often had exactly the opposite effect. Since then, brand-name drug companies routinely file not just one patent on their blockbusters but a series of them spread throughout the life of the first one. These patents are on every conceivable feature of the drug—never mind usefulness, novelty, or non-obviousness, or how remote from the originally approved drug and its approved use. And remember, patents are very easy to get. The result is that generic companies are routinely charged with infringement of one of these secondary patents, which immediately triggers thirty months of additional exclusivity. Companies sometimes try to slow the process still more by filing so-called citizen petitions, in which they pretend to raise safety concerns about a generic drug. And finally, they may even pay a generic company to agree to defer entry into the market. Because of the six-month exclusivity given to the first generic company, this collusion blocks other generic companies. Through such shenanigans, exclusivity can be prolonged for years.[9]

That sort of gaming of the system is not supposed to be possible. Under the law, only challenges to patents listed in the FDA's Orange Book are supposed to trigger the thirty-month delay. To be listed in the Orange Book, patents are supposed to apply only to the drug itself, its formulation, and the use or uses for which it was approved. In other words, they are supposed to be directly relevant. Other patents related to the drug—like those for unapproved uses or for manufacturing processes—are not supposed to be listed. But the FDA does not even attempt to hold drug companies to that restriction. The companies list any patents they choose. For example, there is a patent listed for Neurontin on its use for neurodegenerative diseases, despite the fact that it is not approved for that use. Sometimes companies list virtually the same patent twice. Furthermore, the patents may be listed at any time, even years after original approval. That means there can nearly always be a frivolous patent in effect that can be used as an excuse for suing generic companies, thus triggering the thirty-month additional exclusivity. By filing new patents after the first lawsuit, then suing for infringement of those, drug companies can even obtain successive thirty-month stays. While Hatch-Waxman did indeed boost the generic industry, it did far more for big pharma.

Subsequent congressional actions have added still more exclusive marketing time.[10] In accord with 1994 international trade agreements, Congress increased the basic patent term from seventeen years after issuance to twenty years after filing—which is usually longer. And finally, the Food and Drug Administration Modernization Act of 1997 added six months of protection if drug companies test their drugs in children. One might think that drugs to be used in children should be tested in them anyway, as a condition of FDA approval. But while the agency can require such testing, it seldom does. Instead, Congress offered the industry a gigantic bribe. The result is that drug companies now test their blockbusters, including drugs to treat primarily adult diseases like high blood pressure, in children, just because the extra protection is so lucrative. Less profitable drugs might not be tested in children, even though they are far more likely to be used in them.

Playing the Game

I have described various ways drug companies can extend their exclusive marketing rights on blockbusters, but they don't just select one from the menu. Instead, they use every possible stratagem simultaneously, so that if one fails another might work. First, companies change their top-selling drugs in ways that will add three years' exclusivity, in accord with Hatch-Waxman. Second, they file for multiple patents, staggered over months or even years, which serve as pretexts for lawsuits to trigger thirty-month extensions. Third, nearly every blockbuster is tested in children to get an extra six months of exclusivity, whether the drugs are likely to be used by children or not. Fourth, brand-name companies may collude with generic companies to delay their entry into the market or to keep prices high. And fifth, they may get a new patent and FDA approval for a trivial variation of their blockbuster and promote it as an "improved" version of the original.

In Chapter 5, I showed how the makers of three blockbusters—Prilosec, Claritin, and Prozac—launched virtually identical drugs just as generics were scheduled to come on the market. The idea was to switch users to the new drugs. AstraZeneca patented Nexium, a form of Prilosec, and got three years' FDA exclusivity for it. Schering-Plough patented Clarinex, which is what Claritin turns into in the body, and got five years' exclusivity for that. Eli Lilly launched Sarafem, which is simply Prozac used for premenstrual tension, and got three years' exclusivity for that. (Lilly also patented weekly Prozac.) But what I did not discuss was how these same companies were simultaneously using Hatch-Waxman and the pediatric extension to fend off generic competition. Let's look at that strategy now.

Prilosec

The heartburn drug Prilosec was once the number-one drug in the world, with sales of about $6 billion a year.[11] Patented by a Swedish company that later became part of the British drug giant AstraZeneca, Prilosec was approved by the FDA in 1989. The primary patent was scheduled to expire in October 2001, after a six-month extension for pediatric testing. But the company continued to file more patents, eventually listing eleven in the Orange Book, that would extend patent protection until 2019 (although there was no realistic expectation that these later patents would withstand challenge). And for each of them, the company claimed an additional six months for testing the drug in children, even though heartburn is hardly a top pediatric problem.

When Prilosec's exclusivity approached its end, Astra-Zeneca was loaded for bear. It sued generic companies right and left, charging infringement of these multiple secondary patents. For example, it had obtained a patent on the idea of combining Prilosec with antibiotics, then argued that a generic drug would infringe on that patent because doctors might prescribe it with an antibiotic. It also patented a substance made in the body after Prilosec is swallowed (a metabolite) and claimed people would infringe on that patent if they swallowed a generic. (Note that the culprit would be the hapless consumer, but the generic company would be guilty of contributing to the offense.) Three generic companies were stopped because a court found they had infringed on Prilosec's patent on the capsule's coating. As a result, no generic drug was able to enter the market even after Prilosec's exclusive marketing rights expired. AstraZeneca's CEO, Tom McKillop, was evidently pleased, as well he might have been. He told *The Financial Times* of London, "Our defense strategy has already given us longer exclusivity over the last few months. And now it is likely to give us some months more and maybe even a lot longer than that."[12]

This kind of nonsense is not unique to AstraZeneca. In fact, it is fairly typical. Nothing is too ridiculous to take to court if it will extend exclusivity. Unfortunately, it is hard to appreciate the low comedy, given that such machinations add billions of dollars to the U.S. drug bill. A generic version of Prilosec did not arrive on the market until the end of 2002, and then, because it had six months' exclusivity, its price was almost as high as that of the brand-name drug. Clearly, AstraZeneca had by no means put all its eggs in the Nexium basket.

And the company had one more trick up its sleeve. When the string was finally running out, it petitioned the FDA to convert Prilosec from a prescription drug to an over-the-counter (OTC) product. That was a very shrewd maneuver. According to Hatch-Waxman, switching from prescription to OTC status can buy another three years of exclusivity if it is accompanied by some minimal testing, mainly to show that consumers can understand the instructions for using the drug. On that basis, a slightly modified OTC version of Prilosec came on the market (in conjunction with Procter & Gamble). Other formulations remained available by prescription. (The FDA does not permit identical formulations to be sold both by prescription and over the counter.) The result was that AstraZeneca preserved its monopoly in the prescription market with Nexium, and with Prilosec it accomplished the same thing in the OTC market.

Claritin

Now let's look at how Schering-Plough played the game with its blockbuster Claritin—an antihistamine said to cause less drowsiness than cheaper over-the-counter drugs like Benadryl.[13] Before it lost its exclusivity, Claritin cost $80 to $100 for a month's supply, compared with about one-tenth that for Benadryl. At its peak, it had sales of about $2.7 billion per year. Claritin was patented by Schering-Plough in 1981 but not approved by the FDA until 1993—after much scientific controversy about whether it is any better than a placebo at the low doses necessary to prevent drowsiness. The seventeen-year patent should have expired in 1998, but Hatch-Waxman added two years to make up for the long approval time, the international agreement to extend the duration of drug patents then added twenty-two months, and pediatric testing added another six months. These three extensions amounted to an additional four years and four months of exclusivity—worth many billions of dollars in sales. Starting in 1998, Schering-Plough sued eight generic drug companies for infringement of one or more of the four Claritin patents it had listed in the Orange Book. The company's legal costs were reported to be about $5 million a case— a pittance compared with the stakes.

Schering-Plough patented the active metabolite of Claritin and launched it as Clarinex just before Claritin's exclusive marketing rights expired at the end of 2002. But that left the problem of what to do with Claritin. Like AstraZeneca, Schering-Plough was unwilling to have its blockbuster die in a losing competition with generics. Furthermore, generic drugs might also erode sales of Clarinex (for one thing, the names are too much alike), on which Schering-Plough was pinning its hopes. So in 2002 it did something similar to what AstraZeneca did. It petitioned the FDA to change Claritin from a prescription drug to an OTC product. But unlike AstraZeneca, it moved all formulations of its blockbuster to OTC status, leaving nothing to be sold as a prescription drug. Since identical formulations are not sold as both prescription and OTC drugs, that prevented any generic companies from entering the prescription market. However, Schering-Plough did not get three years' exclusivity for the OTC products, so they face competition. And the company has been much less successful with Clarinex than AstraZeneca has been with Nexium.

Prozac

As Prozac was nearing the end of its exclusivity, Eli Lilly also sued generic makers who hoped to enter the market.[14] One of them, Barr Pharmaceuticals, charged that Lilly had listed essentially duplicate patents in the Orange Book. In 2000, the Court of Appeals for the Federal Circuit agreed. It found that Lilly had "double-patented" Prozac and changed the exclusivity expiration date from December 2003 to February 2001. The U.S. Supreme Court refused to hear an appeal, but Lilly used pediatric testing to extend the time to August 2001. Generic forms of Prozac are now on the market, at much lower prices. Usage has also dropped, as people respond to advertising for similar brand-name (and now more expensive) selective serotonin reuptake inhibitors like Paxil and Zoloft. However, in June 1999, Lilly patented Weekly Prozac, a new formulation (the previous version is taken daily). It was approved by the FDA six months before the Prozac patent expired and had exclusive marketing rights until February 2004.

The most ingenious move to extend the life of Prozac was the creation of Sarafem—the identical drug in the identical dose, but colored pink and lavender instead of green, and taken for a new indication. In 1990 Dr. Richard Wurtman, director of MIT's Clinical Research Center, and his wife, Dr. Judith Wurtman, took out a method of use patent on selective serotonin reuptake inhibitors for the treatment of premenstrual syndrome. According to a CNN report, they tried to license the use to Eli Lilly, but the company was not interested—then.[15] So they licensed it to Interneuron Pharmaceuticals, a small biotechnology company cofounded by Richard Wurtman, which is now called Indevus Pharmaceuticals. In 1997, Lilly, faced with the imminent loss of Prozac's exclusivity, changed its mind. It decided to license Prozac's use for premenstrual syndrome from Interneuron—reportedly for $2 million plus a percentage of sales.

Lilly renamed Prozac "Sarafem" and got FDA approval to market it for "premenstrual dysphoric disorder (PMDD)"—an example of the new move by drug companies to promote diseases for drugs, rather than the reverse. The Wurtmans and MIT get a portion of Indevus's royalties. Sarafem's exclusivity was supposed to last until July 2003, but Lilly received a six-month extension because it tested the drug in children—something I can't imagine would be scientifically illuminating, since these "children" must have been very nearly adults if they were experiencing PMDD. Sarafem was priced slightly higher than the identical drug when it was called Prozac. Now that generic Prozac is on the market, Sarafem costs nearly three times as much—$5.70 per pill at my local drugstore in 2004, compared with $2.00 for the generic. Lilly evidently counts on its marketing to persuade doctors to prescribe the brand-name drug instead of the generic version.

Paxil

The clear champion in the Hatch-Waxman sweepstakes is GlaxoSmithKline and its blockbuster Paxil.[16] This is a me-too drug. Like Lilly's Prozac, it is a selective serotonin reuptake inhibitor to treat depression—now also approved for a variety of other conditions like "social anxiety disorder." It was originally approved by the FDA in 1992. In 1998, a generic company, Apotex, signaled its intention to produce a generic version. GlaxoSmithKline sued it for infringement of its sole patent listed in the Orange Book, and that suit triggered the first thirty-month stay on Apotex. GlaxoSmithKline then began to list nine new patents in the Orange Book. Starting seventeen months into the first thirty-month stay, it sued Apotex successively for infringement of four newly listed patents. Those lawsuits generated four more thirty-month delays, which were staggered, so that altogether GlaxoSmithKline extended its exclusivity by over five years—from 1998 to mid-2003. That represented a gain of billions of dollars in sales for the company. Yet it is highly questionable whether the additional patents met the criteria for listing in the Orange Book.

Reaction

In a damning report issued in July 2002, the Federal Trade Commission (FTC) documented the widespread anticompetitive activities within the pharmaceutical industry.[17] And it implicitly took the FDA to task for failing to enforce legal restrictions on the listing of patents in the Orange Book. The FDA has claimed it doesn't have the resources or expertise (an incredible piece of modesty) to check Orange Book listings, so it relies on the word of the drug companies. The FTC was appropriately skeptical about this honor system, as anyone who had the slightest inkling of how this industry works would be. In sum, the FTC found evidence that Hatch-Waxman is regularly exploited to prevent generic competition, and it has taken antitrust action against several brand-name and generic drug companies that colluded to keep generic drugs off the market. It also criticized the use of bogus "citizen petitions" to slow the approval of generic drugs. Finally, it suggested changes to Hatch-Waxman that would curb the abuse—including limiting drug companies to one thirty-month stay per drug and prohibiting agreements between brand-name and generic companies to delay the entrance of generic drugs to market.

The FTC report caused a brief public outcry, and in 2002 Senators Charles Schumer (D-N.Y.) and John McCain (R-Ariz.) introduced legislation that incorporated the FTC recommendations for reform of Hatch-Waxman. It passed the Senate but died in the House and has not been resurrected. Under pressure, the Bush administration promulgated its own regulations that would limit drug companies to one thirty-month stay for suing generic companies. But these regulations are vague about whether the limitation means one stay per drug or one stay per generic company or one stay per patent, and they seem to introduce a large loophole by imposing no time limitation on when the lawsuit could be filed. Conceivably, a drug company could wait until a generic was approved and on the loading docks before filing. The new regulations also expand the types of patents that can be listed in the Orange Book and, unlike the Senate bill, do not permit generic companies to challenge a listing.[18] In fact, many observers see the administration move as a way to forestall more meaningful reform in Congress. But that is a subject for the next chapter, which will ask just how friendly our government is to the pharmaceutical industry.

11

Buying Influence—How the Industry Makes Sure It Gets Its Way

THE HEAVY HAND OF BIG PHARMA IS felt at all levels of government. Nothing demonstrated that influence more plainly than the prescription drug benefit added to Medicare in late 2003.[1] You will remember that Medicare originally didn't pay for outpatient prescription drugs because when the program was created, in 1965, there was not much need for such a benefit. People didn't take nearly as many prescription drugs back then, and the drugs they did take were much less expensive. But now, senior citizens often take five or six drugs a day, at a cost of thousands of dollars a year out of pocket. Since seniors constitute a strong voting bloc, both political parties were eager to provide a drug benefit before the 2004 elections.

But look at what Congress did. They passed a bill that explicitly prohibits Medicare from using its enormous purchasing power to bargain for low prices. Medicare will have no say in what drug companies are paid, and it will have to cover expensive me-too drugs as well as more cost-effective ones. It isn't even permitted to peg charges to the average wholesale price, as is now the case when Medicare reimburses for drugs administered in hospitals or doctors' offices. To make sure that Medicare will not be able to influence drug prices, the benefit will be administered not by Medicare itself but by multiple private companies with much less bargaining power. Medicare will subsidize these companies but have no other role.

What a bonanza for big pharma! Every other large purchaser—from the Veterans Affairs (VA) system to Aetna and General Motors—negotiates for favorable prices. But not Medicare—potentially the biggest purchaser of them all. That prohibition means not only that the market will expand but that there will be little restraint on prices. As soon as the bill passed, stock prices of the big drug companies shot up, after a long period of decline. Investors knew good news when they saw it.

And the news for senior citizens and the rest of the public? Not so good. The bill originally contemplated expenditures of $400 billion over ten years—or $40 billion a year. About a quarter of that was explicitly earmarked for what can only be called bribes—billions to keep employers from dropping retiree benefits, billions to private insurers to get them to cover seniors, billions to increase fees to doctors and payments to rural hospitals to get the American Medical Association and the American Hospital Association on board, and so forth. That left about $30 billion a year to pay for drugs. How far would that have gone? Not far. In fact, at the current rate of increase, in just a couple of years, rising drug expenditures would have canceled it out altogether. Furthermore, the benefit is so complicated and the scheme of administering it through multiple private payers so daunting that the overhead costs will quickly consume much of what is left.

Within a few weeks of the bill's passage, the White House upped the estimated cost to $530 billion. Later it was reported that the chief actuary of the Centers for Medicare & Medicaid Services had pegged the cost at about $550 billion five months before the bill passed—in plenty of time for Congress to have second thoughts. But the administration reportedly kept this more realistic estimate from Congress until the bill was safely passed.[2]

The fact is that this benefit will provide very little relief for seniors. Even at the outset, many seniors will pay more in monthly premiums and deductibles than they will receive. As costs rise (and they surely will), the deficit-ridden Congress will try to pay for the benefit by wringing it out of the rest of the Medicare program. Seniors may see their monthly part B premiums (taken out of their social security checks) increase, whether they sign up for the drug benefit or not. Deductibles and co-payments will rise. And it is even possible that other Medicare services will have to be curtailed to pay for the drug benefit. But remember, Congress agreed to postpone implementation of the benefit until 2006, when the Bush administration would not have to answer for the consequences. Let the chickens come home to roost then.

All this is not to say we don't need a Medicare prescription drug benefit. We do. But it should be administered through the Medicare program itself, which should be able to negotiate prices like any other large purchaser. All senior citizens should be fully covered for all cost-effective drugs. Medicare should have a formulary of the most cost-effective drugs, just as large private insurers do. Done this way, a Medicare prescription drug benefit would probably cost less than the present one will but provide much better and more efficient coverage. Nearly all of the money would go toward purchasing drugs, not toward windfall profits for the pharmaceutical and insurance industries and the pharmacy benefit management companies (more about them in the next chapter).

If it's that simple, why didn't Congress get it right? The answer is the pharmaceutical industry is so powerful that its interests take precedence over yours. It has essentially hired the government to do its bidding. In the words of Senator Richard J. Durbin (D-Ill.), "PhRMA [the Pharmaceutical Research and Manufacturers of America], this lobby, has a death grip on Congress."[3] That is a serious charge, but the facts bear it out. Big pharma simply would not have permitted a Medicare drug benefit that included price negotiations. Congress was willing to make a useless transfer of billions of extra dollars from taxpayers to the drug companies and pharmacy benefit managers rather than cross big pharma.

The industry is cozy with both Republicans and Democrats and with both the White House and Congress. But most of its attentions are lavished on Republicans, and vice versa. *The New York Times* reported that in 1999, Jim Nicholson, then chairman of the Republican National Committee, wrote to Charles A. Heimbold, then CEO of Bristol-Myers Squibb, "We must keep the lines of communication open if we want to continue passing legislation that will benefit your industry."[4] That lets you know where the public stands. Heimbold is now ambassador to Sweden, and why not? He reportedly gave over $200,000 to Republicans in the 2000 campaign and asked other Bristol-Myers Squibb executives and their spouses to give a thousand dollars apiece to George W. Bush. The total take for the Republicans from the company was $2 million. The "lines of communication" are evidently in super shape.

What It Takes

Big pharma makes its influence felt through a variety of well-worn methods and a few new ones. Lobbying is tried and true, but big pharma employs it on a new scale. In addition, big pharma contributes money to nearly every political campaign that may affect its fortunes. And recently, the industry has put increasing resources into the formation and support of ostensibly "grassroots" organizations to promote its interests in the media. Let's look at these methods in more detail.

Special Lobbyists

The pharmaceutical industry has by far the largest lobby in Washington—and that's saying something. In 2002 it employed 675 lobbyists (more than one for each member of Congress)—many drawn from 138 Washington lobbying firms—at a cost of over $91 million.[5] The job of these lobbyists is to prowl the corridors of power in Washington to promote drug company interests. The industry's trade association, PhRMA, also maintains its offices in Washington, where it had a full-time staff of 120 in 2002, and accounted for $14 million of the lobbying expenditures and 112 of the lobbyists. According to the consumer advocacy group Public Citizen, from 1997 through 2002, the industry spent nearly $478 million on lobbying.

Drug company lobbyists are extremely well connected. In 2002, they included 26 former members of Congress, and another 342 who had been on congressional staffs or otherwise connected with government officials. Twenty had been congressional chiefs of staff, serving such influential members as House Ways and Means Committee Chairman Bill Thomas (R-Calif.) and Senate Judiciary Committee Chairman Orrin Hatch (R-Utah). The lobbyist Nick Littlefield had been chief counsel for Senator Edward Kennedy (D-Mass.), of the Health, Education, Labor and Pensions Committee. Some lobbyists were actually related to members of Congress, including Scott Hatch, son of Senator Orrin Hatch, and former Senator Birch Bayh, father of Senator Evan Bayh (D-Ind.) and also father of the Bayh-Dole Act. Two former chairmen of the Republican National Committee (one now the governor of Mississippi) also joined the ranks of drug company lobbyists. You get the idea. Even without the political contributions (which I will describe next), this revolving door between government and lobbyists guarantees that the industry will have attentive and sympathetic ears in Washington.

No one seems to be concerned about the obvious conflicts of interest. Look at Senator Hatch. From 1991 through 2000, he was the number-one recipient of campaign contributions from the pharmaceutical industry, and has steadfastly championed its causes in the Senate. His son, Scott, worked for many years for a lobbying firm called Parry, Romani, which counted pharmaceutical companies among its clients. In 2002, he opened his own firm—Walker Martin & Hatch—which proved remarkably successful, even in its first year. According to the *Los Angeles Times,* most of its business comes from companies that count on Orrin Hatch for support.[6] Among its clients are PhRMA and GlaxoSmithKline. Now hear what the Hatches have to say about all this. According to the *Times,* the son said, "I don't think I get treated any different in the [congressional and government] offices. I don't get a sense that they're saying, 'Oh, this is Senator Hatch's son.' I think they see three hard-working gentlemen and respect that." Really? The father, in contrast, seems to live in the real world. He told the *Times*, "Scott is my son, so naturally I would expect him to have clients that are interested in what I do."

Generous Contributions

The industry also gives copiously to political campaigns. In the 1999–2000 election cycle, drug companies gave $20 million in direct campaign contributions plus $65 million in "soft" money. Although big pharma used to give roughly equal amounts to both parties, about 80 percent of its contributions now go to Republicans. But there is still enough left for key Democrats. The citizen group Common Cause looked at the top recipients of drug company donations during the 1990s. It found, not unexpectedly, that Senator Hatch led the Senate, followed by Senator Bill Frist (R-Tenn.), who became the Senate majority leader. In the House, Representative Bill Thomas was number one, followed by Representative Nancy Johnson (R-Conn.).[7]

But powerful Democrats from states that are home to major drug companies, such as former Senator Robert Torricelli (D-N.J.) and Senator Joseph Lieberman (D-Conn.), also enjoyed substantial industry favors. As just one example, in 1999, Torricelli introduced a bill to make it easier to extend the patents of Schering-Plough's blockbuster Claritin and a few other drugs. According to Common Cause, this bill was introduced a day after Schering-Plough made a $50,000 contribution to the Democratic Senatorial Campaign Committee, which Torricelli chaired. Senator Hatch held hearings on the bill. He was then a candidate for the Republican presidential nomination and was reportedly being flown around the country on campaign stops in Schering-Plough's Gulfstream executive jet. The company also hired the lobbying firm that employed Scott Hatch. As it turned out, the bill was apparently too embarrassing even for the U.S. Congress, and nothing came of it.

The pharmaceutical industry supports a variety of front groups that masquerade as grassroots organizations. One of these is Citizens for Better Medicare, supposedly a coalition of senior citizen groups. The name sounds like a collection of groups of old folks who came together to try to improve Medicare, yet it is anything but that.[8] Formed in 1999, the group spent an estimated $65 million in the 1999–2000 election campaign fighting against any form of drug price regulation. Its executive director, Tim Ryan, had been PhRMA's advertising director. Members of the "coalition" also had ties to big pharma. United Seniors Association (USA—get it?), for instance, spent about $18 million on "issue ads" in the 2002 election, all of which supported PhRMA positions. Reportedly, its ads were put together by none other than Tim Ryan.[9] As more people become skeptical about the industry itself, drug companies are increasingly hiding behind front groups. The political groups are the counterparts of the patient advocacy groups I discussed in Chapter 8. They are effective precisely because they are not what they seem.

The influence of the pharmaceutical industry on government clearly reaches into the Bush administration. Defense Secretary Donald Rumsfeld was CEO, president, and chairman of G. D. Searle, a major drug firm that merged with Pharmacia, which in turn was bought by Pfizer. Mitchell E. Daniels, Jr., former White House budget director, was senior vice president of Eli Lilly. The first President Bush was on the Eli Lilly board of directors before becoming president. The connections are so close that annual meetings of PhRMA look like Washington power conclaves. The 2003 meeting, for instance, featured the first President Bush, Secretary of Health and Human Services Tommy Thompson, former Food and Drug Administration (FDA) Commissioner Mark McClellan, and the chairman of the Republican Senatorial Campaign Committee, Senator George Allen (R-Va.).[10]

What It Buys

In earlier chapters I discussed some of the many pieces of congressional legislation that have benefited the pharmaceutical industry, beginning with the Bayh-Dole and Stevenson-Wydler Acts of 1980. These, you will remember, enabled drug companies to license, and profit from, research supported by the National Institutes of Health (NIH). Whether the Bayh-Dole Act, which was supposed to encourage the translation of basic discoveries into practical use, is an overall success is debatable. Certainly the number of biomedical patents increased rapidly after it was passed. But many critics say that the effect has often been the opposite of its purpose. By encouraging thickets of licenses on every aspect of new technologies, as well as a proprietary culture of secrecy, it may actually have slowed the sharing of scientific information and the exploration of new scientific leads.[11] And it has certainly done nothing to ensure that drugs licensed from academic institutions are "available on reasonable terms," as called for in the legislation. That stipulation has been totally ignored by the pharmaceutical industry, the academic medical centers, the NIH, and Congress.

I will not enumerate all the favors big pharma has extracted from a compliant Congress. But a few are worth highlighting. As we learned in the last chapter, some of the most lucrative pieces of legislation had to do with extending drug monopolies. Others conferred huge tax breaks, so that now the most profitable corporations in the world pay only a small fraction of their vast revenues in taxes. One favor is much in the news these days. In 1987, under industry pressure, Congress passed a law that prohibits anyone but the manufacturer from importing prescription drugs from another country—even if the drugs were made in the United States. It is this law that is being invoked to stop people from obtaining cheaper drugs from Canada. I will talk more about that in the next chapter.

Other congressional actions target the FDA's ability to regulate the industry. The 1997 Food and Drug Administration Modernization Act, for instance, was a giant giveaway to the pharmaceutical industry. Among other things, it required the agency to lower its standards for approving drugs (sometimes accepting just one clinical trial instead of two, for example). But perhaps most important is what Congress has *not* done. It has not authorized the FDA to require that new drugs be tested against older ones as a condition of approval. The fact that drug companies get away with comparing drugs only with placebos is what makes it possible for the industry to live on me-too drugs. If not for that, drug companies would have no choice but to work on truly innovative drugs.

One of the least-known but biggest gifts Congress gave big pharma was to authorize an industry-supported private company to decide whether Medicaid would pay for off-label uses of prescription drugs.[12] While drug companies are not permitted to market drugs for uses not approved by the FDA, doctors may prescribe drugs for whatever reason they like. That leaves open the question of whether insurers will pay—not a small matter, since as many as half of all prescriptions are written for off-label uses. The question is particularly important for Medicaid, which is the largest government program that pays for outpatient drugs. In 1997, Congress named Drugdex Information Service as one of three organizations that would decide which off-label uses Medicaid would cover. Drugdex lists drugs and their uses in a large directory, which it sells to pharmacists and anyone else who can afford the $3823 annual subscription cost. If a use is listed there, Medicaid must pay for the drug when it is prescribed for that use.

Drugdex is owned by the Thomson Corporation, a multi-

billion-dollar firm that includes medical education and communication companies (MECCs) among its many other divisions.
This creates an incestuous relationship whereby Thomson gains
from putting on continuing medical education courses for drug
companies, while drug companies gain from having their drugs
listed in Thomson's Drugdex. Furthermore, the MECCs "educate" doctors about off-label uses of drugs. With such close connections to industry, it's not surprising that Drugdex authorizes
about twice as many off-label uses as the other two federally
recognized directories, both of which are nonprofit. In 2003,
according to *The Wall Street Journal,* Drugdex listed 203 off-
label uses for the dozen top-selling drugs in the United States.
They included, for instance, 48 off-label uses for Neurontin, the
epilepsy drug.[13] According to the company, Neurontin can be
used for hiccups, nicotine withdrawal, migraine, and just about
anything else you care to name, and Medicaid has to pay for it.

Because Drugdex lists so many more off-label uses than the
other directories, it in effect sets the standards. It cites articles to
support its listings, but the articles are not required to meet any
scientific criteria. Until recently Drugdex even had a drug company advisory board to review its listings. The *Wall Street Journal* reporter David Armstrong wrote that the board was
suddenly dissolved when he started to make inquiries for an article he was writing about Drugdex.[14] So here is a company with
close ties to the pharmaceutical industry that single-handedly
determines coverage for about half of all prescriptions written
for Medicaid recipients. And all at taxpayer expense. That's

quite a gift. Furthermore, since this arrangement bypasses FDA approval, it seems to make the agency's scientific scrutiny almost irrelevant. Whatever the industry can get Drugdex to put in the directory is apparently okay.

An International Embarrassment

Both the Clinton and Bush administrations carried water for the pharmaceutical industry when Third World countries complained that big pharma was pricing HIV/AIDS drugs out of reach. When the World Trade Organization was formed in 1995, members were required to honor twenty-year patents on drugs. At the time, many countries did not even consider drugs patentable. Exceptions were to be allowed for public health emergencies. (In that case, governments could issue "compulsory licenses" to have needed drugs produced by other manufacturers.) Poor countries were given until 2005 to comply. It was in this context that in the late 1990s South Africa—desperate to control its HIV/AIDS epidemic—threatened to produce or import generic drugs to fight it. The pharmaceutical industry adamantly opposed any such move and the Clinton administration, no doubt reflecting the industry's influence in Washington, warned of trade sanctions. Subsequently, the administration was so embarrassed by the public outrage that it backed off. A few drug companies, also embarrassed, announced they would lower prices in parts of Africa, but the reality appears to have fallen far short of the promises. Even the discounted drugs are priced higher than generic drugs made in India, and they have been difficult to obtain.

Later, the Bush administration stood alone among 143 World Trade Organization countries in opposing the relaxation of patent protection in the Third World. The United States would agree only to permit poor countries to manufacture their own generic drugs for a limited number of diseases, not to import them. Since the poorest countries that most need drugs are least able to set up manufacturing plants, that was an empty concession. But more developed countries like India and Brazil, the likely producers of generics, would not risk economic retaliation by defying the United States. The Bush administration then said it might permit some countries to import generic drugs under special circumstances, but the proposal was laden with bureaucratic obstacles. The point is that the United States is generally seen as siding with drug company interests against the needs of millions of HIV/AIDS victims in the Third World.[15] As if to underscore that impression, the administration, as of early 2004, has refused to allow any of the promised $15 billion in federal funds allotted for HIV/AIDS treatment in the Third World to be spent on generic drugs.

In late 2003, South Africa's Competition Commission ruled that GlaxoSmithKline (the major manufacturer of AIDS drugs) and another company had violated the country's Competition Act by charging excessively high prices and refusing to license their patents to generic manufacturers in return for reasonable royalties. Following that ruling, Glaxo agreed to permit four generic companies in South Africa to make three of its AIDS drugs and sell them in all forty-seven sub-Saharan African countries. AIDS treatment now sells for as little as $300 a year in Africa, compared with more than $10,000 in the United States. Yet no one believes the companies are taking a loss there, which gives you some idea of how much they are making here.[16]

Handing the FDA to the Pharmaceutical Industry

Congress also put the FDA on the pharmaceutical industry's payroll. In 1992, it enacted the Prescription Drug User Fee Act, which authorized drug companies to pay user fees to the FDA. These were to be employed only to expedite approval of drugs. Fees originally amounted to about $310,000 per new drug application and soon accounted for about half the budget of the agency's drug evaluation center. That makes the FDA dependent on an industry it regulates. For the drug companies, the user fees are chump change—more than offset by the added income from getting to market sooner.

This act has to be renewed every five years. In the 2002 version, which was tacked on to a bioterrorism bill that swept through Congress without a murmur, the fees were increased to about $576,000 per new drug application. User fees altogether now account for about $260 million a year. Although a small fraction of that can be used for some limited safety monitoring, the lion's share is still earmarked to speed drug approvals. Since the act was passed, about a thousand new FDA employees have been added to handle new drug applications, and another five hundred are called for in the 2002 renewal. Altogether, these industry-paid employees constitute more than half of the FDA staff involved in approving drugs.[17] Yet the faster the approval process, the more likely it is that dangerous drugs will reach the market. Indeed, over the decade since the Prescription Drug User Fee Act was enacted, a record thirteen prescription drugs have had to be withdrawn from the market—after they caused hundreds of deaths.[18]

As I mentioned in Chapter 2, the FDA was once considered too slow and deliberate in approving drugs. Those days are gone. It now generally approves drugs faster than counterpart agencies in Europe and elsewhere. But in its rush, it is demanding less evidence of safety and effectiveness. While shortcuts are sometimes warranted for truly innovative drugs, they are now too frequent. Furthermore, although quick to approve drugs, the FDA is slow to take them off the market when they prove dangerous. For instance, in 1997 Warner-Lambert's diabetes drug Rezulin was taken off the market in Britain because it caused liver failure, but it was not removed from the market in the United States until two and a half years later, by which time it had caused at least sixty-three deaths.[19]

Partly, the problem stems from the fact that the user fees have created an imbalance within the FDA. Since the lion's share can go only to expedite approvals, that area of the agency has grown while staffing and resources in other parts of the FDA have been relatively starved. As drugs enter the market faster, it becomes increasingly difficult for the FDA to perform its other functions—including monitoring drug safety, ensuring manufacturing standards, and regulating marketing. The agency also has a direct interest in satisfying the industry, because that is what Congress expects of it. If the FDA were to displease industry, the user fees might even be discontinued, and many agency employees would probably lose their jobs. When added to the business-friendly pressure from its politically appointed leadership, and from an administration that is generally hostile to regulation, the Prescription Drug User Fee Act has undoubtedly constrained the FDA's independence and influenced its decisions.

Furthermore, the FDA is subject to industry pressures through its eighteen standing advisory committees on drug approvals. These committees, which consist of outside experts in various specialties, are charged with reviewing new drug applications and making recommendations to the agency about approval. The FDA almost always takes their advice. Many members of these committees have financial connections to interested companies. Although there are conflict of interest rules that prohibit participation in such cases, the agency regularly waives them on the unlikely grounds that someone's advice is indispensable. *USA Today* examined FDA hearing records in 2000 and found that "at 92 percent of the meetings at least one member had a financial conflict of interest," and "at 55 percent of meetings, half or more of the FDA advisers had conflicts of interest."[20]

Members of FDA advisory committees are said to command unusually high consulting fees from drug companies. They are certainly in a strong position to do so. They probably don't even have to say, "Pay me if you want your drugs approved." According to the *Washington Times* reporter August Gribbin, "One drug company executive who asked not to be identified referred to the advisory committee members' approaches for obtaining [consulting] work as 'shakedowns' because a company that refused to yield to such requests could doom products that cost tens of millions of dollars to develop." Representative Dan Burton (R-Ind.), head of the Government Reform Committee, charged that certain committees were "dominated by individuals with close working relationships" to drug companies.[21]

Choosing the FDA Commissioner—The Right Stuff

The close connections between the Bush White House and the pharmaceutical industry quite probably had something to do with the last-minute withdrawal of Dr. Alastair Wood's nomination as FDA commissioner in 2002. Wood, a widely respected professor of clinical pharmacology at Vanderbilt University in Nashville (and a former colleague of mine on the editorial staff of *The New England Journal of Medicine*), was reportedly warmly recommended by Senator Bill Frist (R-Tenn.) and Health and Human Services Secretary Tommy Thompson. But he was also known to be a supporter of strong regulatory action by the FDA and had evidently ruffled feathers among drug industry executives and other champions of a "free market" for drugs, including the editors of *The Wall Street Journal*. According to a *Boston Globe* story, the result was behind-the-scenes pressure on the White House, which led to an abrupt change of heart. Senator Frist was quoted as saying, "There was a great deal of concern that he [Wood] put too much emphasis on [drug] safety." (Imagine that!) And Dr. Raymond Woosley, also a distinguished clinical pharmacologist and an earlier candidate for the post (who opted instead for a major academic position), remarked, "It is pretty clear that anyone who has said anything that industry doesn't like isn't going to make it."[22]

When the new FDA commissioner was finally appointed, he could not have been more to the industry's liking. Dr. Mark McClellan, brother of the White House press secretary, Scott McClellan, and son of the Republican comptroller of Texas and former mayor of Austin, has consistently championed drug company causes. In what he called his "first international speech," in Mexico in 2003, he actually put forth the proposition that the answer to the troublesome disparity in drug prices between the United States and other advanced countries was not to lower prices here but to raise them there.[23] He excoriated other wealthy countries for their "overly strict price controls," which he said "are no different than violating the patent directly." He seemed to swallow hook, line, and sinker the fiction that drug prices have to be high to cover research and development costs. "The truth is," he said, "that the main reason prices are higher is that our country is paying the bulk of the costs of developing new treatments." In fact, as we've seen, prices have very little to do with R & D, and everything to do with profits.

McClellan went on to say, without any evidence whatsoever, that "the impact of excessive price controls on R & D is translating into an impact on the development of new products." Nowhere in the speech did the words "excess profits" cross his lips. Nor did he mention the immense marketing budgets, except to say, also without any evidence, that direct-to-consumer advertising "benefits the public health." In short, this was a speech that could have been written by PhRMA. Surely, we ought to expect more from the commissioner of the FDA than acting as a shill for big pharma. And I see no reason why he should even have been discussing drug pricing in his official capacity, since it is not within the FDA's purview. In early 2004, Dr. McClellan was moved to an even bigger job in the Bush administration—head of the Centers for Medicare & Medicaid Services.

I do not want to seem overly critical of the Food and Drug Administration. It performs a vital function, and it is staffed with many conscientious public servants and excellent scientists who are trying their best to do their jobs. But they are constrained by the congressional mandates under which they work, and by the directions that come from their commissioner. They are also constrained by an increasingly antiregulatory climate in Washington, which seems to imagine that the "market" can determine which drugs are safe and effective and which aren't. I have heard that morale in some parts of the FDA is extremely low, and I can certainly understand why it might be. Those staffers who continue to try to do their jobs well despite the fact that the industry they are supposed to regulate sometimes seems to be running their agency are heroes who deserve our gratitude. They stand between us and many more Rezulins.

Plans for More of the Same

In the summer of 2003, *The New York Times* obtained confidential documents from PhRMA that detailed its plans to buy influence in the coming fiscal year.[24] According to the report, spending for that purpose would increase by 23 percent—to $150 million. Of that, $73 million would go for lobbying at the federal level and $49 million at the state level. (The pharmaceutical trade association is moving more of its efforts to the states, which as we will see in the next chapter, are now more threatening to industry interests than the federal government.) Expenditures would include $5 million to lobby the FDA. (Aside from the propriety of an industry lobbying the agency that regulates it, we have to wonder what effect it has on the commissioner's speeches.) More than $12 million would subsidize "like-minded" doctor, patient, academic, and influential racial minority organizations. Another $1 million would be spent on an "intellectual echo chamber of economists—a standing network of economists and thought leaders to speak against federal price control regulations through articles and testimony, and to serve as a rapid response team." There would be $500,000 for "placement of op-eds and articles by third parties." In addition, $18 million would go to fight price controls and protect patent rights in foreign countries. Perhaps the most arrogant allotment was $1 million "to change the Canadian health care system" (do the Canadians know PhRMA thinks they can be bought so cheaply?), and another $500,000 to block the influx of drugs from Canada.

In a 2003 editorial, *The Washington Post* summed up the situation very well. It warned, "Anyone arguing the drug companies' case, no matter how neutral his or her academic or think tank position may seem, should be questioned carefully with regard to sources of income."[25] Too often reporters don't do that. Two reporters for a major newspaper told me that one reason they don't ask is that asking makes it harder to write their stories. If they find out their sources have conflicts of interest, their editors may require them to search for new sources. Or the sources may become indignant at being questioned. So there is an implicit "don't ask, don't tell" policy. But if reporters identify their sources only by their academic credentials, without adding information about relevant commercial ties, they are misleading their readers.

The PhRMA blueprint sounds like crisis planning, and that is exactly what it was. That fact was made clear in a memorandum for the association's board. It said that the industry was facing a "perfect storm" caused by "'expanding government price controls abroad, resulting in politically unsustainable cross-border pricing differences; increasing availability of medicines from abroad via Internet sales'; state ballot initiatives to make drugs more affordable in the United States; increasing state demands for drug discounts in the Medicaid program; and 'false perceptions that drug prices are increasing by 20 percent a year.'"[26] While I might quarrel a little with the list of causes, it is indeed a "perfect storm" that is brewing. We can see the first cracks in the once solid support for the industry in recent congressional efforts to close some of the loopholes in Hatch-Waxman and to permit reimportation of cheaper drugs from Canada. But so far, political support for the industry has held, despite the cracks.

"Our mantra at PhRMA is this," said its president, Alan F. Holmer, at the association's 2002 annual meeting. "We will never allow for failure whenever the political circumstances are at all manageable." And they have been "manageable" so far. As Representative Bernard Sanders (I-Vt.) put it, "Even the New York Yankees sometimes lose, and it has been known that, on occasion, the Los Angeles Lakers lose a ballgame. But one organization never loses, and that organization has hundreds of victories to its credit and zero defeats in the United States Congress. And that is the pharmaceutical industry."[27] In the next chapter, I'll ask whether this astonishing string of victories can continue.

12

Is the Party Over?

THE PHARMACEUTICAL INDUSTRY HAS got to be worried now. If 1980 was the year it started its phenomenal rise, 2000 may be the year it began its slide. It's hard to make the case that an industry as rich and powerful as this one—and fresh from its victory in the Medicare prescription drug benefit—is in trouble, but it is. Some of the trouble can be ascribed to the softening of the economy since its peak in 2000. But in addition, there are specific factors that apply just to this industry, and they are unlikely to be reversible by a general improvement in the economy.

Here is a quick rundown of the problems. People have grown angry about the high and rapidly climbing prices for prescription drugs. They no longer believe that big pharma has to charge stratospheric prices to cover the costs of research and development. Senior citizens are particularly angry, and they are unlikely to be placated for long by the Medicare drug benefit, for reasons I discussed in the last chapter. More and more Americans, even whole towns, are buying their drugs in Canada, where they are much cheaper, and there is pressure on Congress to undo the industry-inspired law that made doing so illegal. Large insurers and state governments are pushing back against drug prices by insisting on steep discounts and using lists of preferred drugs (formularies). In recent years, the industry has also faced a flood of litigation launched by federal and state prosecutors, the Federal Trade Commission, and consumer groups charging multiple offenses. Finally, the much vaunted pipeline is running dry. For all the industry rhetoric about its steady stream of innovative drugs, the truth is that the stream has slowed to a trickle. Profits remain enormous, but sales growth is slowing, drug companies are laying off employees, and some of them have seen steep drops in their share prices over the past year or two. This may indeed be a "perfect storm" brewing.

Now let's look at it in more detail. I won't discuss the Medicare prescription drug benefit further here, because I talked about it in the last chapter. But closely related to it is the controversy over "reimportation" of drugs from Canada. That is something of a misnomer, because what is usually really going on is the importation of drugs approved by the Food and Drug Administration (FDA) that were originally exported to Canada from American and European drug companies. So it's often just a matter of transporting American-made drugs over the same border twice. If you think there's something absurd about that, there is, but it's the only way many Americans can get affordable drugs.

Canada

The United States is the only developed nation that does not regulate drug prices. All the others—Australia, Canada, France, Germany, Italy, Japan, the Netherlands, Spain, Switzerland, Sweden, Britain, and so on—do. The methods vary from country to country. Britain, for instance, does not set prices but instead caps profits. France puts a ceiling on total drug spending. Japan sets reimbursement prices for new drugs based on how they compare with existing ones.

Canada is clearly of most interest to Americans.[1] Its national health insurance program does not cover prescription drugs. Instead, the provinces cover them for senior citizens, as well as for low-income and disabled people, while most other Canadians are covered through their employers. Nevertheless, a federal Patented Medicine Prices Review Board checks twice a year to make sure that prices of patented medicines are "not excessive." The rule is that prices of new drugs may not be higher than the median of their prices in seven other developed nations (the United States, Britain, Switzerland, Germany, Sweden, France, and Italy) or higher than the highest prices of older drugs for the same condition. Once drugs are on the market, prices are permitted to increase no faster than the general inflation rate. Provincial governments establish formularies and negotiate further discounts. Prices for generics, by contrast, are not regulated. Essentially, Canada is saying to brand-name companies, "In return for the patent protection we provide, you owe us reasonable pricing." Prices for brand-name drugs in Canada are roughly half to two-thirds what they are in the United States.

As the disparity between U.S. and Canadian prices grew over the years, Americans near the border began to travel to Canada to fill their prescriptions. Mainly these were senior citizens who had been paying the highest prices in the world out of pocket. They would organize bus trips and make social junkets out of their drug-purchasing trips. Most of the drugs they were buying had been made by major drug companies, based in either the United States or Europe, and approved by the FDA. They were just being brought back across the border. As the price differences became widely known, people all over the United States started to purchase drugs from Internet mail order Canadian pharmacies or from storefront operations that had deals with these pharmacies. Canadian doctors would write the prescriptions or copy U.S. prescriptions. By 2002, over a million Americans bought their drugs from Canada, and it was a $700 million business. In 2003, according to IMS Health, that jumped to $1.1 billion. One poll that year found that 7 percent of respondents had purchased drugs from Canada.[2] There were some 140 Internet pharmacies in Canada, up from 10 in 1999.[3]

There is one problem—buying drugs in Canada is illegal.
You will remember that in 1987, at drug company insistence,
Congress agreed to ban the importation of drugs by anyone except the manufacturers. The reason given is that the ban protects
Americans from counterfeit drugs, but surely another reason is
the industry's insistence that it should be shielded from "unfair"
Canadian price competition. An industry that wraps itself in free
market rhetoric was insisting that competition from other countries be outlawed. It pulled up the drawbridges over the moat
around the United States, so that Americans would not realize
the extent to which they were being overcharged. It worked for
a while, but no longer. A 2003 poll of likely Democratic voters in
New Hampshire found that 83 percent believed it should be legal
to import drugs from Canada; only 7 percent were opposed.

And what of the safety issue? It is true that counterfeit drugs
are an increasing problem. The reasons have to do with the sophisticated technologies available for changing labels and increasingly tortuous supply lines. Often there is not just one
wholesaler but multiple secondary ones. Manufacturing operations themselves are far-flung. In fact, large drug companies
have many plants scattered throughout the world. According to
its website, for instance, in 2003 Pfizer claimed to have sixty
manufacturing plants in thirty-two countries. In addition, many
of the key ingredients in American brand-name drugs come
from foreign suppliers.[4] And remember: About half of the major
drug companies are based in Europe.

At many points along the way, then, it is possible for someone to replace drugs with counterfeits. In one recent case, a wholesaler is alleged to have stolen hundreds of vials of a hormone used to help AIDS patients maintain their weight, substituted counterfeit substances, and resold the hormones over the Internet to bodybuilders.[5] In another case, labels for the anemia drug Procrit were attached to vials of water.[6] But there is absolutely no reason to think counterfeiting is more likely with drugs imported from Canada than with drugs that are sold at home, and some reason to think it is less likely.[7] Counterfeiting of anything is more profitable where prices are higher—and for prescription drugs, that is right here in the United States. Furthermore, when drug companies, no matter where they are based, seek FDA approval to market drugs in the United States, they must meet FDA manufacturing standards and the agency must be given authority to inspect their manufacturing plants— no matter where in the world they are located. So there should be no added concern about the manufacturing standards of imported drugs, as long as they are FDA-approved. We should also remember that the Canadian counterpart of the FDA is every bit as careful as the FDA about the drugs it aproves.

Whole cities and states, faced with the growing strain on their budgets from rising drug prices, now say they are willing to be scofflaws just like the busloads of senior citizens and mail order Internet customers. It began in 2003, when the flamboyant mayor of Springfield, Massachusetts, Michael Albano, offered city employees the option of purchasing their prescription drugs from Canada. Estimating that this practice would cut up to $9 million from the $18 million the city was spending annually on prescription drugs for its 18,000 employees, he made a deal with a Canadian drug supplier, CanaRx. The program is under way, and Mayor Albano remained cheerfully obdurate until his retirement, despite threats from the FDA.[8] His successor has said he will continue the program. That opened the floodgates.

Boston announced that it, too, would begin importing drugs from Canada the following year, and as Albano said modestly, "There's a little bit of a difference when a city like Springfield, Mass., does something and when Boston, Mass., does it."[9] By the end of 2003, officials in about a dozen states had announced their intentions to look into the possibility of importing drugs from Canada for their employees and uninsured residents. The attorney general of Massachusetts wrote to the commissioner of the FDA arguing that, while he did not intend to break the law, imports were necessary to counter the "unrestrained increases" in drug prices and that, if it liked, the agency could easily put safeguards into place. Large health insurers also got into the act. UnitedHealth, the largest of them all, allows 97,000 members of American Association of Retired Persons plans to be reimbursed for drugs they buy overseas, saying the policy is just for the convenience of customers traveling abroad—an unlikely story.[10]

Industry Resistance and Congress Caught in the Middle

Big pharma retaliated.[11] First was GlaxoSmithKline. The British drug giant began to require Canadian pharmacies to agree not to sell Glaxo drugs in the United States—as a condition of receiving shipments. Pfizer followed by demanding that certain Canadian pharmacies order their drugs directly from the company, not from wholesalers. That way the company could track orders and cut off the supply if pharmacies were stocking more drugs than they needed for their local customers. Eli Lilly told wholesalers they would be violating their contracts if they supplied Canadian pharmacies that do business in the United States. AstraZeneca, another British company, said it would limit shipments to Canadian pharmacies placing unusually large orders. And so on. The result is that Canadian pharmacies doing business in the United States have had to try to obtain drugs from other companies, which adds to their expense and drives up the prices they charge their American customers. Worse, it has apparently created shortages of drugs in Canada. Ironically, those shortages could lead to the very thing the drug companies claim they want to prevent—the growth of a market in unregulated drugs from other parts of the world.

The drug companies gave two justifications for their actions. One is the unlikely worry about counterfeit drugs being transported to the United States from Canada—an unpersuasive argument I have already discussed. In addition to being hard to take seriously, this argument implies that even British companies, like GlaxoSmithKline, are more concerned about the safety of Americans than about that of Canadians. The second justification is that drug companies need the high profits from U.S. sales to fund their R & D. That argument, too, is unconvincing, as we have seen. It goes without saying that drug companies do not sell their drugs in Europe and Canada at a loss; it's just that profit margins there are less than in the United States. The fact is that price regulation in other countries comes nowhere close to threatening R & D. Even if drug companies made *no* profits in other countries, given the fact that about half their sales are in the United States, that would cut their profit margins only in half—from 17.0 percent of total sales for the top ten U.S. companies in 2002 to a very respectable 8.5 percent.

You might wonder where Congress has been while this controversy heated up. The answer is: trying to have it both ways. Pulled between voters and the pharmaceutical industry, in 2000 it passed a law permitting "reimportation" of drugs from Canada but stipulated that the secretary of Health and Human Services, with the advice of the FDA, had to certify the practice was safe. Right on cue, the secretary (then Donna Shalala) said she could not give that assurance. In the Bush administration, Tommy Thompson did likewise, sounding the same dire warning that drugs from Canada might somehow turn to poison just by crossing the border. But voters weren't buying it, and Congress was not off the hook.

In the summer of 2003, the House of Representatives, despite the opposition of its leadership and heavy lobbying by big pharma and the FDA, surprised everyone by voting to legalize the importation of FDA-approved drugs from Canada and Europe. And this time there was no requirement that the Department of Health and Human Services certify that the practice was safe. There was no "out." This was a measure of the traction the issue had gained with the public. Alarmed, the Pharmaceutical Research and Manufacturers of America (PhRMA) looked to the Senate to stop the bill. And sure enough, fifty-three senators signed a "Chicken Little" letter to their colleagues warning that legalizing importation from Canada would cause the sky to fall. Later *The New York Times* reported that the letter had been circulated among the senators by PhRMA. In reply, Senator Rick Santorum (R-Pa.) claimed he had initiated the letter but acknowledged that PhRMA had indeed circulated it. "I don't have time to run around and get all these people to sign it," he explained.[12] Later in 2003, there was considerable pressure to permit drug importation from Canada as a part of the Medicare prescription drug benefit, but Congress resisted it and stayed true to big pharma by keeping the requirement for Department of Health and Human Services certification of safety. It did, however, call for the matter to be studied, which opens the door a crack.

Congress would like nothing better than to have this issue go away so it doesn't have to choose between voters and the pharmaceutical industry, but that is not going to happen. Voters are determined to get some relief from the high prices of prescription drugs. In practical terms, there is something absurd about buying drugs from Canada. For one thing, it adds to transaction costs. But the fact that it is still cheaper underscores the basic problem—price gouging in the United States. Importing drugs from Canada is a stopgap way to deal with a problem that shouldn't be there in the first place. It makes far more sense to import Canada's system for holding down drug prices than to import the drugs.

The States Fight Big Pharma

The center of activity to control drug costs is shifting to the states. With the economic downturn in 2001, states found themselves in a real bind. Unlike the federal government, most states do not have the option of running deficits. They must balance their budgets. One of the biggest drains on state budgets is Medicaid, and the fastest-growing component of that is prescription drug spending. States also have to foot the bill for prescription drugs for state employees and, in some states, for some of the uninsured as well. So it was natural for states to target prescription drugs in their efforts to balance their budgets.[13]

The first thing they did was to expand the use of lists of preferred drugs, or formularies. These, you will remember, are the drugs that offer the most bang for the buck. To prescribe drugs not on formularies—that is, more expensive drugs which are usually no better—doctors have to get "prior authorization." That is generally no more than a formality for doctors, but it is enough of a bother that the requirement is still very effective in cutting drug costs. Among the drugs most often excluded from formularies are heavily marketed, high-priced drugs like Nexium and Celebrex. Whereas in 2001, only two states had such programs, two years later, about half the states did. States are also banding together to form purchasing pools that will enable them to get better deals from drug companies.[14]

In 2000, Maine became the first state to legislate a form of price regulation. It was the result of a genuine grassroots movement, spearheaded by senior citizens who rode the buses to Canada to buy their drugs and knew very well how overpriced drugs were in their state. Under the leadership of Democrat Chellie Pingree, then the state's Senate majority leader, now head of the citizen group Common Cause, the legislature passed the "Maine Rx" law. It empowered the state to bargain with drug companies for lower prices for the uninsured. If prices did not come down sufficiently, the state could cap them. The bargaining chip was that if companies refused to deal, their drugs could be excluded from the state's Medicaid formulary. No sooner was the ink dry on Maine Rx than PhRMA challenged the law in federal court, alleging that it violated the Constitution's commerce clause and federal Medicaid law. After three years of legal wrangling, the case reached the U.S. Supreme Court in 2003. The high court refused to block the state and sent the matter back to the lower courts. Whether and when Maine Rx will go into effect is not clear. Vermont passed a similar measure, but it was successfully blocked in the courts by the industry.

Twenty-eight states filed briefs supporting Maine's case, and some of them have proposed or passed their own legislation challenging drug prices, usually involving some variation of requiring discounts or rebates as a condition for being listed on state formularies. Lawyers for PhRMA have sued to stop virtually all of them.

Florida enacted a law that required drug companies to offer discounts or other savings in order to have their drugs included in the Medicaid formulary. This case was particularly interesting because Florida's governor, Jeb Bush, is the brother of President Bush. In a break from family tradition (and in recognition of the political realities in his state), he denounced PhRMA's lawsuit by saying, "Protecting the large profit margins of multibillion pharmaceutical companies is not a priority."[15]

The industry has the money and legal talent to tie the states up in the courts for a long, long time. Yet, because so much is at stake, it is in the states' economic interests to fight back. Once disdainful of state legislatures, big pharma is now aiming its full firepower on them. As I mentioned in the last chapter, PhRMA planned to put $49 million into state lobbying in 2004. Whether the industry will succeed in co-opting state legislatures as it has the U.S. Congress remains to be seen. If it does, that would, of course, dampen the states' enthusiasm to continue their battles in court.

A Thousand Gnats

In just the past couple of years, the pharmaceutical industry has faced a tidal wave of investigations and lawsuits brought by federal prosecutors, state attorneys general, company whistleblowers, and a host of consumer groups and individuals. Nearly every major drug company has faced at least one. Charges have been both criminal and civil. Often they are related to defrauding Medicare and Medicaid by billing for inflated prices, or encouraging providers to do so—which amounts to a kickback, since providers get to keep the difference between the real price and the inflated one. Bayer, for example, was fined $257 million for helping Kaiser Permanente, the giant health maintenance organization, relabel the antibiotic Cipro (in great demand after the anthrax scare) to hide the fact that the government was paying more for it than the HMO.[16]

But defrauding the government by rigging prices and offering kickbacks is not the only charge drug companies are facing. Others involve anticompetitive practices, which the Federal Trade Commission has been aggressively investigating for several years. In its 2002 report, discussed in Chapter 10, the commission documented a widespread pattern of abuse of Hatch-Waxman and fingered several companies for particularly flagrant violations. Numerous lawsuits have been filed to recover money spent on high-priced brand-name drugs while generics were improperly kept off the market.

Other charges include marketing drugs for unapproved uses, as in the Neurontin case described in Chapter 9, and misleading advertising. Still others allege substandard manufacturing practices. And finally, as you might expect in these circumstances, there have been allegations of cover-ups. Some companies have faced a series of different charges. Many involve whistle-blowers from within the companies, who stand to collect a percentage of any settlements and fines.

Federal prosecutors in Boston and Philadelphia have been especially aggressive.[17] More than a dozen drug companies have been the subjects of subpoenas by the U.S. attorneys' offices in those two cities to look into inducements to persuade doctors and health plans to prescribe drugs. State attorneys general have also become very active in prosecuting drug companies for defrauding Medicaid. Finally, consumer groups are banding together to sue drug companies for a variety of alleged offenses. The Prescription Access Litigation Project, for example, is an alliance of seventy consumer groups that has filed suits against more than twenty drug companies. Plaintiffs' attorneys skilled in class actions in the wake of their successes in asbestos and tobacco cases are today setting their sights on drug companies. In fact, you could say that drug companies are now being sued about as often as they sue others—and that's a lot.

Some of the prosecutions have targeted not drug companies but pharmacy benefit management companies (PBMs). These are companies that administer prescription drug benefits for employers, unions, health plans, and public agencies. They now purchase drugs on behalf of some 200 million Americans and have the authority to select formularies and contract with drug companies and retail pharmacies for the best deals. But in fact, they sometimes collude with drug companies to keep prices high. The drug companies pay them "rebates" to list their high-priced drugs. But instead of passing these savings along to health plans and consumers, as they are contractually bound to do, the PBMs pocket them. One of the largest PBMs, originally called Merck-Medco, was owned by the drug giant Merck—an obvious conflict of interest. It accounted for over half of Merck's revenues. When it was spun off by the parent company in 2003, part of the agreement was that Medco Health Solutions (the new name of the PBM) would guarantee a certain market share for Merck drugs.[18] In April 2004, Medco paid $29.3 million to settle state and federal complaints that it violated consumer protection and mail fraud laws by switching patients to drugs that *added* costs for patients and their health plans. The company also agreed to make their arrangements with drug companies transparent.[19]

Whether on balance PBMs lower costs for their customers is impossible to say, since their transactions are anything but transparent. My guess is that they add to costs, since they are just one more hand in the till. But PBMs are now major peripheral players. They will become even bigger with the Medicare prescription drug benefit, since they will administer much of the new coverage and keep a substantial fraction of the billions of dollars earmarked for the program.

Some of the fines and settlements in cases against big pharma have been enormous. Between 2000 and 2003, according to Michael Loucks, chief of the Health Care Fraud Unit in the U.S. Attorney's Office for the District of Massachusetts, eight companies paid out a total of $2.2 billion in fines and settlements. Four of those companies—TAP Pharmaceuticals (discussed in Chapter 7), Abbott, AstraZeneca, and Bayer—pleaded guilty to criminal charges. TAP, the champion so far, paid a total of $885 million, of which $290 million were criminal fines. Loucks pointed out in a speech that the company received $2.7 billion in revenues from Medicare during the 1990s, so it still came out well ahead.[20]

Some companies have faced several legal actions at once. Schering-Plough, for instance, agreed to pay the government $500 million because of its repeated failure to fix problems in its factories and in the manufacture of dozens of drugs in New Jersey and Puerto Rico (not Canada, you'll notice).[21] After an investigation of Schering-Plough by the Federal Trade Commission, consumer groups sued the company for conspiring with generic companies to hold off entering the market. Several coalitions, led by the Prescription Access Litigation Project, also sued Schering-Plough for making misleading claims about Claritin, which they said did not acknowledge that the drug was shown to work only half the time. And as if that were not enough, the company reported in 2003 that it was threatened with indictment for a host of federal charges, including giving kickbacks to doctors, marketing drugs for unapproved uses, submitting false pricing information to Medicaid, and destroying documents related to the investigation. That's quite a plateful.

In general, companies are only too willing to settle cases rather than risk being convicted of a felony and perhaps barred from Medicare and Medicaid. It may be that the fines, huge though some of them are, are more than offset by the extra income generated by drug firms' questionable activities, and the whole thing is shrugged off as just one more cost of doing business. And it may be that many of the charges are frivolous—just a matter of greedy plaintiffs' attorneys going for deep pockets or overeager government lawyers trolling for big settlements. But there is no doubt that litigation is increasing, and the industry is, for the first time, beginning to look vulnerable. Over time it adds up, and it can't be good for public relations. Even gnats in great enough numbers can be a real problem.

A Dry Pipeline and the Reaction of Wall Street

The very worst problem facing big pharma is its dwindling pipeline. Coupled with the cluster of patent expirations since 2001 on many of its biggest blockbusters, and new pressures to modulate prices, this problem may create a major disaster for the industry. And remember, this situation is not just a matter of bad luck. It is the result of a deliberate strategy to leave the risky research to others and concentrate on turning out me-too drugs. In Chapter 4, I discussed the meager output of innovative drugs—defined as newly approved drugs that are both new compounds and classified by the FDA as likely to be improvements over drugs already on the market. Over the four years beginning in 2000, there were just 32 innovative drugs out of a total of 314 approved drugs. Even in this small collection, only seven came from the top ten U.S. drug companies. There were one each from Pharmacia, Merck, and Bristol-Myers Squibb in

2000; one from Merck in 2001; none in 2002; and one each from Pharmacia, Wyeth, and Abbott in 2003. Where was Pfizer? Lilly? Schering-Plough? That paltry output nowhere near justifies all the rhetoric about how innovative the American pharmaceutical industry is, or all the warnings that if we dare regulate prices, we will jeopardize the prodigious flow of lifesaving medicines.

At the end of the third quarter of 2003, *The Wall Street Journal* reported on the performance of the pharmaceutical industry. The story led with a sentence that would have been inconceivable just a few short years ago: "Pharmaceutical companies couldn't look any sicker." It then went on to say, "Drug stocks have been disappointing investors for more than a year, and yesterday's news suggested things are getting worse."[22] Why? "Expired patents on profitable drugs, efforts to curb rising health-care costs, and weak drug pipelines." Merck, once the nation's second-largest drug company, and included in the Dow Jones industrial average, was the biggest share price loser of the thirty blue chips that make up the index.

Companies varied in their bad fortune. Some, like Pfizer, mainly by virtue of its blockbusters Lipitor and Celebrex, did relatively well. Nevertheless, after its acquisition of Pharmacia, Pfizer announced in 2003 that it planned to save $2.5 billion by closing five of its twenty-five research sites worldwide, one in suburban Chicago with 1300 employees.[23] Merck is struggling and in 2003 announced it would lay off as many as 4400 of its 63,000 employees.[24] Bristol-Myers Squibb's share prices plunged nearly 60 percent from 2001 to 2003. Its top-selling drugs, Taxol, Glucophage, and BuSpar (an antianxiety agent), now face generic competition. Furthermore, not one of its top-selling drugs was discovered by company researchers. As Gardiner Harris of *The New York Times* reported, the company "licensed them from elsewhere and relied on its lawyers to defend the drugs from generic competitors, sometimes long after the exclusive marketing rights to the drugs had expired."[25]

While the pharmaceutical industry is still a giant, it's a struggling giant. What will it do? So far, it is searching ever more desperately for drugs to license from small biotechnology companies and universities. It is pushing its me-too drugs harder. It is engaging in a ballet of acquisitions and mergers to combine its dwindling pipeline, swell its marketing staff, and get some economies of scale. And it is filing more lawsuits to extend marketing rights and fight regulation—all the while promoting itself with increasingly extravagant public relations claims. But it cannot long continue on this course for the simple reason that its financial fortunes are predicated on ever increasing prices, and they are simply not sustainable. No one is willing or able to pay those prices anymore. The Medicare prescription drug benefit offers only a temporary reprieve. So big pharma will have to change. But how?

13

How to Save the Pharmaceutical Industry— And Get Our Money's Worth

DESPITE ALL ITS EXCESSES, THIS IS AN important industry that should be saved—mainly from itself. The public is dependent on it, and it should be made to carry out its original purpose of developing important drugs and selling them at reasonable prices. I have shown how the industry, corrupted by easy profits and greed, has deceived and exploited the American people. But that is not to say that everyone who works for big pharma is corrupt or deceitful. In fact, it is my impression that most pharmaceutical employees, even at the highest levels, accept their own public relations. They honestly believe they are part of an innovative industry whose prices are an accurate reflection of the value of its products and the costs of making them. That is a testament to the effects of compartmentalization in big corporations; very few people know the full dimensions of the business. And it is also a testament to human nature. People want to be proud of their work.

But readers will know by now that the pharmaceutical industry, despite its many dedicated employees, has moved a very long way from its original mission. In this chapter I will propose specific reforms that would restore the industry to its purpose and make prescription drugs not only more affordable but better and safer. My intention is to show what needs to change to make the industry function as it claims to—as a source of innovative and affordable drugs to help people lead longer, better lives.

In doing so, I will be painting something of an ideal, in that I will propose reforms even though I know the obstacles to achieving some of them are formidable. In fact, those barriers would vary greatly. Some reforms, like requiring new drugs to be compared with old ones, could be accomplished virtually overnight if the political will were there. Others, like changing patent law or achieving uniform pricing have all sorts of global ramifications and would face almost insurmountable obstacles. But there is value in trying to define the ideal system, so that we can move toward it in the best way possible—unevenly and incompletely, if necessary—but at least with an understanding of where we want to go.

My proposals address seven broad problems that have been discussed in this book. They are listed here with references to the chapters in which they were discussed, in case you want to refresh your memory. I will not address all the problems discussed in the book or all the reforms one might wish for, only those I consider most important.

1. Drug companies produce too many me-too drugs and too few innovative ones. (See Chapters 4 and 5.)
2. The Food and Drug Administration (FDA) is too much in the thrall of the industry it regulates. (Chapter 11)
3. Drug companies have too much control over clinical research on their own products. (Chapters 6 and 9)
4. Patents and other exclusive marketing rights are undesirably long and too elastic. (Chapter 10)
5. Drug companies have too much influence over medical education about their own products. (Chapter 8)
6. Important information about research and development, marketing, and pricing is kept secret. (Chapters 1, 3, and 7)
7. Prices are too high and too variable. (Chapters 1 and 12)

I will discuss the key reforms needed to deal with each of these problems, but it should be understood that the reforms would often have multiple, overlapping effects. For example, anything that shortens exclusive marketing rights will also affect profits and the ability of the industry to influence government and the FDA. But the end result is that nearly all of the changes I propose would lead to better drugs at lower prices, and would loosen the iron lock of big pharma on public policy and the medical profession.

Shift the Emphasis from Me-Too to Innovative Drugs

A number of steps could be taken to stanch the flow of me-too drugs. By default, that would force drug companies to put more of their efforts into developing truly innovative drugs. To start with, *U.S. patent law should be enforced in its original form.* Courts have progressively weakened the requirement that new discoveries or inventions be useful, novel, and non-obvious. There is no possible justification, for instance, for a new patent on Prozac to treat premenstrual tension. Examiners in the U.S. Patent and Trademark Office should not receive bonuses based on how many patent applications they handle. Since it is easier to grant a patent than to deny it, the current payment practice encourages quick approval, whatever the merits. Patent reviewers should be salaried for their time, with appropriate managerial supervision to prevent unreasonable delays.

Food and Drug Administration regulations should require that new drugs be compared not just with placebos but with old drugs for the same conditions. Approval should depend on whether the new drug adds something useful in terms of greater effectiveness, greater safety, fewer side effects, or substantially greater convenience. The FDA should be allowed reasonable flexibility in its judgments, but it should not approve drugs that on balance offer trivial or no advantages over drugs already available, and may even be worse. Overnight, that reform alone would force the industry to concentrate on innovative drugs instead of me-too drugs. *If I could choose only one of the reforms I am suggesting, it would be this one.* This change would have multiple beneficial ripple effects. And this is one that could be accomplished easily by congressional legislation.

There is an ethical issue here, too. It is wrong to compare a new drug with a placebo if there is an effective drug already on the market, because doing so means some human subjects are denied treatment during the trial. For that reason, drug trials for serious diseases, like cancer or HIV/AIDS, almost never have placebo groups. Instead, the new drug is compared with whatever is currently being used. But most new drugs are not for serious diseases. They are for minor conditions, or for conditions that may be *precursors* to serious diseases, like high blood pressure or high cholesterol levels. Here placebo-controlled trials are the order of the day. I have heard one high-ranking FDA official justify them by implying that he didn't really believe the old drugs were effective anyway. If we don't know whether Prozac works, he seemed to be saying, why test Zoloft against it? But that is an argument for higher standards of proof, not for placebo-controlled clinical trials. If there is really doubt about whether a standard treatment is effective, the FDA should require that clinical trials of new treatments have three comparison groups—new drug, old drug, and placebo.

Let's look a little more at the benefits of requiring new drugs to be compared with old ones. First, few me-too drugs would be approved, since it is highly unlikely that each new one is better than the last at comparable doses. Second, as mentioned, drug companies would be forced to concentrate on innovative drugs. Third, they could trim their vast marketing budgets, since most of those expenditures are to convince doctors and the public that one me-too drug is better than another in the absence of evidence. If evidence were required, there would be far less need for marketing, and we wouldn't have to pay the steep markup in prices it adds. Fourth, there would be far fewer clinical trials. A great many clinical trials are now designed to get FDA approval for me-too drugs, to find new uses for them, or (in the case of most Phase IV studies) to jockey for position in a crowded me-too market. In other words, these trials are really marketing tools. If drugs were approved only when they were clearly superior in some way to drugs already on the market, the number of clinical trials would plummet, but each one would be far more important. They would serve the purpose that they are intended to serve and that human subjects are led to believe they serve— to answer a medically important question: Does this drug add something of value to our ability to treat this condition? Not, "Can I create a big market for this drug?"

Strengthen the Food and Drug Administration

The FDA needs to be strengthened as an independent agency. It is now so dependent on the pharmaceutical industry that it has become big pharma's handmaiden. Industry apologists and antiregulatory conservatives still beat up on the FDA publicly (check *The Wall Street Journal*'s editorials on the subject), but that is mainly just an ideological gesture. In fact, the FDA has become extremely accommodating to the industry, as evidenced by the former commissioner's speech (discussed in Chapter 11) urging other countries to allow drug prices to rise. I once heard another high official in the agency say publicly that the job of the FDA's Center for Drug Evaluation and Research is to "facilitate" drug development—something quite different from regulating it. It would seem that the industry, not the public, has become the FDA's client. What should be done to restore the FDA's proper role?

First, the Prescription Drug User Fee Act should be repealed—or allowed to expire in 2007. This act, you will remember, authorizes drug companies to pay "user fees" to the FDA for every drug reviewed. That practice puts the FDA on the industry's payroll, drug by drug. The more drugs the agency reviews, the more money it gets from industry. It's analogous to the incentive of the U.S. Patent and Trademark Office to grant patents. This arrangement creates a powerful conflict of interest for the FDA. Moreover, the very notion that private companies "use" a public regulatory agency is wrong, since the FDA is there to serve the public, not drug companies.

Second, public support should be increased—not just to make up for the loss of user fees but over and above that amount. The FDA is vital to public health, and it needs to be adequately funded. Giving it the resources to do its job properly would pay for itself many times over. Public funding would also restore balance within the FDA. The Prescription Drug User Fee Act required the agency to put too much of its resources into speeding up drug approvals, at the expense of other important functions, like monitoring drug safety, inspecting manufacturing plants, and ensuring truthful advertising. Furthermore, in the rush to approve drugs, the agency is taking shortcuts that lower the standards for safety and effectiveness. Shortcuts may be justified in certain cases—as at the beginning of the HIV/AIDS epidemic—but they should be rare. There is now far too much emphasis on speed at the FDA.

Third, the FDA's advisory committees should not include experts with financial ties to industry. The notion that they are somehow indispensable is not credible. No one is indispensable. The truth is that experts are being co-opted by these deals, just as the FDA is co-opted by user fees.

Create an Institute to Oversee Clinical Testing of Drugs

Drug companies should no longer be permitted to control the clinical testing of their own drugs. There is too much evidence that this practice biases the research in favor of the sponsor's drug. It also distorts the type of research done, since companies are more interested in increasing sales than in obtaining medical knowledge. We really don't need one more study of whether a new drug is better than a placebo for some slightly different use, but drug companies sponsor them because they help to expand the market.

To ensure that clinical trials serve a genuine medical need and to see that they are properly designed, conducted, and reported, I propose that an Institute for Prescription Drug Trials be established within the National Institutes of Health (NIH) to administer clinical trials of prescription drugs. Drug companies would be required to contribute a percentage of revenues to this institute, but their contributions would not be related to particular drugs (as is the case with the FDA user fees). The institute would then contract with independent researchers in academic medical centers to conduct drug trials. The researchers would design the trials, analyze the data, write the papers, and decide about publication. The data would become the joint property of the NIH and the researchers, not be controlled by the sponsoring company. The FDA now assigns responsibility for the conduct of clinical trials to sponsors. That practice would end. Responsibility would lie exactly where it should—with independent researchers and their institutions.

Others have also called for a special NIH institute to evaluate prescription drugs, but they have generally suggested that it would compare drugs that are already on the market (as was done in the ALLHAT study discussed in Chapter 6). While that would be helpful, it would address only the effects of the underlying problem, not the cause. There would be nothing to stop the FDA from continuing to approve large numbers of me-too drugs that were compared with placebos. My proposal is different. It would have the Institute for Prescription Drug Trials oversee clinical trials *before* FDA approval, not afterward. Since drugs would have to be compared with older treatments, many fewer drugs of dubious benefit would come to market in the first place. Important comparisons of drugs already on the market could be done within existing NIH institutes, as was true of the ALLHAT study.

How the institute would administer the trials would have to be worked out carefully. It might prioritize trials on the basis of unbiased expert advice, just as the other institutes at the NIH have expert panels to decide which research to give priority. But the expectation would be that all trials of scientific merit would be carried out, and there would have to be some mechanism to appeal decisions not to carry out a proposed trial. This is not a perfect process, and there may be better alternatives, but the point is that an independent, public agency should administer all clinical trials to ensure that they are properly conducted—both scientifically and ethically. This is too important a matter to leave to private contract research organizations, whose only clients are the drug companies.

Because of reductions in the number of me-too drug trials, there would be many fewer trials altogether, and they could easily be conducted entirely in nonprofit academic settings. There would be no need for a private research industry, which inherently has a conflict of interest. But if academic centers perform the trials, it would be essential that they and their faculty researchers be free from their own financial conflicts. To receive funding, academic institutions should not have equity interest in the pharmaceutical industry, and researchers should have no financial ties to companies whose drugs they evaluate. Similarly, expert advisers to the Institute for Prescription Drug Trials should have no conflicts of interest.

These reforms would eliminate most of the abuses I described in Chapter 6. Unfavorable research results could no longer be suppressed, and papers could not be manipulated to emphasize favorable findings. All clinical trials would be publicly registered, and their results available to everyone.

Curb Monopoly Marketing Rights

The period of exclusivity for brand-name drugs is too long and too easily stretched. That is a major reason for the high costs of prescription drugs and the inordinate profits of big pharma. There is no legitimate reason for generic competition to be delayed so long.

Paradoxically, the first reform I would suggest to curb monopoly marketing rights allows drug companies more time to complete their clinical trials. *I propose that even if patents are granted before clinical testing starts, the clock on the patents should not begin ticking until the drugs come to market.* In other words, a company could patent a new drug before launching clinical trials to protect it from competition, but only after the drug is approved by the FDA and comes to market would the patent's time line begin. Then it might have a duration of, say, six years from the time the drug came to market, instead of twenty years from the time the patent was filed. That way, clinical testing would not eat into sales time, so companies would not be in such a rush to complete it and the research could be done more carefully and thoroughly. (Here I'm assuming there is no National Institute for Prescription Drug Trials.) I am aware that such a change would be difficult to achieve, given the current move to harmonize patent law internationally. But as I said earlier, I am sketching an ideal system, and this change would certainly be an improvement.

The law granting drug companies an extra six months of exclusive marketing rights for testing drugs in children should be repealed. That law is virtual bribery, and it doesn't even accomplish its stated purpose. Drug companies take advantage of the law to test blockbuster drugs in children whether the drugs are meant for this age-group or not. For an investment of a few million dollars or less, they can increase their revenues by hundreds of millions. But, they can opt *not* to test less profitable drugs in children even though they are more likely to be used in this age-group. The FDA now has the authority to *require* pediatric testing as a condition of approval. But it rarely uses it. It should. Imagine the uproar if the FDA let drug companies get away with testing drugs just in men, even though they would probably be used in women as well.

The loopholes in the Hatch-Waxman Act should be closed so that exclusivity cannot be stretched out for years. You will remember from Chapter 10 that drug companies may file for many additional patents on an already patented and approved drug. By suing generic companies for infringement of these secondary patents, they can trigger successive thirty-month stays on generic competition. This should not be possible. The way to stop it is clear. First, Hatch-Waxman restrictions should be enforced. Only patents listed in the FDA Orange Book can be the basis for such lawsuits, and these are supposed to be restricted to patents that pertain to the original drug and its approved use. The FDA completely ignores that restriction and permits drug companies to list whatever secondary patents they wish—no matter how frivolous or far removed from the original drug. That should be stopped, as the Federal Trade Commission urged. It should be the FDA's responsibility to make sure patents are eligible for listing in the Orange Book. Of course, if patent law were strictly enforced, so that patents were granted only for discoveries or inventions that are truly useful, novel, and non-obvious, there wouldn't be so many secondary patents.

There is no reason for a thirty-month stay on generic companies entering the market just because brand-name companies sue them. Even if a brand-name company genuinely believes that a relevant patent would be violated, it could sue the generic company without an automatic extension of exclusive marketing rights. Generic companies would be very wary of violating a valid patent, since they would be liable for the brand-name company's loss of sales. Hatch-Waxman should also be reformed to make it impossible for brand-name companies to make sweetheart deals with generic manufacturers to delay entry into the market. The first generic company to win approval after a lawsuit is given six months' exclusive marketing rights. That exclusivity should be contingent on the generic company bringing a drug to market as quickly as possible. The 2003 Medicare prescription drug benefit law contained some provisions for modifying Hatch-Waxman, but how they will work is still unclear.

Get Big Pharma Out of Medical Education

We need to end the fiction that big pharma provides medical education. Drug companies are in business to sell drugs. Period. They are exactly the wrong people to evaluate the products they sell. I am not saying that all of the information drug companies provide to doctors is false. Some of it is useful and valid. But information from companies comes mixed with hyperbole, bias, and misinformation, and there is often no way to tell which is which. Good education about prescription drugs, like all education, needs to be as objective and critical as possible.

Yet drug companies pour money into medical schools and teaching hospitals, they support most continuing medical education, and they subsidize professional meetings. Wherever clinicians are educated, big pharma is there to help. There is no question that it influences educational content. The result is that doctors not only receive biased information but learn a very drug-intensive style of medicine. They come to believe that there is a drug for everything and that new drugs (of which they have many free samples) are always better than old ones. *Once and for all, we should clarify a simple fact: Drug companies are not providers of education, and they cannot be. No laws, regulations, or guidelines should be based on the idea that they are.*

The medical profession needs to take full responsibility for educating its members. There are a few simple steps to make this happen. *First, medical schools should teach students about drugs, not leave such education to industry-sponsored programs and teaching materials.* Many of our best schools have virtually eliminated the pharmacology courses that used to teach the basic principles of drug actions and uses. *Second, teaching hospitals should regard drug company representatives just as they do other salespeople,* who are not allowed to traipse around at will, promoting their wares and offering gifts and meals to medical students and doctors in training. *Third, the profession needs to take responsibility for continuing medical education.* Just as there should be no private clinical research industry, there should be no private medical education industry hired by the drug companies. This would mean that continuing medical education would be less well financed, but it can be made much less expensive without any loss of quality. *Finally, professional associations should be self-supporting.* If breaking their dependence on drug companies means increased membership dues, so be it. Meetings would benefit by being more modest, serious, and purposeful. But if doctors want to go to a resort in Hawaii for a meeting, let them pay for it.

Many doctors would agree that drug companies should have no input into the content of medical education but argue that it is acceptable for them to support it at arm's length. I disagree. The industry's immense marketing expenditures are tacked on to the prices of prescription drugs. Much of that increased sales income goes toward "education"—remember the missing $35 billion (see Chapter 8)? I believe the public, if asked, would not want to provide such handsome subsidies to doctors. Of course, if educational grants from industry *really* had to be completely at arm's length, such grants would soon largely disappear. These companies are not charities. They expect a return on investment, and they get it—precisely because what they call education is designed to increase sales. As concern grows about marketing masquerading as education, some companies may create separate education budgets. But no matter what you call it, the overall purpose is the same—to sell drugs.

Drug companies sometimes contend that direct-to-consumer advertising is also educational, but it is even less educational than company-sponsored meetings for doctors in Hawaii. There is no way consumers can evaluate clinical claims in a thirty-second TV advertisement. The purpose and the effect of these commercials is to increase pressure on doctors to prescribe the latest, most expensive me-too drugs. *Direct-to-consumer advertising should be prohibited in the United States just as it is in other advanced countries.* At the very least, it should be regulated more stringently. Big pharma and the advertising agencies, which have a huge financial stake in the ads, would strongly resist, so any such action would probably require a congressional mandate. For reasons of public health and safety, however, the

FDA is acknowledged to have authority over pharmaceutical advertising, so there is no question of an unfettered "right to commercial free speech" in this case. The issue is how, and how much, it should be regulated.

Open the Black Box

Big pharma badly needs some transparency. It gets away with exploiting the public in part because of its extraordinary secrecy. Drug companies reveal very little about the most crucial aspects of their business. Yet, unlike other businesses, they are dependent on the public for a host of special favors—including rights to NIH-funded research, long periods of market monopoly, and multiple tax breaks that almost guarantee a profit. *Because of these special favors and the importance of its products to public health, as well as the fact that government is a major purchaser of its products, the pharmaceutical industry should be regarded much as a public utility. Its books should be open.*

We ought to know exactly what drug companies spend on R & D and how it is broken down, not only by function but by individual drugs once they are patented and enter clinical trials. We should know the relative amounts spent on preclinical, clinical, and market research. Expenditures on clinical trials for each drug should be separated into their various phases, including Phase IV studies. And we should know how much drug companies spend on marketing research, and where that money is budgeted.

The enormous black box known as "marketing and administration" also needs to be opened. Where do those tens of billions of dollars really go? How much for top executive compensation? How much for lawyers? How much for "educating" doctors and the public? All of these categories should be broken down into their components. These expenditures produce a huge markup on drugs, and the public is entitled to know the details about them.

Price reform is discussed in the next section, but prices are also a big part of the industry's secrets. It is extremely difficult to find out what various purchasers actually pay for their prescription drugs. Drug companies publish their average wholesale prices, supposedly the prices they recommend wholesalers charge pharmacies. But in practice, the average wholesale price means little. In fact, AWP is sometimes said to stand for "Ain't What's Paid." Different customers are charged very different prices, and exactly what any given customer pays is often obscured by discounts and rebates. Those who pay something close to the average wholesale price are mainly people with no insurance, although prices may still vary from pharmacy to pharmacy. Most prosecutions of drug companies have had to do with defrauding Medicaid or Medicare by inflating prices, sometimes in conjunction with offering kickbacks to doctors or pharmacy benefit managers. It is only by virtue of the secrecy, complexity, and great variability of pricing arrangements that drug companies can get away with bilking their biggest customer—the government—and exploiting individuals without bargaining power.

Establish Reasonable and Uniform Pricing

Drug prices should be not only transparent but reasonable and as uniform as possible for all purchasers. The great disparities that now exist, with the most vulnerable people paying the highest prices, are unfair. Prices need to be regulated in some way to make them generally affordable. Pharmaceutical profits could still be very high, even with significantly lower prices, especially if marketing expenditures were greatly reduced. Since the biggest single purchaser of prescription drugs is the government, it could negotiate or regulate prices on behalf of everyone, much as the governments of other advanced countries do. For people who are too poor to afford needed drugs, there could be subsidies, but prices should not vary, only the payer. Uniform prices would prevent the current chaos that serves as a cover for fraud, kickbacks, and price gouging. It would also be desirable if prices were roughly the same in all developed countries, as well as within the United States, since big pharma is a global industry and great disparities create problems across borders (as we are now seeing with Canada).

That does not mean other developed countries should allow prices to climb to match U.S. prices, which former FDA Commissioner Mark McClellan seemed to recommend, apparently with the backing of the Bush administration. Instead, based on full knowledge of the industry's profits and expenditures, we should try to converge toward a reasonable price. The industry and its apologists claim that the higher prices Americans pay are to cover R & D costs, but that ignores the fact that the big drug companies are profitable all over the world and their total profits actually exceed their total R & D expenditures. They are not just squeaking by, as industry apologists imply, but in recent years are making three to six times the profits earned by other Fortune 500 companies. One might just as well argue that Americans should pay higher prices to cover marketing costs, or to ensure that the top ten U.S. drug companies continue to make their extraordinary profits—more total profits than all the other Fortune 500 companies put together in 2002.

Unfortunately, with the passage of the Medicare reform bill in 2003, public policy has moved in exactly the opposite direction from any reasonable brake on pharmaceutical prices. The prescription drug benefit expressly forbids Medicare to use its purchasing power to bargain for lower prices. That provision was tantamount to writing a multibillion-dollar check—signed by taxpayers—to big pharma. (Not for nothing does this industry have the largest lobby in Washington.) Expenditures on drugs will quickly rise to exceed the value of the benefit. Worse, the money diverted to drug companies, pharmacy benefit management companies, and private insurers will have to be squeezed out of taxpayers, and the most likely way that will be done is by cutting other Medicare services or raising premiums and charging higher deductibles and co-payments. *This bill should be repealed, and replaced by a simple measure that guarantees all Medicare beneficiaries appropriate coverage of their drug costs, with government-negotiated payments to industry and a medically based formulary.*

The Medicare bill also stipulated that prescription drugs cannot be imported from Canada without the approval of the Department of Health and Human Services, something that has so far not been forthcoming, although there are some signs that that position may be softening. Yet there is no reason to believe that drugs imported from Canada are any less safe than other drugs, and some reason to suppose they are safer than those bought in the United States, since the high-profile counterfeiting cases have occurred here. But importation is best seen as a temporary measure, pending other reforms that would lead to more uniform pricing across borders. It treats the symptoms, not the disease.

Some Final Thoughts

Prescription drugs are an essential part of modern medical care. Americans need good new drugs at reasonable prices. Yet the pharmaceutical industry is failing to meet that need. There is a widening gap between its rhetoric and its practices. Driven by its lust for profits, it seems almost bent on eventual self-destruction. Its current way of doing business is not sustainable. Both the federal government and the medical profession have been co-opted by big pharma's wealth and power, but sooner or later that will have to change. The Medicare prescription drug benefit will give the industry a huge boost, but it cannot last. Those who pay for drugs—government, insurers, and individuals—simply do not have the money to continue to support the industry in its present form. And the public is angry.

In thinking about reform, it is useful to consider the industry in terms of its functions. Which does it do well, which badly, and which shouldn't it be performing at all? The industry supposedly discovers, develops, tests, manufactures, distributes, and promotes drugs. We have seen that it contributes much less to discovery and early development than it claims but instead feeds off the NIH, and universities and smaller companies in the United States and abroad. Maybe we should simply accept that fact. But then it makes no sense to continue to reward big pharma as though it were the major source of innovation. Clinical testing could continue to be the industry's responsibility, but it should be conducted at arm's length, preferably through an Institute for Prescription Drug Trials. The industry should play no role whatsoever in medical education. What remains is what this industry could do very well, if it redirected its efforts—the development of promising drug candidates, manufacturing, distribution, and a reasonable amount of marketing. This would bring the industry into line with reality, which is very different from its pretensions.

We need to remember that much of what we think we know about the pharmaceutical industry is mythology spun by the industry's immense public relations apparatus. In this book, I have set out to expose the most important of those myths—the claims that big pharma's prices reflect its R & D costs, that it is innovative, and that it is a shining example of American free enterprise. As we have seen, this industry actually spends far more on marketing and administration than on R & D. It is not innovative. And it lives on government favors and shrinks from competition. If you know that, you should be immune to the kind of threat the pharmaceutical industry specializes in: "Give us everything we want, or we might have to stop producing miracle drugs."

Finally, in this chapter, I suggested how the industry could be reformed. Those suggestions were not meant to be comprehensive but to deal with what I believe are the most important problems. As I said at the outset, nearly all would lead to better drugs at lower prices. Most of the changes could be achieved with simple congressional legislation. That is where you come in. Your representatives in Congress will not deviate much from the industry script unless you force them to. We saw a sad demonstration of that fact with the 2003 Medicare reform bill, which was made to order by and for big pharma. Your representatives will stand up to the industry only if you demand that they do. I have tried to arm you with the facts. Yes, the pharmaceutical industry has enormous clout, but what finally matters most is concerted public pressure.

Afterword

CLEARLY, THE PHARMACEUTICAL INDUSTRY AND the medical profession need thoroughgoing reform, and Congress and the Food and Drug Administration need to be reminded that they exist to serve the public, not drug companies. In the meantime, what can you as an individual do to protect your interests? Here are a few specific suggestions.

1. **When your doctor prescribes a new drug, ask him or her these questions:**

What is the evidence that this drug is better than an alternative drug or some other approach to treatment? Has the evidence been published in a peer-reviewed medical journal? Or are you relying on information from drug company representa-

tives? Insist on getting a straight answer and, if necessary, a reference to a journal article or a medical textbook.

Is this drug better only because it is given at a higher dose? Would a cheaper drug be as effective if it were given at an equivalent dose? Sometimes the best course is simply to increase the dose of an older drug. Remember, there is usually no reason to think new drugs are better than old ones, and the older the drug, the better its safety record is likely to be.

Are the benefits worth the side effects, the expense, and the risk of interactions with other drugs I take? Every drug has side effects, and it may be better not to treat self-limited or trivial ailments.

Is this a free sample? If so, is there a generic drug or an equivalent drug I can use that is cheaper when the free samples run out? Free samples are a false economy. They are designed to get you and your doctor hooked on the newest, most expensive drugs.

Do you have any financial ties with the company that makes this drug? For example, do you consult for the company? Other than free drug samples, do you receive gifts from drug companies? Are you being paid to put me on this drug and enroll me in a drug company study? Do you make time for visits from drug company representatives? If the answer to any of these questions is yes, you should consider changing doctors. You need to know your doctor's decisions are based solely on what is best for you. And doctors need to be weaned from their dependence on drug company largesse.

2. And ask your senators and representatives in Congress this question:

Do you receive campaign contributions from the pharmaceutical industry, and if so, how much are they? There is no doubt that this industry largely writes its own ticket in Washington, and you have to put a stop to that.

3. Pay no attention to direct-to-consumer ads for prescription drugs.

These are meant to sell drugs, not educate consumers, and they only add to the prices you pay.

Finally, remember the admonition of the *Washington Post* editorial, quoted on page 215, to question those arguing big pharma's case about their sources of income. I can think of no better advice. Nowadays, even the most distinguished and apparently unbiased academics may be on the pharmaceutical industry's payroll. If they are, you need to be especially skeptical about their pronouncements.

Acknowledgments

I AM INDEBTED ABOVE ALL TO DR. ARNOLD S. (Bud) Relman, with whom I share my life. Together we wrote an extended article about the pharmaceutical industry called "America's Other Drug Problem—The Insatiable Greed of the Pharmaceutical Industry." It was published in the December 16, 2002, issue of *The New Republic,* and received the 2002 George Polk Award for magazine reporting. In outline, the present book largely follows that article. We also collaborated on a related essay, "Patents, Profits and American Medicine," which was published in the spring 2002 issue of *Daedalus* (the journal of the American Academy of Arts and Sciences), and we wrote an op-ed piece for *The Washington Post,* "Prescription for Profit," which was published on June 20, 2001. But even before these joint endeavors, we had written separately about various aspects of the pharmaceutical industry. We were both editors of *The New England Journal of Medicine* (our tenures spanned the years 1977 to 2000), a position in which the industry figures prominently, and we had both warned in editorials of its growing and disturbing power. It is not surprising, then, that Bud's influence is present throughout this book. In addition, he was, as always, an exacting editor.

I am also deeply indebted to my daughters, Dr. Lara Goitein and Elizabeth Goitein, Esq. They read the book carefully and gave me the benefit of their considerable expertise, their uncompromising commitment to clear writing, and their loving encouragement. Drs. Steffie Woolhandler, David Himmelstein, and Joseph Gerstein were also kind enough to read the book in its entirety. Their suggestions and corrections were invaluable, and I am grateful to them. I also benefited from conversations with Dr. Sidney Wolfe of Public Citizen's Health Research Group and James Love of the Consumer Project on Technology. Love read sections of the book and offered helpful comments. Both of their organizations have been at the forefront of efforts to inform the American public about the pharmaceutical industry.

Random House was enthusiastic and supportive throughout the project. In particular, I thank Jonathan Karp, Jonathan Jao, and Amelia Zalcman for their careful attention to me as well as to the book. Finally, I salute Alice Martell, my agent. She is everything an agent should be, and in addition a smart, warm, and witty friend.

Notes

Introduction: Drugs Are Different

1. There are several sources of statistics on the size and growth of the industry. One is IMS Health (www.imshealth.com), a private company that collects and sells information on the global pharmaceutical industry. See www.imshealth.com/ims/portal/front/articleC/0,2777, 6599_3665_41336931,00.html for the $200 billion figure. Others include FamiliesUSA, "Out-of-Bounds: Rising Prescription Drug Prices for Seniors," July 2003 (www.familiesusa.org); Public Citizen Congress Watch, "2002 Drug Industry Profits: Hefty Pharmaceutical Company Margins Dwarf Other Industries," June 2003 (www. citizen.org); Henry J. Kaiser Family Foundation, "Prescription Drug Trends," November 2001 (www.kff.org); National Institute for Health Care Management Foundation, "Prescription Drug Expenditures in 2001: Another Year of Escalating Costs," May 6, 2002 (www.nihcm.org). While figures differ slightly from source to source, they are reasonably close.
2. For a full picture of the special burden of rising drug prices on senior citizens, see FamiliesUSA, "Out-of-Bounds."

3. Sarah Lueck, "Drug Prices Far Outpace Inflation," *Wall Street Journal,* July 10, 2003, D2.
4. FamiliesUSA, "Out-of-Bounds."
5. FamiliesUSA, "Out-of-Bounds."
6. On ABC Special with Peter Jennings, "Bitter Medicine: Pills, Profit, and the Public Health," May 29, 2002.
7. For the top ten companies and their recent mergers as of 2003, see www.oligopolywatch.com/2003/05/25.html.
8. Lueck, "Drug Prices."

1. The $200 Billion Colossus

1. These figures come from the U.S. Centers for Medicare & Medicaid Services, Office of the Actuary, National Health Statistics Group, Baltimore, Maryland. They were summarized in Cynthia Smith, "Retail Prescription Drug Spending in the National Health Accounts," *Health Affairs,* January–February 2004, 160.
2. Center for Policy Alternatives, "Playing Fair: State Action to Lower Prescription Drug Prices," 2000.
3. My figures are culled from several sources. They include:
   a. IMS Health, a private information company and the principal source for data on global sales (www.imshealth.com).
   b. U.S. Centers for Medicare & Medicaid Services (www.cmms.gov).
   c. The annual report of the industry's trade group, the Pharmaceutical Research and Manufacturers of America, "Pharmaceutical Industry Profile 2002" (www.phrma.org).
   d. National Institute for Health Care Management Foundation, "Prescription Drug Expenditures in 2001: Another Year of Escalating Costs," May 6, 2002 (www.nihcm.org).
   I also checked the annual reports of the largest drug companies.
4. For excellent summaries of public contributions to drug company research, see Public Citizen Congress Watch, "Rx R & D Myths: The Case Against the Drug Industry's R & D 'Scare Card,' " July 2001 (www.citizen.org); NIHCM, "Changing Patterns of Pharmaceutical Innovation," May 2002 (www.nihcm.org).
5. This is probably an underestimate. One source that indicates it is at least this is CenterWatch, www.centerwatch.com, a private company owned by Thomson Medical Economics, which provides information

to the clinical trials industry. See *An Industry in Evolution,* 3rd ed., ed. Mary Jo Lamberti (Boston: CenterWatch, 2001), 22.

6. FamiliesUSA, "Out-of-Bounds: Rising Prescription Drug Prices for Seniors," July 2003 (www.familiesusa.org).

7. Public Citizen Congress Watch, "Rx R & D Myths."

8. "The Fortune 500," *Fortune,* April 15, 2002, F26.

9. Public Citizen Congress Watch, "2002 Drug Industry Profits: Hefty Pharmaceutical Company Margins Dwarf Other Industries," June 2003 (www.citizen.org/documents/Pharma_Report.pdf). The data are drawn mainly from the Fortune 500 lists in *Fortune,* April 7, 2003, and April 5, 2004, and drug company annual reports.

10. Henry J. Kaiser Family Foundation, "Prescription Drug Trends," November 2001 (www.kff.org).

11. FamiliesUSA, "Profiting from Pain: Where Prescription Drug Dollars Go," July 2002 (www.familiesusa.org/site/DocServer/PReport.pdf?docID=249).

12. Vasella spoke at the AARP International Forum on Prescription Drug Policy in Washington, D.C., June 10, 2003.

13. Patricia Barry, "More Americans Go North for Drugs," *AARP Bulletin,* April 2003, 3.

14. Chandrani Ghosh and Andrew Tanzer, "Patent Play," *Forbes,* September 17, 2001, 141.

15. Gardiner Harris, "Schering-Plough Is Hurt by Plummeting Pill Costs," *New York Times,* July 8, 2003, C1.

16. For key information about the numbers and kinds of drugs approved each year, see the website of the U.S. Food and Drug Administration (FDA), www.fda.gov/cder/rdmt/pstable.htm.

17. Sheryl Gay Stolberg and Gardiner Harris, "Measure to Ease Imports of Drugs Is Gaining in House," *New York Times,* July 22, 2003, A1.

18. Alice Dembner, "Drug Firm to Pay $875M Fine for Fraud," *Boston Globe*, October 4, 2001, A1.

2. The Creation of a New Drug

1. For an overview of the process of drug R & D as well as of NIH contributions to basic research, see Public Citizen Congress Watch, "Rx R & D Myths: The Case Against the Drug Industry's R & D 'Scare Card,' " July 2001 (www.citizen.org).

2. See the annual report of the industry's trade group, the Pharmaceutical Research and Manufacturers of America, "Pharmaceutical Industry Profile 2002," 20 (www.phrma.org).

3. For the story of AZT, see Philip J. Hilts, *Protecting America's Health: The FDA, Business, and One Hundred Years of Regulation* (New York: Alfred A. Knopf, 2003), 236. See also "Approval of AZT," March 20, 1987, www.fda.gov/bbs/topics/NEWS/NEW00217.html.

4. "Mitusya, Weinhold, Yarchoan, Bolognesi, Broder, Credit Government Scientists with Developing Anti-AIDS Drug," *New York Times,* September 28, 1989. The letter is available at http://lists.essential.org/pharm-policy/msg00106.html.

5. For a thorough and readable account of the detailed workings of the FDA by a former chief medical officer, see Suzanne Parisian, *FDA: Inside and Out* (Front Royal, Va.: Fast Horse Press, 2001); also see Public Citizen Congress Watch, "Rx R & D Myths," appendix A.

6. The best source of information on CROs and the clinical trials industry is CenterWatch, a private company owned by Thomson Medical Economics (www.centerwatch.com). For an overview, see CenterWatch, *An Industry in Evolution,* 3rd ed., ed. Mary Jo Lamberti (Boston: CenterWatch, 2001). CenterWatch also publishes a monthly newsletter. The 80,000 figure is CenterWatch's estimate. The 2.3 million figure is drawn from IMS International, the FDA, and the NIH; see Naomi Aoki, "Trials and Errors," *Boston Globe,* June 12, 2002, D1.

7. One of many sources for this statement is "Shifts in the Foundation of Drug Development," *CenterWatch Monthly,* January 2004, 8.

8. Department of Health and Human Services, Office of Inspector General, "Recruiting Human Subjects: Pressures in Industry-Sponsored Clinical Research," June 2000, OEI-01-97-00195, 17.

9. Chris Adams, "FDA Inundated Trying to Assess Drug Ad Pitches," *Wall Street Journal,* March 14, 2002, B1.

10. Melody Petersen, "FDA Lets Others Inspect Plants Again," *New York Times,* April 3, 2002, C3.

11. For reviews of the history of the FDA, see Parisian, *FDA: Inside and Out;* Hilts, *Protecting America's Health;* "FDA Backgrounder: Milestones in U.S. Food and Drug Law History," May 3, 1999 (http://vm.cfsan.fda.gov/mileston.html).

12. "Revolution at the FDA," *Wall Street Journal,* February 19, 2003, A14.

13. Washington Legal Foundation advertisement, "In All Fairness," *New York Times,* December 16, 2002, A27.

3. How Much Does the Pharmaceutical Industry
Really Spend on R & D?

1. Alan F. Holmer on National Public Radio, *Talk of the Nation,* hosted by Juan Williams, January 2, 2001.
2. William Safire, "The Doughnut's Hole," *New York Times,* October 27, 2003, A23.
3. Robert Pear, "Research Cost for New Drugs Said to Soar," *New York Times,* December 1, 2001, C1.
4. For industry figures on R & D expenditures, see the annual report of the industry's trade group, the Pharmaceutical Research and Manufacturers of America, "Pharmaceutical Industry Profile 2002," table 1 (www.phrma.org); for the number of drugs approved by year, see the FDA website www.fda.gov/cder/rdmt/pstable.htm.
5. For an excellent and detailed analysis of the true costs of drug company R & D, plus references to other analyses, see Public Citizen Congress Watch, "Rx R & D Myths: The Case Against the Drug Industry's R & D 'Scare Card,' " July 2001 (www.citizen.org).
6. Naomi Aoki, "R & D Costs for Drugs Skyrocket, Study Says," *Boston Globe,* December 1, 2001, C1.
7. Aoki, "R & D Costs."
8. Pear, "Research Cost for New Drugs."
9. Joseph A. DiMasi, Ronald W. Hansen, and Henry G. Grabowski, "The Price of Innovation: New Estimates of Drug Development Costs," *Journal of Health Economics,* vol. 22 (2003), 151–85.
10. Pear, "Research Cost for New Drugs."
11. See FDA website.
12. DiMasi et al., "Price of Innovation," 173.
13. DiMasi et al., "Price of Innovation," 151.
14. DiMasi et al., "Price of Innovation," 161.
15. The orphan drug act and a list of orphan drugs are available on the FDA website www.fda.gov/orphan/taxcred.htm. For a summary, see Larry Stevens, "Big Gains, Some Strains," *American Medical News,* August 4, 2003, 5.
16. For information about drug company taxes, see Common Cause, "Prescription for Power: How Brand-Name Drug Companies Prevailed over Consumers in Washington," June 2001, 13 (www.commoncause.org); also see annual reports of companies.
17. Aoki, "R & D Costs."

18. Public Citizen Congress Watch, "2002 Drug Industry Profits: Hefty Pharmaceutical Company Margins Dwarf Other Industries," June 2003 (www.citizen.org/documents/Pharma_Report.pdf).
19. FamiliesUSA, "Profiting from Pain: Where Prescription Drug Dollars Go," July 2002 (www.familiesusa.org/site/DocServer/PReport.pdf?docID=249).
20. Alan Sager, Professor of Health Services at Boston University School of Public Health, quoted in BusinessWeek Online, July 9, 2001 (www.businessweek.com).
21. Arnold S. Relman and Marcia Angell, "America's Other Drug Problem," *New Republic*, December 16, 2002, 32.

4. Just How Innovative Is This Industry?

1. Vicki Kemper, "Drug Industry Poised to Recap Political Dividends," *Los Angeles Times*, November 8, 2002, A15.
2. To find the members of the Pharmaceutical Research and Manufacturers of America, see www.phrma.org/whoweare/members; also the PhRMA annual report, "Pharmaceutical Industry Profile 2002."
3. To find the names and manufacturers of drugs approved by the FDA, go to www.fda.gov/cder/rdmt/ndaaps02cy.htm and check by year; to learn more about the drugs, see *Physicians' Desk Reference*, 58th ed., (Montvale, N.J.: Thomson PDR, 2004) or (www.PDR.net).
4. This is my best estimate, based in part on CenterWatch, www.centerwatch.com, *An Industry in Evolution*, 3rd ed., ed. Mary Jo Lamberti (Boston: CenterWatch, 2001), 22; and Gautam Naik, "GlaxoSmithKline Actively Pursues Drug Licenses," *Wall Street Journal*, February 13, 2002, B2.
5. Naik, "GlaxoSmithKline Actively Pursues Drug Licenses."
6. Naik, "GlaxoSmithKline Actively Pursues Drug Licenses."
7. The most complete source on the Taxol story is provided by the watchdog group Consumer Project on Technology: Susannah Markandya and James Love, "Timeline of Paclitaxel Disputes," August 23, 2001 (www.cptech.org). See also Public Citizen Health Research Group's Health Letter, "Taxol: How the NIH Gave Away the Store," August 2003, 12; Peter Landers, "U.S. Recoups Modest Sum on Taxol," *Wall Street Journal*, June 9, 2003, B7; Common Cause, "Prescription for Power: How Brand-Name Drug Companies Prevailed over Consumers in Washington," June 2001, 13 (www.

commoncause.org); Eliot Marshall, "Universities, NIH Hear the Price Isn't Right on Essential Drugs," *Science,* April 27, 2001, 614 (www.sciencemag.org).

8. To find information on FDA approval and exclusivity terms and patent numbers, visit the FDA website www.fda.gov/cder/ob. To find information on patents, visit the U.S. Patent and Trademark Office website, www.uspto.gov; the original patent number for Taxol, for example, is 5,157,049, and it was patented by the U.S. Department of Health and Human Services on October 20, 1992. For Florida State University royalties, see Florida State University Office of Research, Office of Technology Transfer (www.techtransfer.fsu.edu).

9. For the story of Epogen, see Arnold S. Relman and Marcia Angell, "America's Other Drug Problem," *New Republic,* December 16, 2002, 31. Also Merrill Goozner, "The Price Isn't Right," *American Prospect,* September 11, 2000 (www.prospect.org); Paul Elias, "Suit Against Columbia Highlights Issue of University Patents," *Boston Globe,* April 28, 2003, A7; Naomi Aoki, "Biotech Firms Sue Columbia University," *Boston Globe,* July 16, 2003, C1; Anthony Shadid, "A U.S. Share of Royalties on Research Proposed," *Boston Globe,* August 22, 2001, A1.

10. For the story of Gleevec, see Relman and Angell, "America's Other Drug Problem," 31. This was based in part on personal conversations between Relman and Dr. Brian J. Druker. Also see James Love, Consumer Project on Technology (www.cptech.org/ip/health/gleevec); Charles L. Sawyers, "Medical Progress: Chronic Myeloid Leukemia," *New England Journal of Medicine,* April 29, 1999, 1330 (www.nejm.org).

11. The ad appeared, for example, in *The New Yorker,* February 9, 2004, 25. Also, for the Novartis view, see Daniel Vasella, with Robert Slater, *Magic Cancer Bullet: How a Tiny Orange Pill Is Rewriting Medical History* (New York: HarperCollins, 2003); and a review by Arnold S. Relman, *Journal of the American Medical Association,* October 22/29, 2003, 2194.

12. Darren E. Zinner, "Medical R & D at the Turn of the Millennium," *Health Affairs,* September–October 2001, 202.

13. Public Citizen Congress Watch, "Rx R & D Myths: The Case Against the Drug Industry's R & D 'Scare Card,' " July 2001 (www.citizen.org).

14. U.S. Congress, Joint Economic Committee, "The Benefits of Medical Research and the Role of the NIH," May 2000, http://jec.senate.gov.

15. Alice Dembner, "Public Handouts Enrich Drug Makers, Scientists," *Boston Globe,* April 5, 1998, A1.
16. Merrill Goozner, *The $800 Million Pill: The Truth Behind the Cost of New Drugs* (Berkeley: University of California Press, 2004).
17. Vasella, with Slater, *Magic Cancer Bullet.*
18. For difficulties in getting access to Gleevec, see Love, www.cptech. org/ip/health/gleevec; Stephanie Strom and Matt Fleischer-Black, "Questions on Choice of Foundation for Drug Program," *New York Times,* June 5, 2003, C7; IANS, "Novartis Stops Donation of Cancer Drug to India," June 6, 2003, (www.newindpress.com); the complaint was made to Daniel Vasella by a member of the audience at the AARP International Forum on Prescription Drug Policy in Washington, D.C., June 10, 2003.
19. For the story of Cerezyme, see Goozner, "Price Isn't Right."
20. For the story of Fuzeon, see Vanessa Fuhrmans, "Costly New Drug for AIDS Means Some Go Without," *Wall Street Journal,* January 13, 2004, A1.
21. For a summary of this legislation, see Council on Governmental Relations, "The Bayh-Dole Act: A Guide to the Law and Implementing Regulations," October 1999 (www.cogr.edu/docs/Bayh_Dole.pdf). Also see Peter S. Arno and Michael H. Davis, "Why Don't We Enforce Existing Drug Price Controls?" *Tulane Law Review,* vol. 75, no. 3 (2001); Eyal Press and Jennifer Washburn, "The Kept University," *Atlantic Monthly,* March 2000, 39.
22. For the NIH response, see Department of Health and Human Services, National Institutes of Health, "NIH Response to the Conference Report Request for a Plan to Ensure Taxpayers' Interests Are Protected," July 2001 (www.nih.gov/news/070101wyden.htm).

5. "Me-Too" Drugs—The Main Business of the Pharmaceutical Industry

1. For an excellent overview of the industry's shift from innovative to me-too drugs, see the National Institute for Health Care Management Foundation, "Changing Patterns of Pharmaceutical Innovation," May 2002 (www.nihcm.org).
2. See the FDA website www.fda.gov/cder/rdmt/pstable.htm.
3. The relevant law, the Kefauver-Harris Drug Amendment of 1962, required manufacturers to show their new drugs were safe and effective; it did not say what they should be compared with, but it has

since been taken literally to mean new drugs need not be compared with anything.

4. Gardiner Harris has done superb work reporting on Prilosec and Nexium. See his "As a Patent Expires, Drug Firm Lines Up Pricey Alternative," *Wall Street Journal,* June 6, 2002, A1; and "Two Fronts in Heartburn Market Battle," *New York Times,* August 20, 2003, C12. See also Neil Swidey, "The Costly Case of the Purple Pill," *Boston Globe Magazine,* November 17, 2002, 11; information on approval for all FDA-approved drugs is on the FDA website www.fda.gov/search/databases.html.

5. For a summary of the trials, see *Physicians' Desk Reference,* 56th ed. (Montvale, N.J.: Thomson PDR, 2002), p. 621 (www.pdr.net).

6. Harris, "Two Fronts."

7. For an excellent and detailed account of the Claritin saga, see Stephen S. Hall, "Prescription for Profit," *New York Times Magazine,* March 11, 2001, 40. For the switch to Claritin, see Gardiner Harris, "Schering-Plough Wins New Approval for Allergy Drug," *Wall Street Journal,* February 12, 2002, B10, and "Schering-Plough Faces a Future with Coffers Unfortified by Claritin," *Wall Street Journal,* March 22, 2002, A1.

8. Christopher Rowland, "Ad Spending Soars as Cholesterol Fighters Duel," *Boston Globe,* July 30, 2003, D1; Francesca Lunzer Kritz, "Statins, at the Heart of a New Cholesterol Campaign," *Washington Post,* July 31, 2001, F6. Manufacturer information about individual drugs is available in *Physicians' Desk Reference,* 58th ed.

9. David Brown, "Cholesterol Drug Taken Off the Market," *Washington Post,* August 9, 2001, A1.

10. Ron Winslow, "Study Signals How Low to Go on Cholesterol," *Wall Street Journal,* November 13, 2003, D1.

11. Alicia Ault, "A Statin Too Far?" *Washington Post,* August 12, 2003, F5.

12. The list of the top ten drugs in the world is available from IMS Health, "World Review for 2002," data released February 25, 2003 (www.imshealth.com).

13. See Arnold S. Relman and Marcia Angell, "America's Other Drug Problem," *New Republic,* December 16, 2002, 38, for the story of Prozac and Sarafem; for a rundown on Prozac's competitors, see Erica Goode, "Researchers Scramble for the Next Prozac," *Seattle Times,* June 30, 2002, A7. Manufacturer information about individual drugs is available in the *Physicians' Desk Reference,* 58th ed.

14. Denise Grady, "U.S. Guidelines Are Reassessing Blood Pressure," *New York Times,* May 15, 2003, A1.

15. Melody Petersen, "Advertising," *New York Times,* July 18, 2003, C5.

16. Shankar Vedantam, "Drug Ads Hyping Anxiety Make Some Uneasy," *Washington Post,* July 16, 2001, A1.

17. Vedantam, "Drug Ads Hyping Anxiety."

18. Maureen Dowd, "Aloft on Bozoloft," *New York Times,* July 3, 2002, A23.

19. Gardiner Harris, "2 Cancer Drugs, No Comparative Data," *New York Times,* February 26, 2004, C1.

20. For reports of shortages, see Melody Petersen, "Drug Shortages Become a Worry at Hospitals Around the Country," *New York Times,* January 3, 2001, A1; Julie Appleby, "Hospitals, Patients Run Short of Key Drugs," *USA Today,* July 11, 2001, 1A; Gardiner Harris, "CDC Warns Vaccine Supply Is in Jeopardy," *Wall Street Journal,* February 11, 2002, A3.

21. Appleby, "Hospitals, Patients Run Short."

22. Petersen, "Drug Shortages."

6. How Good Are New Drugs?

1. The ALLHAT Officers and Coordinators for the ALLHAT Collaborative Research Group, "Major Outcomes in High-Risk Hypertensive Patients Randomized to Angiotensin-Converting Enzyme Inhibitor or Calcium Channel Blocker vs. Diuretic," *Journal of the American Medical Association,* December 18, 2002, 2981. For detailed media accounts, see Ron Winslow and Scott Hensley, "Study Questions High-Cost Drugs for Hypertension," *Wall Street Journal,* December 18, 2002, A1; Lawrence K. Altman, "Older Way to Treat Hypertension Found Best," *New York Times,* December 18, 2002, A1.

2. The list of the top ten drugs in the world is available from IMS Health, "World Review for 2002," data released February 25, 2003 (www.imshealth.com).

3. Winslow and Hensley, "Study Questions High-Cost Drugs."

4. Altman, "Older Way."

5. FamiliesUSA, "Bitter Pill: The Rising Prices of Prescription Drugs for Older Americans," June 2002 (www.familiesusa.org).

6. Winslow and Hensley, "Study Questions High-Cost Drugs."

7. Altman, "Older Way."

8. Lindon M. H. Wing et al., "A Comparison of Outcomes with Angiotensin-Converting-Enzyme Inhibitors and Diuretics for Hypertension in the Elderly," *New England Journal of Medicine,* February 13, 2003, 583.

9. I focus on Harvard Medical School and its teaching hospitals only because they are most familiar to me, and I touch on just a few of the arrangements. For media coverage, see Liz Kowalczyk's reports: "Beth Israel Seeks Deal with Drug Company," *Boston Globe,* February 14, 2001, A1; "Harvard to Use Caution with Merck," *Boston Globe,* August 1, 2001, A1; "Lucrative Licensing Deals with Drug, Biotech Firms Are Raising Ethics Issues for Hospitals," *Boston Globe,* March 24, 2002, C1. Also see Raja Mishra, "Harvard May Ease Rules on Faculty Ties to Drug Firms," *Boston Globe,* June 9, 2003, A1. The Millennium deal was spelled out in a request for applications sent to faculty at Partners.

10. See Justin E. Bekelman et al., "Scope and Impact of Financial Conflicts of Interest in Biomedical Research," *Journal of the American Medical Association,* January 22–29, 2003, 454.

11. Kevin A. Schulman et al., "A National Survey of Provisions in Clinical Trial Agreements Between Medical Schools and Industry Sponsors," *New England Journal of Medicine,* October 24, 2002, 1335.

12. This was reported by Alison Bass, "Drug Companies Enrich Brown Professor," *Boston Globe,* October 4, 1999, A1; and by Douglas M. Birch and Gary Cohn, "Of Patients and Profits: Standing Up to Industry," *Baltimore Sun,* June 26, 2001, 1A.

13. David Willman, "Stealth Merger: Drug Companies and Government Medical Research," *Los Angeles Times,* December 7, 2003, A1.

14. "Subverting U.S. Health" editorial, *Los Angeles Times,* December 7, 2003, M4.

15. For an excellent overview of bias in clinical research, see Thomas Bodenheimer, "Uneasy Alliance: Clinical Investigators and the Pharmaceutical Industry," *New England Journal of Medicine,* May 18, 2000, 1539.

16. Bekelman et al., "Scope and Impact."

17. H. T. Stelfox et al., "Conflict of Interest in the Debate over Calcium-Channel Antagonists," *New England Journal of Medicine,* January 8, 1998, 101.

18. The *British Medical Journal* published an excellent issue on industry sponsorship and bias in clinical research. The papers are accessible at

the journal's website, www.bmj.org. See in particular Silvio Garattini et al., "How Can Research Ethics Committees Protect Patients Better?" *British Medical Journal*, May 31, 2003, 1199; see also Frank van Kolfschooten, "Can You Believe What You Read?" *Nature*, March 28, 2002, 360.

19. Bodil Als-Nielsen et al., "Association of Funding and Conclusions in Randomized Drug Trials," *Journal of the American Medical Association*, August 20, 2003, 921.

20. Susan Okie, "Missing Data on Celebrex: Full Study Altered Picture of Drug," *Washington Post*, August 5, 2001, A11.

21. This case was fully covered in the press. See, for example, Philip J. Hilts, "Company Tried to Bar Report That HIV Vaccine Failed," *New York Times*, November 1, 2000, A26; Richard Saltus, "AIDS Drug Researchers Say Firm Pressured Them," *Boston Globe*, November 1, 2000, A3; Thomas M. Burton, "Unfavorable Drug Study Sparks Battle over Publication of Results," *Wall Street Journal*, November 1, 2000, B1; Carol Cruzan Morton, "Company, Researchers Battle over Data Access," *Science*, November 10, 2000, 1063. I also spoke with one of the authors and had access to some of the documents, including the agreement between the authors and the company.

22. This was reported in Birch and Cohn, "Of Patients and Profits."

23. This study of Prozac-type antidepressants was unique in that it analyzed all clinical trials of antidepressant drugs from the FDA, whether published or not. See Irving Kirsch and Thomas J. Moore, "The Emperor's New Drugs: An Analysis of Antidepressant Medication Data Submitted to the U.S. Food and Drug Administration," *Prevention & Treatment*, July 15, 2002.

24. See Wayne Kondro and Barbara Sibbald, "Drug Company Experts Advised Staff to Withhold Data About SSRI Use in Children," *Canadian Medical Association Journal*, March 2, 2004; "Depressing Research," editorial, *The Lancet*, April 24, 2004.

7. The Hard Sell . . . Lures, Bribes, and Kickbacks

1. For statistics on free samples and sales representative visits to doctors, see Tyler Chin, "Drug Firms Score by Paying Doctors for Time," *American Medical News*, May 6, 2002, 1 (www.amednews.com);

Scott Hensley, "As Drug-Sales Teams Multiply, Doctors Start to Tune Them Out," *Wall Street Journal,* June 13, 2003, A1.

2. The U.S. General Accounting Office issued a critical report on direct-to-consumer prescription drug advertising in 2002, which contained the industry's assertions about its promotional spending. See U.S. General Accounting Office, "Prescription Drugs: FDA Oversight of Direct-to-Consumer Advertising Has Limitations," October 2002, GAO-03-177 (www.gao.gov).

3. Christopher Rowland, "Pats Ink Levitra Marketing Deal," *Boston Globe,* September 12, 2003, D1.

4. Rowland, "Pats Ink Levitra Deal."

5. Melody Petersen, "A Respected Face, but Is It News or an Ad?" *New York Times,* May 7, 2003, B1; Reuters, "Film Production Company Sues Cronkite," *New York Times,* September 20, 2003, B4.

6. For the story of Lauren Bacall and other celebrity promoters, see Melody Petersen, "Heartfelt Advice, Hefty Fees," *New York Times,* August 11, 2002, C1; Alex Kuczynski, "Treating Disease with a Famous Face," *New York Times,* December 15, 2002, section 9, 1; Lawrence Goodman, "Celebrity Pill Pushers," Salon.com, July 11, 2002.

7. Petersen, "Respected Face."

8. See Arnold S. Relman and Marcia Angell, "America's Other Drug Problem," *New Republic,* December 16, 2002, 27. For the decade 1990 to 2000, the ten largest companies spent about 35 percent on "marketing, general and administrative"; see Henry J. Kaiser Family Foundation, "Prescription Drug Trends," November 2001 (www.kff.org). For data on the top ten U.S. companies in 2002, see Public Citizen Congress Watch, "Drug Industry Profits: Hefty Pharmaceutical Company Margins Dwarf Other Industries," June 2003 (www.citizen.org).

9. For this type of information, visit company websites and check their annual reports; for example, www.novartis.com.

10. Pharmaceutical Research and Manufacturers of America, "Pharmaceutical Industry Profile 2002" (www.phrma.org).

11. See glossary, employment definitions, PhRMA, "Pharmaceutical Industry Profile 2002," 95 (www.phrma.org).

12. See U.S. GAO "Prescription Drugs"; also Robert Pear, "Investigators Find Repeated Deception in Ads for Drugs," *New York Times,* December 4, 2002, A22.

13. U.S. GAO, "Prescription Drugs," 3.

14. Pear, "Investigators Find Repeated Deception."

15. For background, see Francis B. Palumbo and C. Daniel Mullins, "The Development of Direct-to-Consumer Prescription Drug Advertising Regulation," *Food and Drug Law Journal,* vol. 57, no. 3 (2002), 423. For background and information on the shift to television, see U.S. GAO, "Prescription Drugs."

16. For such evidence, see Meredith B. Rosenthal et al., "Deman Effects of Recent Changes in Prescription Drug Promotion," Henry J. Kaiser Family Foundation, June 2003 (www.kff.org); Meredith B. Rosenthal et al., "Promotion of Prescription Drugs to Consumers," *New England Journal of Medicine,* February 14, 2002, 498; U.S. GAO, "Prescription Drugs"; Pear, "Investigators Find Repeated Deception"; Vanessa Fuhrmans and Gautam Naik, "In Europe, Prescription-Drug Ads Are Banned—and Health Costs Lower," *Wall Street Journal,* March 15, 2002, B1.

17. Chris Adams, "FDA Inundated Trying to Assess Drug Ad Pitches," *Wall Street Journal,* March 14, 2002, B1.

18. The go-slow policy at the FDA has been well reported in the media. See, for example, Melody Petersen, "Who's Minding the Drugstore?" *New York Times,* June 29, 2003, section 3, 1; Alice Dembner, "FDA Action on Drug Ads Declining," *Boston Globe,* October 19, 2002, A1; Michael Kranish, "FDA Counsel's Rise Embodies U.S. Shift," *Boston Globe,* December 22, 2002, A1.

19. See U.S. GAO, "Prescription Drugs," 21.

20. See Alan F. Holmer, "Direct-to-Consumer Advertising—Strengthening Our Health Care System," *New England Journal of Medicine,* February 14, 2002, 526.

21. Katharine Greider, *The Big Fix: How the Pharmaceutical Industry Rips Off American Consumers* (Cambridge, Mass.: Perseus Books, 2003).

22. Chin, "Drug Firms Score by Paying Doctors for Time."

23. Liz Kowalczyk, "Drug Firms Increasingly Barred from Exam Rooms," *Boston Globe,* July 28, 2003, A1.

24. "Drugmakers' Gifts to Doctors Finally Get Needed Scrutiny," editorial, *USA Today,* October 14, 2002, 14A.

25. American Medical Association Council on Ethical and Judicial Affairs, "Clarification of Gifts to Physicians from Industry," addendum 2, opinion 8.061, December 2000. Department of Health and Human Services, Office of the Inspector General, "Compliance Program

Guidance for Pharmaceutical Manufacturers," April 18, 2003 (http://oig.hhs.gov/authorities/docs/03/050503FRCPGPharmac.pdf), see *Federal Register,* vol. 68, no. 86 (May 5, 2003), 23738. Also see Robert Pear, "Drug Industry Is Told to Stop Gifts to Doctors," *New York Times,* October 1, 2002, A23.

26. Liz Kowalczyk, "Drug Companies' Secret Reports Outrage Doctors," *Boston Globe,* May 25, 2003, A1.

27. Some of the TAP/Lupron story is based on presentations and handouts at the Pharmaceutical Regulatory and Compliance Congress and Best Practices Forum in Washington, D.C., November 12–14, 2003, in particular those by Michael Loucks, Chief of the Health Care Fraud Unit, Assistant U.S. Attorney, U.S. Attorney's Office for the District of Massachusetts. I am also indebted to one of the whistle-blowers in the case, Dr. Joseph Gerstein, for talking with me at length. For media accounts, see Alice Dembner, "Drug Firm to Pay $875M Fine for Fraud," *Boston Globe,* October 4, 2001, A1; Alice Dembner, "$840M Penalty Is Expected for Drug Company," *Boston Globe,* May 28, 2001, A1; Bruce Japsen, "Doctors' Outrage Stings TAP," *Chicago Tribune,* October 7, 2001, C1; Anne Barnard, "Ailing Hospitals, Pharmaceutical Deals, Ethics Put to Test," *Boston Globe,* November 23, 2002, B1; Shelley Murphy, "Drug Sale Said Tied to Favors at Lahey," *Boston Globe,* November 9, 2002, A1.

8. Marketing Masquerading as Education

1. Department of Health and Human Services, Office of the Inspector General, "Compliance Program Guidance for Pharmaceutical Manufacturers," April 18, 2003 (http://frwebgate6.access.gpo.gov/cgi-bin/waisgate.cgi?WAISdocID=861841312951+0+0+0&WAISaction=retrieve); see *Federal Register,* vol. 68, no. 86 (May 5, 2003), 23738.

2. Arnold S. Relman, "Defending Professional Independence: ACCME's Proposed New Guidelines for Commercial Support of CME," *Journal of the American Medical Association,* May 14, 2003, 2418.

3. "Concepts in Professional Education and Communications, Why Should You Invest in Medical Education?" (http://www.citizen.org/publications/release.cfm?ID=6731), as quoted in a letter from Joseph Ross, Peter Lurie, and Sidney M. Wolfe to the ACCME.

4. See Liz Kowalczyk, "Drug Firms and Doctors: The Offers Pour In," *Boston Globe,* December 15, 2002, A1.

5. For a sobering look at the world of drug company speakers' bureaus, see Sue Pelletier, "Pulling the Strings? How Pharma's Big Bucks Are Influencing Your CME Speakers," *Medical Meetings*, September–October 2002, 39 (www.meetingsnet.com).

6. One source for this figure is a press release from Quintiles Transnational, "Rx's and RSVP's: Pharmaceutical Companies Holding More Physician Meetings and Events," July 9, 2001.

7. I came upon this catchy phrase in Ray Moynihan, "Who Pays for the Pizza? Redefining the Relationships Between Doctors and Drug Companies," *British Medical Journal*, May 31, 2003, 1189 (www.bmj.com). He attributed it to Dana Katz et al., "All Gifts Large and Small: Toward an Understanding of the Ethics of Pharmaceutical Gift Giving," in press at the time.

8. See Martin B. Keller et al., "A Comparison of Nefazodone, the Cognitive Behavioral-Analysis System of Psychotherapy, and Their Combination for the Treatment of Chronic Depression," *New England Journal of Medicine*, May 18, 2000, 1462 (www.nejm.org). In the same issue, see my editorial, "Is Academic Medicine for Sale?" 1516. The letter to the editor was from Thomas J. Ruane, *New England Journal of Medicine*, August 17, 2000, 510. Nefazodone was subsequently withdrawn from the market in Europe because of adverse reactions.

9. Ellen Barry, "Psychiatrists Become Drug Firms' Targets," *Boston Globe*, May 28, 2002, C5.

10. Barry, "Psychiatrists Become Targets."

11. "PhRMA Code on Interactions with Healthcare Professionals," 2002, obtainable from www.phrma.org/publications/policy/2004-01-19.391.pdf.

12. DHHS, "OIG Compliance Program Guidance," 23738.

13. Mary Riordan, quoted by Tamar Hosansky, "No Turning Back," *Medical Meetings*, July–August 2003, 21 (www.meetingsnet.com).

14. The Patient Channel was described by Vincent Bzdek, "Tube Feeding," *Washington Post*, July 8, 2003, HE01; also Suzanne Vranica, "GE's Upstart TV Network Plans to Pitch Drugs to the Bedridden," *Wall Street Journal*, September 25, 2002. Bzdek reported the protest from Gary Ruskin, cofounder of the citizen group Commercial Alert and the letter from Dennis S. O'Leary, President of JCAHO, to General Electric Medical Systems, a copy of which I obtained. Vranica was the source of the quotation from Kelly Peterson.

15. Robert O'Harrow, "Grass Roots Seeded by Drugmaker," *Washington Post,* September 12, 2000, A1.
16. Alex Beam, "The Biggest Drug Dealer on Campus," *Boston Globe,* October 17, 2002, D1. Also see the program's website: www. goonandlive.com/goal_news.asp?newsID=4.

9. Marketing Masquerading as Research

1. This case was extensively reported in the media. For an excellent review, see Melody Petersen, "Court Papers Suggest Scale of Drug's Use," *New York Times,* May 30, 2003, C1.
2. Liz Kowalczyk, "Use of Drug Soars Despite Controversy," *Boston Globe,* November 25, 2002, A1; Melody Petersen, "Suit Says Company Promoted Drug in Exam Rooms," *New York Times,* May 15, 2002, C1.
3. Liz Kowalczyk, "Drug Company Push on Doctors Disclosed," *Boston Globe,* May 19, 2002, A1.
4. Associated Press, "Court Files Show Drug Company Strategy for Marketing Drug to Doctors," May 19, 2002 (www.businesstoday.com).
5. Melody Petersen, "Doctor Explains Why He Blew the Whistle," *New York Times,* March 12, 2003, C1.
6. Kowalczyk, "Use of Drug Soars"; and Liz Kowalczyk, "Drug Firm Seen Skirting FDA OK," *Boston Globe,* November 4, 2002, A1.
7. Gardiner Harris, "Pfizer to Pay $430 Million over Promoting Drug to Doctors," *New York Times,* May 14, 2004, C1.
8. Clinical Trials Advisor, "Peri-Approval Clinical Trials on Increase; FDA Focuses on Post-Marketing Safety," August 15, 2002, 4 (www. clinicaltrialsadvisor.com).
9. "A Phase IV Market Accelerates," *CenterWatch,* October 2003, 1 (www.centerwatch.com). CenterWatch is a private company, owned by Thomson Medical Economics, that provides information to the clinical trials industry; until 2004, it was also the name of the monthly newsletter.
10. Mike Mitka, "Accelerated Approval Scrutinized: Confirmatory Phase 4 Studies on New Drugs Languish," *Journal of the American Medical Association,* June 25, 2003, 3227.
11. "Phase IV Market Steams Ahead," *CenterWatch,* October 2002, 1 (www.centerwatch.com).

12. Ann Davis, "Tactic of Drug Makers Is Raising Questions About Use of Research," *Wall Street Journal,* January 7, 2002, A1.
13. "Phase IV Market Steams Ahead."
14. "Phase IV Market Steams Ahead."
15. "Phase IV Market Steams Ahead."
16. Melody Petersen, "Madison Ave. Plays Growing Role in Drug Research," *New York Times,* November 22, 2002, A1; Vanessa O'Connell, "Agencies Join in Drug Development," *Wall Street Journal,* March 13, 2002, B1.
17. Petersen, "Madison Ave. Plays Growing Role."
18. For an excellent and detailed newspaper account of this, see Antonio Regalado, "To Sell Pricey Drug, Lilly Fuels a Debate over Rationing," *Wall Street Journal,* September 18, 2003, A1. For those interested in the scientific evidence, see the original trial on which FDA approval was based: Gordon R. Bernard et al., "Efficacy and Safety of Recombinant Human Activated Protein C for Severe Sepsis," *New England Journal of Medicine,* March 8, 2001, 699. And for the scientific controversy, see the ensuing articles and correspondence in the same journal, September 26, 2002, 1027, 1030, 1035.
19. Kimberly Atkins, "Diet Called Key in Type 2 Diabetes Risk," *Boston Globe,* August 9, 2001, A2.
20. Liz Kowalczyk, "Cost and Consequence," *Boston Globe,* June 22, 2003, E1.

10. Patent Games—Stretching Out Monopolies

1. For a valuable discussion of these two types of exclusivity, see Rebecca S. Eisenberg, "The Shifting Functional Balance of Patents and Drug Regulation," *Health Affairs,* September–October 2001, 119.
2. Milt Freudenheim, "Generic Drug Sales Flourish Thanks to Big Companies," *New York Times,* November 2, 2002, B16; David Gross, "Issue Brief: Generic Drugs," AARP Public Policy Institute, 2003 (www.aarp.org/ppi).
3. Gardiner Harris and Chris Adams, "Drug Manufacturers Step Up Legal Attacks That Slow Generics," *Wall Street Journal,* July 12, 2001, A1.
4. For a quick review of standards for patents on prescription drugs, see U.S. Federal Trade Commission, "Generic Drug Entry Prior to Patent

Expiration: An FTC Study," July 2002, 41. See also the website of the U.S. Patent and Trademark Office, www.uspto.gov.

5. For an analysis of the relaxation of patent standards in biomedicine, see Arti K. Rai and Rebecca S. Eisenberg, "Bayh-Dole Reform and the Progress of Biomedicine," *Law & Contemporary Problems,* vol. 66, no. 1 (2002), 289. Also available at http://www.law.duke.edu/journals/66LCPRai.

6. Visit the FDA website for details of FDA-granted exclusivity: "Frequently Asked Questions for New Drug Product Exclusivity" (www.fda.gov/cder/about/smallbiz/exclusivity.htm); for the criteria for Orange Book listing, see the FTC study "Generic Drug Entry"; to access the electronic Orange Book, see www.fda.gov/cder/ob/default.htm.

7. Kathleen D. Jaeger, President and CEO, Generic Pharmaceutical Association, testimony to the U.S. Senate Commerce Committee, April 23, 2002 (www.gphaonline.org/policy/pdf/2002-04-23-testimony.pdf).

8. For the basics on Hatch-Waxman, see the FDA website www.fda.gov/cder/about/smallbiz/patent_term.htm. Also www.fda.gov/cder/about/small biz/generic_exclusivity.htm. For a fuller analysis, see Eisenberg, "Shifting Functional Balance."

9. For a thorough analysis of both Hatch-Waxman and its abuses, see the FTC study, "Generic Drug Entry." This is the single best source of information for understanding the current machinations of the pharmaceutical industry.

10. See Eisenberg, "Shifting Functional Balance," for other legislation; for pediatric exclusivity, see Robert Steinbrook, "Testing Medications in Children," *New England Journal of Medicine,* October 31, 2002, 1462.

11. For the story of Prilosec/Nexium, see Gardiner Harris, "As a Patent Expires, Drug Firm Lines Up Pricey Alternative," *Wall Street Journal,* June 6, 2002, A1; I checked the number of patents on Prilosec in the Orange Book on August 8, 2002.

12. Neil Swidey, "The Costly Case of the Purple Pill," *Boston Globe Magazine,* November 17, 2002, 31.

13. For Claritin patent games, see Gardiner Harris, "Schering-Plough Faces a Future with Coffers Unfortified by Claritin," *Wall Street Journal,* March 22, 2002, A1; also Stephen S. Hall, "Prescription for Profit," *New York Times Magazine,*" March 11, 2002, 40.

14. For Prozac patent games, see Arnold S. Relman and Marcia Angell, "America's Other Drug Problem," *New Republic,* December 16,

2002, 38; also James Vicini, "Supreme Court Rejects Lilly's Prozac Patent Appeal," *Reuters News Service,* January 14, 2002.

15. Jeff Swiatek, "MIT Benefits from New Prozac Use," CNN.com, July 13, 2000 (www.cnn.com/2000/LOCAL/eastcentral/07/13/isn.prozac/).

16. See the FTC study "Generic Drug Entry," 49, 51, A-33.

17. FTC, "Generic Drug Entry."

18. For reactions to the FTC study, see *Los Angeles Times,* "Curb the Drug Patent Tricks," editorial, July 10, 2002, B12; Markian Hawryluk, "Patent Law's Impact on Patients Debated," *American Medical News,* May 13, 2002, 5 (www.amednews.com). And for the Bush administration response, see Patricia Barry, "Speeding Up Generics," *AARP Bulletin,* January 2003, 13; Richard W. Stevenson, "Bush Announces an Easing of Rules on New Generic Drugs," *New York Times,* June 13, 2003, A28.

11. Buying Influence—How the Industry Makes Sure It Gets Its Way

1. This is an enormously long and complicated law, called the Medicare Prescription Drug, Improvement, and Modernization Act of 2003 (Public Law 108-173). It is available on the congressional website, thomas.loc.gov, as PL 108-173. For good summaries, see Patricia Barry, "The New Law—And You," *AARP Bulletin,* January 2004, 16; Jacob S. Hacker and Theodore R. Marmor, "Poison Pill," *Boston Globe,* December 7, 2003, D1; Drew E. Altman, "The New Medicare Prescription-Drug Legislation," *New England Journal of Medicine,* January 1, 2004, 9 (www.nejm.org); for the increase in estimated costs, see Robert Pear, "Bush's Aides Put Higher Price Tag on Medicare Law," *New York Times,* January 30, 2004, A1.

2. Robert Pear, "Democrats Demand Inquiry into Charge by Medicare Officer," *New York Times,* March 14, 2004, A1.

3. Robert Pear, "Drug Companies Increase Spending on Efforts to Lobby Congress and Governments," *New York Times,* June 1, 2003, section 1, 33.

4. Sheryl Gay Stolberg and Gardiner Harris, "Industry Fights to Put Imprint on Drug Bill," *New York Times,* September 5, 2003, A1.

5. For comprehensive documentation of industry lobbying, including names of drug companies, lobbying firms, and lobbyists, see the report of the citizen group Public Citizen Congress Watch, "The Other

Drug War 2003: Drug Companies Deploy an Army of 675 Lobbyists to Protect Profits," June 2003 (www.citizen.org). This report provides an invaluable look at the influence of the pharmaceutical industry on public policy.

6. Chuck Neubauer, Judy Pasternak, and Richard T. Cooper, "A Washington Bouquet: Hire a Lawmaker's Kid," *Los Angeles Times,* June 22, 2003, A1.

7. See the report from Common Cause, "Prescription for Power: How Brand-Name Drug Companies Prevailed over Consumers in Washington," June 2001 (www.commoncause.org).

8. Thomas B. Edsall, "High Drug Prices Return as Issue That Stirs Voters," *Washington Post,* October 15, 2002, A8.

9. Public Citizen Congress Watch, "Citizens for Better Medicare: The Truth Behind the Drug Industry's Deception of America's Seniors," June 2000 (www.citizen.org); Public Citizen Congress Watch, "Other Drug War"; also see Larry Lipman, "Political Groups Woo Seniors," *Atlanta Journal and Constitution,* November 1, 2002, 17A.

10. See Public Citizen Congress Watch, "Other Drug War," 6; also see biographical sketches of administration officials through an Internet search engine.

11. See, for instance, Arti K. Rai and Rebecca S. Eisenberg, "Bayh-Dole Reform and the Progress of Biomedicine," *Law & Contemporary Problems,* vol. 66, no. 1 (2002), 289 (www.law.duke.edu/journals/66LCPRai).

12. For a detailed look at this giveaway, see David Armstrong, "How Drug Directory Helps Raise Tab for Medicaid and Insurers," *Wall Street Journal,* October 23, 2003, A1.

13. Armstrong, "How Drug Directory Helps Raise Tab."

14. Armstrong, "How Drug Directory Helps Raise Tab."

15. The story of Third World struggles to gain access to affordable prescription drugs is laid out in Roger Thurow and Scott Miller, "As U.S. Balks on Medicine Deal, African Patients Feel the Pain," *Wall Street Journal,* June 2, 2003, A1; Elizabeth Becker, "Pact to Help Poor Nations Obtain Drugs Is Delayed," *New York Times,* August 29, 2003, C1; John Donnelly, "Deal Paves Way for Generic HIV Drugs," *Boston Globe,* December 11, 2003, A8; also see Brook K. Baker and Michael Hochman, "Death Sentence," *American Prospect,* December 20, 2002 (www.prospect.org/webfeatures/2002/12/baker-b-12-20.html).

16. Donnelly, "Deal Paves Way for Generic HIV Drugs."

17. Jeffrey Krasner, "FDA Rule Changes in Contention," *Boston Globe,* March 21, 2002, D1.

18. See Marc Kaufman, "Critics Fear Conflicts," *Washington Post,* May 23, 2002, A1; also Baker and Hochman, "Death Sentence."

19. David Willman, "FDA Post-Mortem Finds Drug Approval Problems," *Los Angeles Times,* November 16, 2000, A1.

20. Dennis Cauchon, "FDA Advisors Tied to Industry," *USA Today,* September 25, 2000, 1A.

21. August Gribbin, "House Investigates Panels Involved with Drug Safety," *Washington Times,* June 18, 2001.

22. Michael Kranish, "Drug Industry Costs Doctor Top FDA Post," *Boston Globe,* May 27, 2002, A1; see also Christiane Culhane, "Favor of the Month," *New Republic* online, March 18, 2002 (http://ssl.tnr.com).

23. For background on Mark McClellan, see Christopher Rowland, "FDA's Economist in Chief," *Boston Globe,* January 18, 2004, E1; for his speech, go to the FDA website www.fda.gov/oc/speeches/2003/genericdrug0925.html.

24. Pear, "Drug Companies Increase Spending."

25. "Behind the Lobbying Curtain," editorial, *Washington Post,* June 9, 2003, A20.

26. Pear, "Drug Companies Increase Spending."

27. Both quotations come from Edsall, "High Drug Prices Return."

12. Is the Party Over?

1. For a summary of Canadian price regulation, see Patricia Barry, "Why Drugs Cost Less Up North," *AARP Bulletin,* June 2003, 8; also Abigail Zuger, "Rx: Canadian Drugs," *New England Journal of Medicine,* December 4, 2003, 2188 (www.nejm.org).

2. Gardiner Harris, "Cheap Drugs from Canada: Another Political Hot Potato," *New York Times,* October 23, 2003, C1.

3. Tamsin Carlisle, "What's Left for Canadians if Americans Buy Their Drugs?" *Wall Street Journal,* November 4, 2003, D3.

4. According to one report, foreign suppliers provide most of the key ingredients for American and European companies; see Donald G. McNeil, Jr., "Selling Cheap 'Generic' Drugs, India's Copycats Irk Industry," *New York Times,* December 1, 2000, A1.

5. Christopher Rowland, "Officials Take Steps to Curb Fake Drugs," *Boston Globe,* October 13, 2003, C1.

6. Denise Grady, "FDA Outlines Plans to Counter Growing Trade in Counterfeit Pharmaceuticals," *New York Times,* October 3, 2003, A21.

7. Christopher Rowland, "Canada Vows Drugs Sent to U.S. Are Safe," *Boston Globe,* July 26, 2003, C1.

8. Anna Wilde Mathews, "FDA Warns Cities, States About Buying Canadian Drugs," *Wall Street Journal,* August 27, 2003, B1.

9. Stephen Smith, "City Looks to Get Drugs via Canada," *Boston Globe,* December 9, 2003, A1.

10. For other reports about city, state, and insurer efforts to obtain prescription drugs from Canada and the FDA response, see "States Look at Buying Drugs from Canada," Nationline, *USA Today,* December 12, 2003, A2; Christopher Rowland, "AG Pushes for Medicine from Canada," *Boston Globe,* October 14, 2003, A1; Thomas M. Burton, "The FDA Begins Cracking Down on Cheaper Drugs from Canada," *Wall Street Journal,* March 12, 2003, A1.

11. For the story of big pharma's retaliation, see Burton, "FDA Begins Cracking Down"; Gardiner Harris, "Canada Fills U.S. Prescriptions Under the Counter," *New York Times,* June 4, 2003, A1; Carlisle, "What's Left for Canadians"; Tamsin Carlisle, "Canada Cools to U.S. Drug Flow," *Wall Street Journal,* December 26, 2003, A9.

12. Sheryl Gay Stolberg, "Drug Lobby Pushed Letter by Senators on Medicare," *New York Times,* July 30, 2003, A15.

13. For an excellent review of the struggle between the states and the pharmaceutical industry, see Michelle M. Mello et al., "The Pharmaceutical Industry Versus Medicaid—Limits on State Initiatives to Control Prescription-Drug Costs," *New England Journal of Medicine,* February 5, 2004, 608. See also Alice Dembner, "Drug Firms Fend Off Discount Initiatives," *Boston Globe,* January 21, 2003, A1.

14. Richard Perez-Pena, "Twenty-two States Limiting Doctors' Latitude in Medicaid Drugs," *New York Times,* June 16, 2003, A1; Russell Gold, "Six States Plan to Pool Purchases to Limit Prescription Drug Costs," *Wall Street Journal,* October 17, 2001, B6.

15. Robert Pear, "U.S. Backs Florida Plan to Cut Drug Costs," *New York Times,* September 19, 2001, A14.

16. See Melody Petersen, "AstraZeneca Pleads Guilty in Cancer Medicine Scheme," *New York Times,* June 21, 2003, B1.

17. For accounts of federal and state prosecutions, see Bloomberg News, "Drugmakers Under Scrutiny," *Boston Globe,* May 22, 2002, C1; Alex Berenson, "Trial Lawyers Are Now Focusing on Lawsuits Against Drug Makers," *New York Times,* May 18, 2003, A1. In addition, I used information provided at the Pharmaceutical Regulatory and Compliance Congress and Best Practices Forum in Washington, D.C., November 12–14, 2003, in particular the presentations and handouts of Michael Loucks, Chief of the Health Care Fraud Unit, Assistant U.S. Attorney, U.S. Attorney's Office for the District of Massachusetts.

18. See Barbara Martinez, "Spinoff to Promote Merck's Drugs," *Wall Street Journal,* May 30, 2003, B4; Associated Press, "U.S. Says Firm Favored Use of Merck Drugs," *Boston Globe,* June 24, 2003, D9; also Milt Freudenheim, "Drug Middlemen Are Facing Pressure over Rising Prices," *New York Times,* January 5, 2002, B1. For more general commentary, see Milt Freudenheim, "Pharmacy Benefit Companies Won't Disclose Fees," *New York Times,* January 10, 2003, C3; Milt Freudenheim and Robert Pear, "More Disclosure for Drug Plans," *New York Times,* July 19, 2003, B1.

19. Milt Freudenheim, "Medco to Pay $29.3 Million to Settle Complaints of Drug Switching," *The New York Times,* April 27, 2004, C1.

20. Loucks, Forum, Nov. 12–14, 2003.

21. Some of Schering-Plough's troubles were reported in Denise Gellene, "Lawyers Take Aim at Drug Industry," *Boston Globe,* June 10, 2001; Christopher Newton, "Groups Sue Allergy Drug Maker over Ads," *Boston Globe,* August 10, 2001; Melody Petersen, "Big Drug Company May Face Charges for Its Marketing," *New York Times,* May 31, 2003, A1.

22. Gregory Zuckerman and Ken Brown, "Good Prognosis for Drug Makers," *Wall Street Journal,* October 23, 2003, C1.

23. Theresa Agovino, "Pfizer to Shut Sites, Transfer Jobs," *Boston Globe,* April 30, 2003.

24. Kenneth N. Gilpin, "Merck, Its Income Shy of Estimates, Plans to Cut Jobs," *New York Times,* October 23, 2003, C1.

25. Gardiner Harris, "Will the Pain Ever Let Up for Bristol-Myers?" *New York Times,* May 18, 2003, section 3, 1.

Index

ABOUT THE AUTHOR

The former editor in chief of *The New England Journal of Medicine* and a physician trained in both internal medicine and pathology, Marcia Angell is a nationally recognized authority in the field of health care and an outspoken proponent of medical and pharmaceutical reform. *Time* magazine named her one of the twenty-five most influential people in America. Dr. Angell is the author of *Science on Trial*.

ABOUT THE TYPE

This book was set in Sabon, a typeface designed by the well-known German typographer Jan Tschichold (1902–74). Sabon's design is based upon the original letterforms of Claude Garamond and was created specifically to be used for three sources: foundry type for hand composition, Linotype, and Monotype. Tschichold named his typeface for the famous Frankfurt typefounder Jacques Sabon, who died in 1580.